The High Peak, from the Ordinance Survey map, 1906.

The Discovery of the
PEAK DISTRICT

From Hades to Elysium

Chee Tor on the River Wye, engraved by I. Greig from a drawing by Henry Moore for Beauties of England and Wales, *1802.*

The Discovery of the
PEAK DISTRICT

From Hades to Elysium

Trevor Brighton

Phillimore

2004

Published by
PHILLIMORE & CO. LTD,
Shopwyke Manor Barn, Chichester, West Sussex, England

ISBN 1 86077 314 1

Printed and bound in Great Britain by
CAMBRIDGE PRINTING

Contents

List of Illustrations

Frontispiece: Chee Tor

Acknowledgements

As with most writers I am indebted to a good number of professional and private people for their assistance in my researches. The list below will, I trust, serve as some note of gratitude for help received. I would, however, begin by giving particular thanks to people living and working in the area covered by this book. I would especially record my gratitude to the late Andrew Cavendish, 11th Duke of Devonshire for his interest and encouragement and to the Trustees of the Chatsworth Settlement. On the many occasions I have been allowed free access to the Chatsworth archives and collections I have received unfailing help from Peter Day, Keeper of the Collections, and from his present successor, Charles Noble. Ian Fraser-Martin and Diane Naylor have assisted me in selecting illustrations of the House and its treasures.

To Rosalind Westwood, Derbyshire Museums Manager on behalf of Derbyshire County Council, I am particularly indebted for her time and patience in guiding me through the fine collection of pictures and prints in the archives of the Buxton Museum and Art Gallery. To my colleagues in the Bakewell and District Historical Society thanks are due for making available the artefacts and publications in the Society's Old House Museum in the town. The Derbyshire Record Office and the Derbyshire Local Studies Library, both at Matlock, have been invaluable sources, as have the Local Studies archives in both the Derby and Sheffield City Libraries.

Ray Manley, photographer, of the Peak District National Park Authority, Bakewell, took time in showing me the Authority's photographic archives as well as his own contemporary records.

Jim Dickinson, the respected dealer in maps and prints in Bakewell, has obtained some items which I have used to illustrate this book.

As one who still writes in an archaic, copper-plate hand, I relied entirely on Liese Cooper and, latterly, Jane Bradbury, for word processing the manuscript. This was painstakingly read by my wife, Pat, who made invaluable suggestions.

The author and publisher are most grateful to the following owners and trustees of copyright for their permission to publish these images: Bakewell and District Historical Society (Old House Museum), 39, 49, 70; British Museum, London, 4, 17, 18, 23, 25, 78; Bodleian Library, Oxford, 26, 27, 28, 30, 66, 67; Derby Museums and Art Gallery, 50, 51, 52; Derbyshire County Council (Buxton Museum and Art Gallery), 33, 38, 40, 43, 47, 60, 82, 92, I, III, IV, VII, X, XVI; Devonshire Collections, Chatsworth Settlement Trustees, 41, 61, 62, 63, 65, 68, 69, V, VI, IX; Fitzwilliam Museum, Cambridge, XII, XIII; High Peak Borough Council (Buxton Museum and Art Gallery), XVI; National Gallery, Prague, XIV; Peak District National Park Authority, Bakewell, 101, 102, 104, 105, 106, 108, 109, 110, 111, 112; Severn Trent Water Board, X; Tate Gallery, London, 35, 48, 59, 85, 87; Victoria and Albert Museum, London, 5, 16, 73; Whitworth Art Gallery, University of Manchester, 12; York Museums' Trust (York Art Gallery), XI. Private owners: Ms S Hartley (Buxton Museum and Art Gallery), 43; Mr Ray Manley, 97; Mr Peter Robinson, 53; Lord Sandys, 79.

Introduction

Today the Peak District is well known throughout Britain and around the world. In 2003, for instance, Chatsworth House, the premier attraction in the Peak, drew almost 700,000 visitors. In 1996 the Peak District National Park Authority recorded that two million visitor-days were spent in the Park. Add to this the numbers thronging to those parts outside the National Park – Buxton, the Matlocks and Ashbourne – and one can reckon that some five million visitors come to the Peak District annually.

Tourists today are well aware of what they will see and experience before they leave home. Travel agencies, information centres, leaflets, videos and the internet have provided for every exigency. This book is not concerned with the modern 'packaged' tourist but looks for the first time at those who were prepared to venture into a 'no go' area in the centre of England. These early 'explorers' wrote their own travel experiences in poems, letters and diaries, many of which were published. How many of today's tourists communicate activities beyond a postcard on the weather or a few portrait snapshots?

Printed tourist literature from the 17th to the 19th centuries inspired many writers. Jane Austen could describe the Peak and Chatsworth in *Pride and Prejudice* without ever having been there. Similarly, Mary Shelley could use Matlock Bath as a location in *Frankenstein*. The poets Gray and Wordsworth, well known collectors of travel literature, certainly came to the Peak, as did Charlotte Brontë. Her novel *Jane Eyre* (1847) was inspired by her stay at Hathersage.

The Peak was the first of the British wildernesses to be discovered, long before the Lake District, Wales or the Scottish Highlands were fashionable. This was largely due to the lure of the Seven Wonders of the Peak. These natural mysteries, Chatsworth excluded, instilled dread and superstition until Defoe began to deprecate them in the early 18th century.

Thereafter the old fears changed, by degrees, into the gothick 'horror' of the romantic period. The aristocracy, gentry and professional classes, deprived of the Grand Tour during the French and Napoleonic Wars, found the Peak District a substitute for the Alps and the Apennines. Here they could have presentiments of awe, grandeur and the sublime, such as the Peak is said to have inspired in Mrs Radcliffe's *The Italian* and the *Mysteries of Udolpho*. Almost all of the great English romantic landscape painters made at least one tour of the Peak. By the pictures they exhibited and the books they illustrated they heightened the public's imagination and its desire to visit what seemed another world. Antiquaries and archaeologists came to probe into its past and geologists strove to deduce from the rocks and minerals how and when the earth was formed.

As its mysteries were unravelled and the turnpike roads penetrated its inner fastnesses, so its rocky ravines and rivers became the 'cradle of the Industrial Revolution'. The mills and factories were included in the 'grand tour' of the Peak. Initially they were hailed as the 'new wonders' that would make Britain prosperous, but some tourists, especially John Byng, were soon questioning their impact on the rural population and on the landscape. The cry was then taken up by Ruskin who deplored the air pollution emanating from the new ring of industrial towns and the desecration of the dales by the railways.

Ruskin, Morris and their followers advocated the escape into the Peak for the industrial workers, whether on foot or by bicycle. Thus began the outdoor movement and the belief in the right to roam which were in no small degree instrumental in the creation of Britain's first National Park.

All trippers and shoppers will find much to divert them in the Peak District. Yet to those prepared to put on a pair of boots, and carry a waterproof and a rucksack, the moors and dales contain more fleeting wonders than can be enjoyed in a lifetime of shop window gazing. As this book goes to press an Act of Parliament, extending the right to roam in the countryside, has opened up new tracts of the Peak District to be discovered.

I

'In Monte vocato Pec'

(Henry of Huntingdon, Historia Anglorum)

Few places in Britain are as evocative and shrouded in myth and mystery as the curious region in the centre of England known as the Peak. Its very name has been redolent of mountain ranges, caves, precipices and torrents – a fastness at the foot of the Pennine range. This historical vision lingered into the 19th century and was finally laid to rest when accurate, contoured cartography provided the true statistics of steepness, altitude and distance. Only then did it become common knowledge that Kinder Scout, the highest feature in the Peak, is neither a mountain nor a peak. Instead it is a plateau some four miles in extent, east to west, whose highest point is 2,088 feet above sea level.

Early English cartographers had neither the means to calculate, nor the interest in knowing, statistics of altitude. The location of towns and rivers was of prime importance. The first maps to depict hills and mountains were those of Christopher Saxton and John Norden in the Elizabethan period and those of John Speed in the reign of James I. Their clusters of uniform mounds, like molehills in a meadow, largely anonymous, served equally for the Peak, Cumbria, Wales, Scotland and Ireland (see page 4).

Few if any climbed mountains or scaled rock faces for curiosity or for pleasure and Charles Cotton's account in *The Wonders of the Peak* (1681) of the rash fool who managed, by a hair's breadth, to scale the scree-strewn face of Mam Tor must be a very rare example of the urge to conquer peaks. Nor were artists and writers drawn to the grandeur of mountain ranges which only interested the painter as the second half of the 18th century approached. Before this the descriptive inspiration of writers dealing with the works of Nature drew largely on the classical poets' portrayals of the landscapes of Greece and Italy. Thus Thomas Hobbes, the philosopher, who was tutor to three Earls of Devonshire at Chatsworth, began his Latin poem, *De Mirabilibus Pecci*, with the following hyperbole:

> *Alpibus Angliacis, ubi Pecci nomine surgit*
> In the English Alps, where the Peak by name does rise

Charles Cotton, the poet of Beresford Hall on the Staffordshire edge of the Peak, wrote in his own *Wonders of the Peak* that 'the scorn'd Peak rivals proud Italy'.

Yet these, and many other early writers on the Peak, had never seen the Alps and had not been on the Grand Tour to Italy. Foreigners, of course, were not so impressed as the exaggerations continued in the writings and assertions of the early Romantics. An Italian, Gabriel Mario Piozzi, the second husband of Mrs Hester Thrale, Dr Johnson's old friend, biographer and correspondent, reacted strongly. In 1787 Mrs Thrale noted in her diary, 'Mr Piozzi liked Matlock, it put him in mind of Savoy, as he said; but the Rocks of Dovedale looked too despicable to people who had just crossed the Alps'.[1] Conversely, another foreigner who settled in England and became a Royal Academician, Philip James de Loutherbourg (1740-1812) painted Dovedale as a sublime Alpine ravine and the River Dove as a mountain torrent (see plate XI).[2]

Nevertheless, despite Defoe's scorn for the Wonders of the Peak and Piozzi's disparaging censure, Englishmen still extolled and exaggerated the grandeur of the Derbyshire hills. Samuel Johnson, lured by Boswell to view the magnificence of the Scottish Highlands, remarked with faint praise that they would have surprised him greatly had he not already seen the Peak![3] Even the inveterate European wanderer Byron could ask his friend, the poet Thomas Moore, if he had ever seen Dovedale and add that 'there are things in Derbyshire as noble as Greece or Switzerland'.[4]

By Byron's time, of course, Romanticism had ennobled Nature's wild creations, unsullied by man. In stark contrast had been Cotton's literal denigration of his native hills as 'ignoble jet', 'impostumous boils' and 'the warts and pudenda of nature'. Ignorant of geology, mineralogy and the earth's structure, pre-romantic writers attributed the chaotic landscapes to the gods, biblical or

Terrā castelli Willi peurel tenueř Gernebern 7 Hundinc.
Hi habueř ibi.ii.car træ ad gld.Tra.e.ii.cař.Ibi nc in
dnio.iiii.cař.7 iii.uilt cu.i.cař.7 viii.ac pti.T.R.E.uat.xl.fot.
m.l.fot.

1 *Domesday Book, 1086. The entry for Peak's Arse and the castle at Castleton.*

In PEAK'S ARSE Arnbern and Hundling held the land of William Peverel's castle. They had 2c. off land taxable. Land for 2 ploughs.
Now in lordship 4 ploughs;
   3 villagers with 1 plough.
   Meadow, 8 acres.
Value before 1066, 40s; now 50s.

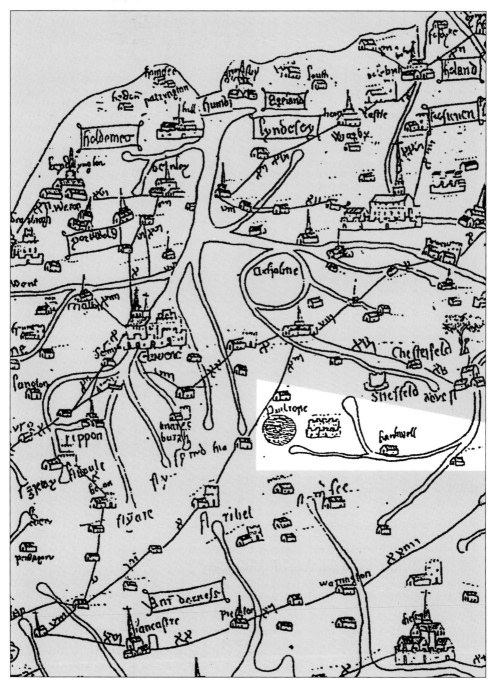

2 *The Gough Map, c.1360. The highlighted detail shows Peak's Arse and the castle. Gough was unable to read their Latin labels, which are* 'puteus pek' *and* 'castrum', *which mean 'Peak's Hole' and 'castle'.*

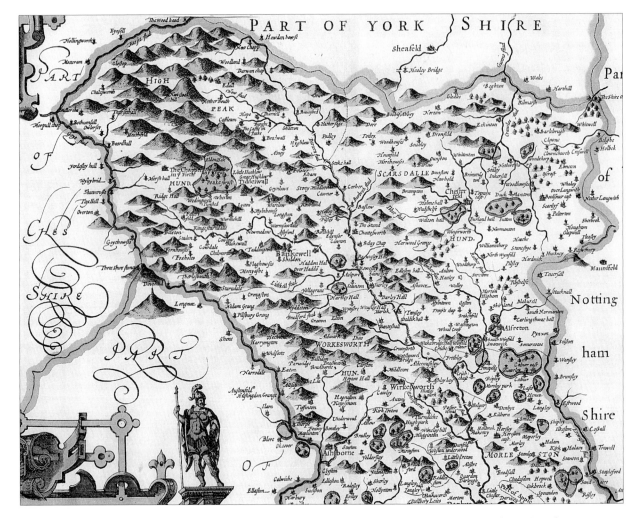

3 *Derbyshire by John Speed, 1610 (later hand-colouring). Detail showing the High Peak and Wirksworth Hundreds.*

classical. Thus Dr Charles Leigh, who, in 1700, published the first scientific study of the Peak and its formation,[5] considered that the mountains, caves and boulder-strewn ravines were the products not of an earthquake but of the Flood. William Stukeley, the first major antiquary to visit the region sought analogies, if not answers, in the Roman poets. His description of the Peak or, as he called it, 'the British Alps', was liberally interspersed with lines from Virgil's *Aeneid* and on sighting Cratcliff Tor, near Winster, he proclaimed it 'a monstrous parcel of gigantick rocks, seemingly pil'd one a top of another as in the wars of the gods' (see plate 44, p.85).[6]

Yet the Peak was never hailed by early writers as Mount Olympus; rather it was to the classicist the site of Hades – the residence of Pluto – or to the Christian the abode of the Devil. The latter association with the Lord of Evil had its origins at least as early as the Anglo-Saxons when Peak Cavern was considered the Devil's Arse whose passage led to Hell. Here, over the centuries, had congregated the criminal elements of society, mythological and real, to sup with the Devil. Traditionally it was the gathering place of gypsies, rogues and vagabonds and here the prince of thieves, Cock Lorel, had his lair. Similarly Poole's Cavern, near Buxton, was the haunt of a legendary robber called Poole. Evil-doers abounded. Cotton tells us of a gang of footpads who threw their hapless victim to perdition down the bottomless pit called Eldon Hole. Writing as late as 1824, Ebenezer Rhodes recounts an atrocious murder in the Winnats Pass.[7] Here, amid the huge rocks of the narrow defile, whose scenery was described by the Reverend Richard Warner[8] as 'hideous' and by Rhodes himself as 'sublimely terrible', five local brigands were said to have brutally killed a young lady and gentleman as they rode, unattended, through the pass. Their bodies were discovered a few days later, hidden in a cave amid the crags. Such were the lurid tales with which the Peakrils, as Cotton called them, regaled the traveller down to the 19th century.

Yet the diabolical tales concerning Peak Cavern stretch back a thousand years or more and were purveyed in literary circles in those highly credulous and superstitious times before and after the Norman Conquest. The Norman historian, Henry of Huntingdon, described the Devil's Arse as the first wonder of England in his *Historia Anglorum*:

> *… quod ventus egreditus de cavernis in monte vocato pec tanto vigore ut vestas rejectas repellat et in altum elevatas procul rejaciat.*

> … because half a gale leaves the caverns in the mountain called Peak with such force that clothing cast in its path is blown aloft and jettisoned a good way off.

One can imagine this exaggerated tale being recounted at feasts and in the great halls of English castles and especially in Peak Castle itself, perched high above the mouth of the cave. The story is repeated in the *Chronicle of the History of England* by Robert of Gloucester, in the anonymous *De Mirabilibus Britanniae* and in the *Polychronicon* of Ranulf Higden.

However, under the pen of Gervase of Tilbury the story of the great cave took a unique turn and received European attention. Gervase, a cosmopolitan scholar and courtier, a kinsman of the Earl of Salisbury, had studied and taught at the University of Bologna. Returning to England he entered Henry II's household and then passed into the service of the Archbishop of Rheims.

After attendance at the court of William II of Sicily he served the Emperor Otto IV as marshal of the Kingdom of Arles. His claim to fame derives from his *Otia Imperialia*, a compendium of history, natural history and geography which he dedicated to Otto IV shortly after 1215. Above all it is a catalogue of marvels, especially the third book in which he deals with Peak Cavern. Having repeated the tale of the vent of wind issuing from the cave Gervase then relates the following story which he claims was told to him by 'a most religious man, Robert, Prior of Kenilworth, who came from that region' (i.e. the Peak).

> In Great Britain there is a castle situated among certain mountains which local folk call Pech … One day, when the noble William Peverel held that invaluable castle with the adjacent lordship, … his swineherd, who was lazy and negligent, lost a very well-bred, pregnant sow from his master's breeding stock. Fearing the severe censure of his lord he pondered whether, by chance, the sow might have entered the famous and, till then, unexplored hole of the Pech.
>
>   … He entered the cave which, at that time, was at peace from the blast and, after a long trek, at length came out of the darkness into a shining place and the freedom of a wide meadow plain. Crossing the broad cultivated acres he met harvesters picking ripe fruit and spied among the bending ears of corn his sow which was now in farrow. Overjoyed at recovering his sow, the incredulous swineherd gathered it and restored it to his herd. A wondrous affair: returning from subterranean harvests to the wintry frosts that persisted in our hemisphere.[9]

This strange story may have been told around the courts of 12th- and 13th-century Europe but it appears to have had scant attention from English chroniclers. William Camden, the celebrated antiquarian and historian, dismissed Gervase's tale, saying he wrote it 'whether for want of knowing truth, or upon a delight he had in fabling'.[10]

Camden had travelled England in search of information for his famed *Britannia* (1586) and almost certainly came to Derbyshire. He roundly disparaged those who continued the myth of the vents of wind issuing from Peak Cavern and was quick to reprove his older contemporary, Roger Ascham, private tutor to Elizabeth I. Ascham held that these 'Aeolian winds' also burst forth from nearby Eldon Hole![11]

So much for hyperbole and fantasy; in conclusion, the meaning and etymology of the term 'Peak' requires some discussion. It has been suggested that the word 'Pec', 'Pech' or 'Peac' may well be of pre-Saxon origin and have had a much more precise topographical association than was later the case. In the first instance, there is a conjecture that 'Pec' could be a monster or dragon of pre-Saxon mythology which eventually became identified with the Devil in Christian times. This could account for Pechesers (Peak's Arse) recorded in

4   *Beeley, 22 August 1694. Watercolour by Jan Siberechts. This gives an early impression of Peak scenery. The Derwent flows towards its confluence with the Wye in the centre of the picture.*

Domesday Book (1086). Secondly, the name 'Pech' could have referred to a particular hill – the one on which Peverel's Castle stood by 1086 – and this would concur with Huntingdon's reference to caves 'in monte vocato Pec' (in the mountain called Peak).[12]

However, most etymologists would now agree that 'Pec' has always been a more general, regional term and would cite its earliest occurrence in the *Tribal Hideage* of the seventh century. Here the expression 'Pecsaetna lond' means the territory of the Peak settlers. This regional term occurs again in the Anglo Saxon Chronicle (924) where Bakewell is said to be in 'Peak lond'. It would seem that from early Saxon times this land was within and around the triangle formed by the settlements of Castleton, Buxton and Bakewell.

By the late Saxon period the administrative unit known as Peak Hundred, within the county of Derbyshire, had developed from this earlier unit of settlement. By 1196 it was referred to as 'Alto Pech' and by the late 15th century as 'Hye Peak'. Speed's map of Derbyshire (1610)[13] labels it as the High Peak and by this time Castleton, which had declined by the 14th century, had been replaced by Bakewell as the administrative capital or hundred town. To the south the wapentake or hundred of Wirksworth, whose name derives from

5   *Edensor. Watercolour sketch by John Constable, 1801. This gives an impression of a typical Peak village before it was rebuilt in the 1830s with a new church in 1869.*

its principal town, was, by the late middle ages, referred to as the Low Peak. Jointly, the two hundreds together have long been known as the Peak.

Finally, more modern divisions based on geological strata have provided two further names which are still in use – the White Peak and the Dark Peak. The former relates to those areas characterised by rocky outcrops, dales and caves of carboniferous limestone. The latter is the upland peat moors and edges of the dark gritstone. The vernacular architecture of the villages and the dry stone walls of the enclosed fields accentuate the contrast, as do the varying trees and plants and the differing nature of the streams and rivers.

The Peak, then, is contained in the north-west confines of Derbyshire. Nevertheless, it has always had affinities with the southern Pennines in Cheshire where the hills fall away to Macclesfield and the Cheshire Plain. More importantly akin to the Derbyshire Peak, both in its landscape and its people, is the area north of Leek in Staffordshire. Known as the Moorlands it has high, jagged gritstone outcrops like Hen Cloud and the Roaches. Gradually it falls away towards Ashbourne in the limestone hills and dales on the banks of the Dove. This river constitutes much of the boundary between Staffordshire and Derbyshire from Dovehead to the Trent Basin.

2

The Hazards of the Ways

Few travelled around England simply for the sake of discovery or for pleasure before the end of the 16th century. Perhaps Thomas Platter, albeit a Swiss Protestant visiting England, was one of the earliest, in 1599, who described his objective as 'mere curiosity to see'.[1] Tourism was in its very infancy and travel was still synonymous with travail, or the labour of journeying. It was a determined man who set out to cover any distance, bearing in mind the state of the roads, or the lack of them, the paucity and poverty of inns beyond cities and towns and the lack of clear maps, signposts and directions.

Although the Gough map of Britain (*c*.1360) outlined the basic network of England's roads and the distances in miles between its principal towns, no road whatsoever is shown in the Peak.[2] Roads were not generally included on maps until county maps were engraved in the Elizabethan and Stuart periods – and then not universally. The absence of accurate road maps was, to a small degree, remedied by chapter XVI of Ralph Holinshed's *Chronicles* published in 1578. Entitled *Of our Innes and Thorowfares,* it provided a table of roads with the mileage between towns and a guide to some of the inns and hostelries along the way. This must have had very limited circulation. More useful were the maps of John Norden (1548-1625?) who engraved a few county maps of the south of England, on which roads were indicated for the first time. Of particular value to the traveller was his *England. An Intended Guyde for English Travailers* which appeared in 1625 and included 40 plates of triangular tables of distances between towns – a form of information still used in modern motoring atlases. One of the plates by Jacob van Langeren covered Derbyshire and this was subsequently published in Thomas Jenner's *Directory for the English Traveller* (1643). It was included in later editions of Camden's *Britannia*, giving distances, but no routes, to the Peakland towns (see plate 9, p.17).

However, the travellers of the late 17th and 18th centuries owed most to John Ogilby (1600-76) who in 1675 printed his *Britannia … a Geographical and Historical Description of the Principal Roads.* This was a landmark in the

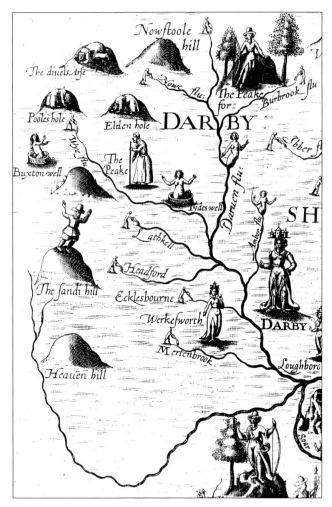

6 *Map to accompany Poly-Olbion by Michael Drayton, 1622 (detail of the Peak).*

accurate description of the country's roads, based on his own journeys on foot. The 100 folio plates, produced at the request of Charles II, depicted the roads as strips and gave brief notes on the route itself and its surrounding countryside. *Britannia* established the statute mile (1593) of 1,760 yards, instead of the old British mile of ten furlongs, went into numerous editions and served the traveller until the end of the 18th century.

Though these various aids might help the intending traveller to reach the Peak, they could direct him to its confines and little further. A ring of towns on the periphery was accessible, even in the vagaries of winter. In the north were Chesterfield and Sheffield; on the west at the foot of the Pennine passes lay Glossop, Stockport, Macclesfield and Leek; whilst from the south lay the entry points of Derby and Ashbourne. Otherwise the roads from London passed by on the east and the west. The London wagons, for instance, penetrated as far as Ashbourne before turning west to Leek and then northwards via Manchester to Carlisle. Ogilby does give one route across the Peak – that from Derby to Manchester, via Buxton, in 1675. This was the way taken by Defoe and the route Stukeley took into Cheshire from Buxton. For much of its distance it followed the Roman road which, in parts, had overlain much earlier tracks. It was an upland route, quite different from the modern A6 on the stretch from Derby to Buxton. This, using the turnpike roads of the 18th and early 19th centuries, penetrated the rising hills along the valleys of the River Derwent and its tributary the River Wye.

Ogilby marks two Low Peak villages as his track descends across the largely unenclosed limestone hills to Derby – Brassington and Hognaston. Along the way he signs the cross-roads to Chelmorton, Flagg and Monyash and the larger one to Ashbourne and Wirksworth. The road negotiates anonymous hills placed across it in the manner of John Speed's mounds. The way would have been difficult, especially in winter and the anxious traveller is assisted by the marking of rocky outcrops. Only one tavern – *Pipers Inn* – is signed between Buxton and Derby but this, probably a farmhouse, cannot be identified today. Apart from Buxton Well none of the other six 'Wonders of the Peak' is shown. In a sense, then, this is not a tourist's road-map so much as a businessman's guide.

Nevertheless, Ogilby's Manchester to Derby road through the High and Low Peak was the only road which Herman Moll considered important enough to include on his map of Derbyshire, first published in 1724. Apart from this and a decorative view of the interior of 'Poole's Hole', the rest of the map differs little from Christopher Saxton's.

Until the second half of the 18th century the Peak was a very difficult area for the stranger on foot or horseback to enter. Very few stretches could accommodate wheeled vehicles and rarely merited the title of road. Some of the peakland tracks had their origins in prehistoric times, such as the Portway and Doctor's Gate. The former carried traffic from the regions of Nottingham and Derby into the highlands over Harthill Moor, by Bakewell to Ashford and then via Wardlow into Edale, or over the passes and out of the Peak through Chapel-en-le-Frith. Doctor's Gate is still clearly discernible north of Hope rising up the Ashop Valley and descending out of the Peak towards Glossop.

The Romans had also laid down roads into the hills to bring out the lead and to provide communications with their baths at Buxton and their forts at Brough and Melandra. Parts of this network were still used and are evident today in the fields, over the moors or under modern tarmac.

These old tracks and roads radiated to a network of minor byways during ensuing centuries. They were worn to the rock surface and channelled through meadow and moorland bog by the countless pack-horse trains which trudged along them and were to do so in some areas of the Peak until the beginning of the 19th century. For this reason, and because many of the tracks followed the high ground above the old fields of the villages, the Peak is rich in fossil tracks.

Early travellers groped their way into and out of the Peak. Asking directions from the folk of these parts was not always advisable. There was a suspicion on their part of strangers and many, especially the womenfolk, travelled little beyond their own hamlets. The broad dialect of the natives was often incomprehensible to strangers. As late as 1805 the artist Edward Dayes, having been given wrong directions at a local farm, or having misunderstood them, had recourse to a pocket compass to find his way out of Dovedale![3]

In September 1622 Edward Browne, later physician to Charles II, travelled from Norwich to see the 'Wonders of the Peak' and reached an inn at Chesterfield. Fortunately he fell in with some Bakewellians and used them as guides on their return journey over East Moor to take him via Chatsworth to Bakewell.[4] Here he spent his first uncomfortable night in the Peak. Celia Fiennes, bravely travelling the same way on horseback in 1698, agreed with Browne's descriptions of 'this strange, mountainous, misty, moorish, rocky wild country' with its 'craggy ascents, the rocky unevenness of the roade, the high peaks and the almost perpendicular descents.' She described her difficulties when she first spied Bakewell from the top of Ball Cross Hill:

> Thence we came to Bankwell [sic] a pretty neate market town, it stands on a hill yet you descend a vast hill to it, which you would think impossible to go down and we was forced to fetch a great compass, and by reason of the steepness and hazards of the Wayes – if you take a wrong Way there is no passing – you are forced to have Guides as in all parts of Darbyshire, and unless it be a few that use to be guides the common people know not above 2 or 3 mile from their home, but they of the country will climbe up and down with their horses those steep precipices … but indeed all Darbyshire is but a world of peaked hills which from some of the highest you discover the rest like steeples or tops of hills as thick as can be, and tho' they appear so close yet the steepness down and up takes up the time that you go it, as if so many miles, and were the ground measur'd would be in length as much as miles on a plane.[5]

Celia's contemporary, the actor, dramatist and poet laureate, Colley Cibber, had struggled to Chatsworth to see the 'Palace of the Peak' and the sculptures his father, Caius Gabriel Cibber, had wrought there. On his departure he took his leave of the Duke of Devonshire with typical feeling and theatricality:

> My Lord, I thought I should have broken my neck to get here; I am sure I shall break my heart to get away.[6]

William Stukeley, his neck intact, felt no such heartache as he finally departed the Peak from Buxton by way of the Goyt Valley, 'the very centre of desolation'. 'At length,' he says, 'we entered the pleasant country of Cheshire, as into a new world; wondering that people are found who can content themselves with the poverty and horror of the Peak, so near riches and delight.'[7]

Although strangers found the ways hazardous and had recourse to local guides, there were those who needed to find their way about the hills to earn their living. Such were the leadminers who could ride well over the terrain and kept strings of pack horses to transport lead ore to the smelters. Lead merchants too, living in middling houses in Wirksworth, Buxton, Castleton and Bakewell, used the same means to carry the pigs of lead to surrounding towns or, via Chesterfield, to the ports of Bawtry and Hull. Considerable numbers of

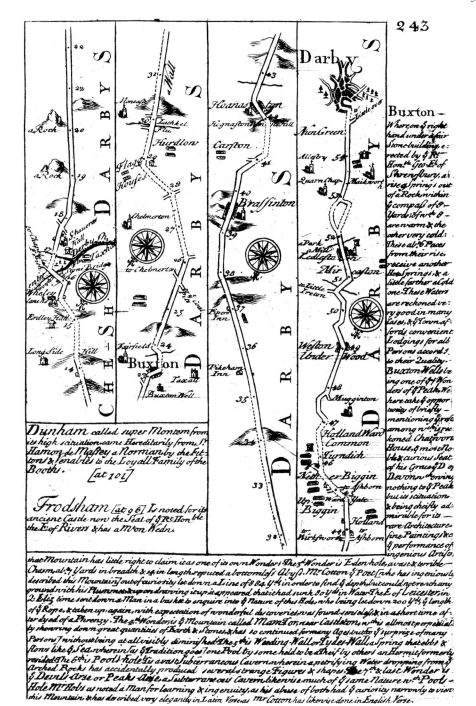

7 *Peak road maps (Buxton to Derby) by Owen and Bowen, after John Ogilby. issued in*
Britannia Depicta, c.1700. A description of the 'Wonders of the Peak' has been added.

8 *Peak guidestone reading 'Chesterfiel Rude',*
1699, between Bakewell and Edensor.

horses were kept in the Peak for this traffic. In 1549, for instance, 132 pack horses were employed to bring 64 loads of ore from Bonsall Dale to Sir George Vernon's smelter at Haddon.[8]

The trackways of the Pennines were pounded by strings of horses with loaded panniers conducted by jaggers or chapmen. They carried varying loads; blocks of salt from Cheshire, scythes and sickles made in the Hallamshire villages of the High Peak and Scarsdale hundreds; sacks of lime from the kilns, even small millstones were carried by packhorses.[9] Their belled harness announced their coming across mist-bound moors and encouraged many a lonely or lost traveller to tag on behind. Jags, or droves of pack-horses, continued to be employed in some parts until the beginning of the 19th century. Farey writing in 1811 tells us they were still to be seen 'about Buxton, Hathersage and the mountainous parts'.

The ways were further churned and rutted by other animals such as shoed and yoked oxen which were used into the 18th century to haul blocks of stone and millstones from the gritstone edges and quarries. Such teams were used to pull sleds and drugs with stone from Bakewell Edge for the building of the 4th Earl (later 1st Duke) of Devonshire's Chatsworth in the late 17th century.[10] Add to this traffic that of the drovers herding their sheep and cattle to the markets as far afield as Cheshire, Lincolnshire and the Midlands as well as the gypsies and horse dealers driving their animals to the fairs.

Thus on the softer ground the tracks became holloways and trenchways and on the rocky surfaces smooth and treacherously slippery passages. No carriages could negotiate such routes and carts had a very limited range beyond farms and villages. They could ford the rivers in the dry season, as could pack-horse trains, but when the snows of the Peak melted the rivers, especially the Derwent, could only be crossed by a few stone bridges. Defoe described the Derwent as 'a fury of a River' and 'a frightful creature when the hills load her current with water'.[11]

Standard signposts were non-existent. Wooden markers across the moors no longer exist though some stone waymarkers still survive, none of which bears any information. To assist the increase in trade and travel along remote highways and byways Parliament, in 1697, authorised JPs to erect guideposts or stoops at crossroads removed from towns and villages. The JPs acted promptly and Celia Fiennes recorded how the new crossroad signs aided her journey. They were not in place when she travelled through the Peak. The Derbyshire JPs did not act until 1709 when they instructed the overseers of the highways that

> For the better convenience of travelling, where two or more cross Highways meet in your said Liberty, you are required forthwith … to erect or fix … in the most convenient place, where such ways join, a Stone or Post with an inscription thereon in large letters containing the Name of the next Market Town to which each of the said joining Highways leads.

Many of these stout, four-sided gritstone posts survive in and around the Peak, and especially in the old moorland tracks to Sheffield and Chesterfield. They stand tall to give their boldly incised directions above the snow-lines, together with a date for 1709 or for subsequent years.[12]

Perhaps the anxieties aroused in the stranger as he entered the Peak on horseback for the first time are best portrayed in the 1676 edition of the *Compleat Angler*. The kindly squire of Beresford Hall, Charles Cotton (Piscator), has met a fellow angling enthusiast (Viator) and invites him to enjoy the hospitality of his house and fishing lodge in Dovedale. The traveller, from Essex, on his way to Lancashire, had never ridden over such terrain.

PISC.   … and therefore prepare yourself to be a little frightened.

VIAT.   Sir, I see you would fortify me, that I should not shame myself: but I dare follow where you please to lead me; and I see no danger yet; for the descent, methinks, is thus far green, even, and easy.

PISC.   You will like to worse presently, when you come to the brow of the hill; and now we are there, what think you?

VIAT.   What do I think? Why I think it is the strangest place that, ever sure, men and horses went down; and that, if there be any safety at all, the safest way is to alight.

PISC.   I think so too for you, who are mounted upon a beast not acquainted with these slippery stones; and though I frequently ride down, I will alight too to bear you company, and to lead you the way; and, if you please, my man shall lead your horse.

VIAT.   Marry, Sir, and thank you too: for I am afraid I shall have enough to do to look to myself; and, with my horse in my hand should be in a double fear, both of breaking my neck, and my horse's falling on me; for it is as steep as a penthouse.

PISC.   To look down from hence it appears so, I confess; but the path winds and turns, and will not be found so troublesome.

VIAT.   Would I were well down though! Hoist thee! There's one fair 'scape! I think I were best lay my heels in my neck, and tumble down.

PISC.   If you think your heels will defend your neck, that is the way to be soon at the bottom; but give me your hand at this broad stone, and then the worst is past.

VIAT.   I thank you, Sir, I am now past it, I can go myself. What's here the sign of a bridge? Do you use to travel with wheelbarrows in this country?

PISC.   Not that I ever saw, Sir. Why do you ask that question?

VIAT.   Because this bridge certainly was made for nothing else; why a mouse can hardly go over it: 'tis not two fingers broad.[13]

Charles Cotton's descriptions of the Peak in winter, the landscape that Defoe called 'a howling wilderness', are particularly graphic. *A Journey into the Peak* which he dedicated to his cousin, Sir Aston Cockayne of Ashbourne, describes the rigours endured by man and beast as do his lines *To my dear and most worthy Friend Mr Isaac Walton*:

> Whilst in this cold and blust'ring Clime
> Where bleak winds howl and Tempests roar,
> We pass away the roughest time
> Has been of many years before
>
> Whilst from the most tempestuous Nooks
> The chillest Blasts our peace invade,
> And by great Rains our smallest Brooks
> Are almost navigable made;
>
> Whilst all the ills are so improv'd
> Of this dead quarter of the year,
> That even you, so much belov'd,
> We would not now wish with us here;
>
> In this estate, I say, it is
> Some comfort to us to suppose,
> That in a better Clime than this
> You our dear Friend have more repose;
>
> And some delight to me the while,
> Though nature now does weep in Rain,
> To think that I have seen her smile,
> And haply may I do again.
>
> If the all-ruling Power please
> We live to see another *May*,
> We'll recompence an Age of these
> Foul days in one fine fishing day:[14]

Cotton looked forward to May, though winter did not always end there. Spring was often minimal and snow sometimes fell in June. Hibernation was an accepted way of life, often for a third of the year. The aristocracy and gentry could, of course, break out and stay at one of their other seats further south or combine business with pleasure and reside for a spell in London. Sir George Vernon of Haddon Hall, for instance, left Haddon for London on 26 January

DARBYSHIRE	Darby	Ashborne	Wirkesworth	Alfreton	Chesterfield	Tiddeswell	Castle in Peak	Chaple in Firth	Buxton	Banckewell	Hereston Cas.	Chattsworth	Hartley Hall	Chaberinÿ For.	Norbury	Newton Soncy	Croxall	Cubley	Harrington	Clowne Church	Eckington	Darley	Swarston	Somershall	Codnor Cas.	Boulsouer Cas.
Edall N.W.	26	20	19	20	15	6	3	5	8	10	24	11	13	5	22	30	35	24	14	18	15	14	30	26		18
Boulsouer Ca.NE	16	17	12	7	4	16	17	21	19	12	13	10	12	18	20	22	28	21	17	3	5	10	19	23	9	
Codnor Ca. NE	8	12	7	3	10	18	20	22	20	13	4	12	11	20	14	13	20	14	15	12	13	10	10	16	132	
Somershall S.W.	10	6	11	16	21	19	23	22	18	16	12	17	14	21	4	8	10	2	12	25	25	15	11	120		
Swarston S.E	4	12	12	13	10	24	27	28	25	20	7	20	17	20	12	5	10	10	18	22	13	17	122			
Darley N.W.	13	9	5	7	7	8	11	13	11	4	10	3	2	10	12	17	23	13	7	12	11	98				
Eckington N.	20	20	15	11	5	14	14	18	18	12	17	10	12	16	22	25	32	23	17	3	118					
Clown Church N.W.	19	20	15	10	0	17	17	21	20	14	15	12	14	16	23	25	31	24	19	121						
Harrington N.W.	15	7	8	13	13	8	11	10	7	6	14	8	5	9	8	17	21	11	120							
Cubley W.	9	4	9	14	19	18	22	21	18	15	10	16	23	27	3	7	11	111								
Croxall S.W.	12	15	18	21	28	29	32	32	26	25	16	26	23	50	13	7	120									
Newton Soncy SW	6	10	12	15	21	24	27	27	24	20	9	20	17	26	10	111										
Norbury W.	10	4	8	14	18	16	19	18	15	13	11	14	11	17	113											
Chaberinÿ Fo.NW	22	16	15	17	14	2	3	3	4	7	20	8	9	130												
Hartley Hall N.W.	14	8	6	9	8	7	10	12	0	3	12	3	119													
Chattesworth NW	16	11	8	9	6	6	8	11	9	3	13	120														
Horeston Ca.NE	4	9	6	6	12	19	21	23	20	14	106															
Banckewell N.W.	16	10	8	11	9	5	8	9	7	121																
Buxton N.W.	22	14	14	18	16	4	6	3	130																	
Chaple in Firth NW	24	17	17	20	17	5	5	131																		
Castle in Peak NW	24	17	16	18	13	4	130																			
Tiddeswell NW	21	14	13	16	12	127																				
Chesterfield N.	16	15	10	7	117																					
Alfreton N.	9	11	6	108																						
Wirkesworth NW	8	5	112																							
Ashborne N.W.	8	111																								

DERBYSHIRE sends IV Members to Parliament, has IX Market Towns, and 106 Parishes; is divided into 6 Hundreds, containing about 1920000 Acres of Ground, 56000 Houses, and near 283000 Inhabitants, being in Circumference 200 Miles.

The Arms of Derby

9 *Chart of mileage between towns and villages in Derbyshire. Magna Britannia, vol. I, 1720.*

1553 and returned on the 18th of the following month. He took with him his lawyer, a servant and a string of horses including at least a spare one for himself and a sumpter or pack horse. He travelled the usual way out of the Peak when bound for the capital and slept that night in Derby; crossing the Trent at Wilne Ferry he spent the second night in Leicester. The next night's stay was at Northampton and the fourth at Dunstable. Thus he reached London in five days and spent his time there prosecuting a suit in Star Chamber and, when not so engaged, shopping for himself and his family in Cheapside.[15]

The journey was naturally faster in summer. In August 1557, Sir George Vernon's near neighbour, Lady Elizabeth Cavendish (Bess of Hardwick), travelled from newly rising Chatsworth House to London by horse-litter, with three wagons for her luggage and accompanied by over 40 attendants on nags. She took the same route out of the Peak, resting at Loughborough, Northampton and St Albans, a journey of three nights and four days.[16]

The chance of finding a reasonable inn increased the nearer the traveller approached London. In the Peak the hostelries were generally abysmal. When Edward Browne reached Bakewell he declared his horse was better accommodated in the stable than he was in the inn. Celia Fiennes fared no better in Buxton, even in the most prestigious establishment in the town:

> The house thats call'd Buxton Hall which belongs to the Duke of Devonshire its where the warme Bath is and Well, its the largest house in the place tho' not very good, they are all entertaining houses and its by way of an Ordinary, so much a piece for your dinners and suppers and so much for our Servants besides; all your ale and wine is to be paid besides, the beer they allow at the meales is so bad that very little can be dranke, you pay not for your bed room and truely the other is so unreasonable a price and the Lodgings so bad, 2 beds in a room some 3 beds and some 4 in one roome, so that if you have not Company enough of your own to fill a room they will be ready to put others into the same chamber, and sometymes they are so crowded that three must lye in a bed; few people stay above two or three nights its so inconvenient: we staid two nights by reason one of our Company was ill but it was sore against our wills, for there is no peace nor quiet with one Company and another going into the Bath or coming out; that makes so many strive to be in this house because the Bath is in it.[17]

3

The Peakrils

Quite apart from the indignities of accommodation which Celia Fiennes endured at Buxton Hall, the foul beer was unforgivable in the Peak. Derbyshire ale was nationally celebrated, especially in Derby itself, which was hailed as a brewing centre for centuries before Burton-on-Trent supplanted it. The excellent water and local barley contributed to its reputation and it was brewed with equal flavour and potency throughout the Peak. It was an early tourist attraction in its own right. Cotton recommended that made just across the River Dove in the Staffordshire Moorlands. Defoe, who came to the bath at Buxton to ease his ailments,[1] found the local ale equally to his liking and applauded the qualities of northern beer in general, and that of Yorkshire above all.

Everyone drank ale and beer, men and women, at meals or not. Ale houses abounded in towns and villages in Derbyshire especially in the Peak where they were frequented by lead miners, limestone burners and the industrial workers of the hills long before the Industrial Revolution. The county's JPs of the early 17th century were under pressure from growing Puritan indignation among the authorities to reduce the large number of ale houses and thus the amount of drunkenness and associated crime. The JPs argued that such action would promote dangerous riots, especially among the volatile lead miners. Defoe, again, remarked how the lead miner, to whom he and his friend gave money, promptly headed into Brassington to spend it on 'pale Derby'. Women drank hard too, and matched their menfolk in their lurid language and lewd behaviour. James Plumptre, a fellow of Clare Hall, had barely entered Derbyshire to begin his tour of the Peak in August 1793 when he was shocked by the following encounter:

> … We met a party of Drunken women from Harvest-work. No shameless rout of Bacchalian women ever behaved with more indecency than did these; swearing and using every indecent term they could think of. Alas! that there should be any of a sex formed for modesty and grace, so far forgot themselves, and riot thus shameless with bacchanalian revel in the broad face of day'.[2]

These are certainly not the sober, even elegant, agricultural workers portrayed in the rural idylls of that time by Stubbs and his fellow artists. These women may well have been harvesting the ingredients of next year's Derby ale which would, again, be part of the harvest boons!

Apparently the brew had always been thick and strong and the praise of such ale was sung as early as the 13th century when Henry of Avranches penned these cautionary Latin hexameters:

> Nescio quod stygia monstrum conforme paludi,
> Cervisiam plerique vocant: nil spissius illa
> Dum bibitur, nil clarius est dum mingitur, unde
> Constat, quod multas faeces in ventre relinquit.
>
> Of this strange drinke, so like to Stygian lake,
> (Most tearme it Ale) I wot not what to make:
> Folke drinke it thicke, and piss it passing thin,
> Much dregges therefore must needs remaine within.[3]

Camden, who quotes this witticism, goes on to agree with Turnebus 'that most learned Frenchman who maketh no doubt, but that men using to drink heereof [i.e. ale], if they could avoid surfeiting, would live longer than those that drinke wine: and that from hence it is, that many of us drinking Ale live an hundred yeeres.'[4]

It would seem that some Peakrils enjoyed such longevity; whether from the ale or the air, or whatever, is uncertain (see plate 60, p.121). Parish registers record interesting examples of old age but how much more than those of gentler regions is not known. The Reverend Richard Warner, who toured the Peak about 1800, was confronted by old women as he was about to enter Poole's Cavern, a mile from Buxton. He describes them as follows:

[Poole's Cavern] belongs to the Duke of Devonshire, and is kindly granted by him to nine old women, resembling the Muses indeed in number, but hardly approaching to the female race in any thing else; dried with age and as rugged as the rocks amongst which they dwell. But though living like the Troglodytes of old, in caverns of the earth (for their dwellings are not of an higher order) and exposed to the variations of the seasons and ragings of the storm, they exhibit a longevity unknown to the population of the more civilised parts of the kingdom. One of the old ladies (for there were ten of them) … died last year at the age of ninety-two. Nor was this considered as a rare instance of protracted life.[5]

Against this must be set the health hazards of living and working among the mineral deposits in the limestone (see plate 1). The lead miners, their families and their livestock frequently suffered and died from lead poisoning by handling the ore, inhaling the smelter's fumes and polluting the springs and the pastures with waste (see plare 13 p.20). The symptoms were not difficult to see. Celia Fiennes found the miners 'generally look very pale and yellow'[6] whilst Defoe described a Brassington miner as being 'as lean as a skeleton, pale as a dead corpse, his hair and beard a deep black, his flesh lank and ... something of the colour of the lead itself.'[7] Further details of the afflictions of the lead miners are given by Defoe's contemporary, the local historian William Woolley:

> There is a corrosive sulphur in the ore, which flies up into the smelting – which occasions a disease among the smelters called the 'belland' known by difficulty of breathing, loss of appetite, yellowness of complexion, a dry cough and hoarseness, attended with swelling limbs and joints which are rendered useless; which is taken by working in the lead mines or the smell of the fumes of the ore in smelting. This distemper falls upon the horses and cows that eat grass or drink water at the mill. The other disease which is incident to them is called the 'byon'; the first is mostly incurable.[8]

Whether greater care was taken as the 19th century progressed or whether better treatments were available to these rough folk is difficult to detect. In 1793, however, James Plumptre was conducted down the Odin Mine near Castleton and saw various processes to produce lead employed by the miners with the assistance of their womenfolk. He portrays one of the miners as 'one of the stoutest men I ever saw; the very picture of health, well proportioned, and his muscles seemed of Herculean strength. It does not appear from what we saw, that working in the mines is, as has been said, prejudicial to the health of either man or woman.'[9]

However, some women living in the spring-line villages of the limestone uplands did suffer from a disfiguring ailment known as goitre, or more commonly as 'Derbyshire neck' on account of the pronounced swelling that occurred about the throat. This was a disorder of the thyroid induced by deposits in the local spring water and was still in evidence until the beginning of the 20th century.

Despite these health hazards and the great fortitude necessary to live in

10 *A medieval leadminer. Carved stone in St Mary's Church, Wirksworth.*

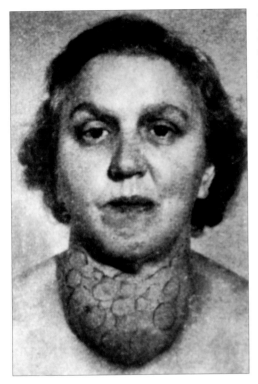

11 *A sufferer from multinodular goitre.*

the High and Low Peak, both these hundreds had higher populations, until the 18th century, than those in the south of the county. At the time of the Civil War, for instance, the population of the County has been estimated at 68,000, including 4,000 who lived in the largest town of Derby.[10] Yet a concentration of 70 per cent of this figure dwelt in the three northern hundreds of High and Low Peak and Scarsdale.

Lead mining was the principal reason for inflating the population. The free miners of the Peak included a good number of poor folk who came into the area as prospectors. In the 17th century it is reckoned that there were 4,000 miners at work with a further 21,000 dependent on the industry – that is, more than a third of the county's population.[11] Other industries also existed in the Peak – limestone burning and coal mining near Buxton, marble quarrying, cutting and polishing at Ashford and later at Bakewell, millstone and grindstone cutting along the gritstone edges from Baslow to Hathersage (see plate 16, p.30). Many employed in these industries often had dual or triple occupations and worked in farming, carrying and other trades.

Add to these people the groups of beggars who frequented the tourist centres of Buxton and Castleton and the sites of the various Wonders of the Peak. Gypsies were also mendicants who gathered annually to sell their dogs and horses. The following *Gipsies' Song* which was set to music in 1673 goes back much further in time.

> From the famous peak of Darby
> and the Devil's A ---- that's hard by;
> Where we yearly make our musters;
> There the Gypsies throng in clusters.
> Be not frighted with our fashion,
> Though we seem a tatter'd nation;
> We account our Raggs our Riches,

So our tricks exceed our stitches;
Give us Bacon, Rinds of Walnuts,
Shells of Cockels and of Small Nuts:
Ribonds, Bells, and Saffron Linnin;
And all the World is ours to win in.[12]

Derbyshire has long had a reputation for the coarse manners of its inhabitants, especially in the north of the county. The traveller from the south of England often found their bearing and dress somewhat daunting – miners' wives, for instance, wore trousers, caps and chewed tobacco and smoked clay pipes – whilst the dialect of Peakrils might well have been the language of another country. A wry, sarcastic humour, even wit, often lay behind the information given to the unwary visitor. Charles Cotton knew them well and was wise to their rough banter and jocular ways. He portrays them with good humour and appropriate verse in his *Wonders of the Peak*. Defoe, conversely, could neither appreciate the humour and poetry of Cotton nor the strange ways of the Peak dwellers. The latter he described as 'a rude, boorish kind of people'. However even he, it seems, was taken in by their stories. He tells us, for instance, that the Duke of Devonshire, whilst constructing the gardens at Chatsworth, 'removed and perfectly carried away a great mountain' … 'to make a clear vista or prospect beyond into the flat country, towards Hardwick, another seat of the same

12 *The Odin Lead Mine and Mam Tor, Castleton. Watercolour by John Webber, 1789.*

owner …'[13] The Duke, in fact, removed a slope to make way for a canal and Hardwick never came into the view or the reckoning.

The inhabitants of the Peak gave directions to travellers in what Cotton called 'peakish miles' – no doubt a variable unit of measurement! Indeed, the word 'peakish', or 'peaky', though almost archaic today, was long used to denote uncouthness or stupidity and, latterly, to describe a pale or sickly countenance. In this latter sense 'peaky' or 'peeky' is occasionally used in the north of England today and may derive from the grim conditions in which the Peakrils lived.

Many dwelt, as they worked, in, or below, the ground. They were the last cave dwellers in England. Tourists were amazed and horrified to find humans living like animals in dens. The poorer lead miners lived in old workings or caves in the limestone. Defoe's is the best and most moving description of such a lead miner's dwelling near Brassington when he and his fellow travellers were invited inside. Defoe engaged the lead miner's wife as follows:

> … says I, good wife, why, where do you live. Here, sir, says she, and points to the hole in the rock. Here! says I; and do all these children live here too? Yes, sir, says she, they were all born here. Pray how long have you dwelt there then? said I. My husband was born here, said she, and his father before him. Will you give me leave, says one of our company, as curious as I was, to come in and see your house, dame? If you please, sir, says she, but 'tis not a place fit for such as you are to come into, calling him, your worship, forsooth; but that by the by. I mention it, to show that the good woman did not want manners, though she lived in a den like a wild body.
>
> However, we alighted and went in. There was a large hollow cave, which the poor people by two curtains hanged cross, had parted into three rooms. On one side was the chimney, and the man, or perhaps his father, being miners, had found means to work a shaft or funnel through the rock to carry the smoke out at the top … The habitation was poor, 'tis true, but things within did not look so like misery as I expected. Every thing was clean and neat, though mean and ordinary. There were shelves with earthen ware, and some pewter and brass. There was, which I observed in particular, a whole flitch or side of bacon hanging up in the chimney, and by it a good piece of another. There was a sow and pigs running about at the door, and a little lean cow feeding upon a green place just before the door, and the little enclosed piece of ground I mentioned, was growing with good barley; it being then near harvest.[14]

Peak Cavern and Poole's Cave had been dwellings since earliest times (see plate 17, p.33); prehistoric animal remains have been found in the former and its known human occupancy can be traced historically to the 16th and 17th centuries (see plate 19, p.37). The latter had probably been used by Neolithic man, was certainly an abode, and possibly a workshop, in Romano-British times and was finally used as a robber's den, according to tradition, by one Poole in the 14th or 15th centuries. Continuous habitation took place in Peak

13 *Lead Smelting House in Middleton Dale by Francis Chantrey, ARA, 1818. Engraved by W.B. Cooke.*

Cavern until about 1845. The cave dwellers there lived 'in poor little houses built of stone or clay … and thatched like little styes'.[15] These troglodytes were employed in twine and rope making from hemp – an industry that finally ended in 1969 – and most tourist accounts from the 17th century described the wheels, pulleys and gallows-like equipment essential to the tasks.

Living under rocky overhangs also provided shelter for the poor. Celia Fiennes described such a feature at Stanedge on her way from Chesterfield to Chatsworth. Cottages exist there to this day, as they do under the base of the cliffs near Stoney Middleton (as illustrated in plate 84, p.160). These last are the descendants of the hovels of the lime burners of Calver and Middleton Dale whose furnaces lit up the long gorge at night and in the day the smoke and the dust blanched the hanging vegetation.

It was around Buxton, however, from Axe Edge and Fairfield to Grin Low, above Poole's Cavern, that the lime burners had produced the most grotesque hovels, more akin to ant hills, within their own lime kilns and spoil heaps (see plate 15, p.29). Both Jewitt and Rhodes drew attention to these singular communities, the latter in the following words:

It is hardly possible to conceive a prospect more cheerless and forbidding than the hills around Buxton present. They had now lost the grandeur which darkness had thrown over them the preceding evening, and their unpleasant detail was obtruded on the eye. With the exception of one or two small plantations of Scotch fir and larch, and a few meadows separated from each other by angular stone fences, that are carried along the sides of the hills with a tiresome monotony, scarcely any thing but sterility is to be seen. From Fairfield the lime hills beyond Buxton have a curious and delusive effect; they appear like an assemblage of tents, placed on a steep acclivity, in regular stages one above another, and they strangely disfigure the scene: as a feature in landscape, they are very unpleasant, yet they are not the least extraordinary places in the vicinity of Buxton. Many of them have been excavated, and they now form the habitations of human beings. Some of them are divided into several apartments, and one aperture serves to carry off the smoke from the whole. The roofs of these humble dwellings are partially covered with turf and heath, and not unfrequently a cow or an ass takes a station near the chimney, on the top of the hut, amongst tufts of fern and thistles, which together produce a very singular and sometimes a pleasing effect. One conical hill that I observed, contains within it five or six different habitations, and to the whole there appears but one or two chimneys: by what contrivance these are made to answer the common purposes of so many families, I have not been informed.[16]

The incredulous Frenchman, Faujas de St Fond, likened the two hundred or so inhabitants to rabbits in a warren, which was jokingly alluded to as a 'burrow' without a corporation![17] The ten old ladies who, as we have seen, acted as guards and guides at Poole's Cavern lived in these holes and, if longevity is a product of contentment, they were 'probably ... no less happy than the inhabitants of the finest houses in Buxton, over whom they command a superior view.'[18]

Most Peakrils lived in the better comfort of their small towns and hamlets. Here their low-level vernacular cottages shambled along the narrow unpaved streets. There was no great tradition of timber framed housing; the woodland, as in the tree-less Peak Forest had been cut for smelting lead, burning lime or propping mines. Traces of cruck-framed structures survive in Bakewell, Wirksworth and Castleton but there is little evidence of box-framed timber houses. There was such an abundance of easily obtainable stone that it was used to build the settlements and enclose the fields from earliest times in the White and the Dark Peak. Much building, especially for the poorer folk, was largely dry-stone built and therefore low. Two storeys were seldom exceeded except in manor houses and these were of modest proportions.

As late as 1801 the Duke of Devonshire's estate village of Edensor was depicted in sketches by John Constable as one of low stone cottages, covered in straw thatch, huddling down the street to its insignificant low church (see plate 5, p.8).[19] Gritstone slates were used on the more important buildings and local lead on the roofs of the largest houses and churches.

14 *Sketch of Cave Dale, Castleton by Sir James Thornhill, c.1699. Limestone burners are operating a primitive kiln.*

Churches, whose steeples and bells were so often a guide to the traveller in the flatter parts of England, were few, small and largely invisible among the hills and dales of the Peak. Apart from Bakewell, Wirksworth and Ashbourne, the principal and largest parishes, together with the fine 14th-century 'cathedral of the Peak' at Tideswell, the rest were largely insignificant. However, they did serve as points of interest to the travelling antiquary in the 17th and 18th centuries.

Monasticism never took root in the Peak. One might have expected an order like the Cistercians to have sought its solitude, but the lack of communications made the area too uncivilised a backwater and the bleak climate was no encouragement to communal living. Hence the tradition of hospitality to the wayfarer which vanished generally at the Dissolution had never been a feature of the Peak or of Derbyshire as a whole. Between the two 12th-century premonstratensian houses of Beauchief in the very north of the county and Dale Abbey, near Derby, monasticism was only represented by some fifty granges, the property of various religious houses, many of which operate as farms today.

The monastic granges must have been among the most prosperous agricultural units in this largely barren region. The medieval monks had specialised in sheep farming on the carboniferous limestone uplands and had grazed some cattle in the bottoms of the dales. Some granges, like Meadow Place, south of Over Haddon had been involved in arable farming and other granges at lower altitudes probably increased their ploughlands when they became established farms after the Reformation. Indeed monasticism must have played an important part in establishing the uplands as sheep, cattle and arable areas in that order. The two great houses of Haddon Hall and Chatsworth made a similar contribution and increased their prosperity with the profits from lead mines and, in Chatsworth's case, coal pits. As Piscator informed his amazed friend Viator, 'These hills, though high bleak and craggy, breed and feed good beef and mutton above ground and afford good store of lead within.' [20]

Grain crops were grown in the less shaded valleys but struggled on the slopes as the soil cover thinned. The produce was often meagre from oats which were the chief cereal used for porridge and oat cakes and, of course, to feed the numerous horses. Some barley was grown, which found its way to the maltsters and a little wheat to make coarse bread. Neither crop was of high quality before the 18th century and Peak wheat in the 16th century was regarded as the worst type, having, according to Fitzherbert, 'a red eare ... and oftymes it is flyntered, that is to say, small corne, wrynkeled and dryed'. The poor of the Peak relied on such doubtful crops and obtained some of their milk, as Fitzherbert also states, by milking their ewes. [21]

The villages of the region were not usually like the nucleated villages with their surrounding three or four fields, typical of the Midland plain and some parts of South Derbyshire. Strip farming with ridge and furrow ploughlands can be found in parts of the Peak but there is much debate about the standardisation of farming practices at different periods. [22] Some villages like Chatsworth and Nether Haddon had vanished by the 15th century, emparked by the growing estates of the wealthy. [23] A few may have succumbed after the Black Death (1348) whilst others struggled to survive with tiny populations, swelled by lead-mining families, and an agricultural economy based on a one- or two-field system.

The agricultural economy in general progressed over the ensuing centuries following the increase of enclosures and the farming improvements of the 18th century. Certainly in the Peak the gentry and aristocracy followed the national trend. Arthur Young, the renowned agricultural commentator, praised such Derbyshire landowners following his visit to the Peak in 1771. He was pleasantly surprised by what he saw.

From Chatsworth to Tideswell the country is nineteenths of it enclosed and cultivated; this surprized me, as I expected to find the chief part of the Peak waste land; but such great improvements have been carried on in this country, that even sheep walks too rocky to plough, let at 5s an acre … Around Tideswell for many miles, has been worked as great improvements as in any part of England: all this country was a black ling but a few years ago, and common land. It is now inclosed by act of parliament. As this improvement is very curious, and practised I believe in no other country, I was particular in my enquiries, being very desirous to know the means of effecting such profitable undertakings. … The first work was the inclosure, which was done at the landlord's expence, but no more than the ring fence; the subdivisions were made by the tenants; it is all done by dry walling; the stones taken out of pits … It lasts 20 years before any repairs are necessary …

These improvements are also carried on all the way to Castleton, and around that town. In the road from Tideswell by Elden Hole are very many large closes of good grass gained … from the moors; all of which are full of very large herds of cows fattening … and it is very remarkable that the grass is equally good to the tops of the highest mountains. At the summit of Mam Tor, which is the highest mountain in Derbyshire, is an excellent pasture … All these hills have been improved in the manner above mentioned with lime alone.[24]

By the beginning of the 19th century the landscape of the Peak had changed for ever as farming in the uplands began to prosper. This made travellers notice bad farming practices all the more. The poet Wordsworth, riding into the Peak from Manchester on Guy Fawkes's Day, 1830, remarked upon 'a starveling field or two of corn' at Peak Forest and 'fields of corn in the sheaf'.[25]

15   *Limestone burner's or leadworker's cottage. Watercolour, early 19th-century.*

16 *Millstone quarry (near Grindleford). Pen and wash sketch by John Constable, 1801.*

Apparently this was not an uncommon sight as autumn passed into winter. John Farey observed almost 20 years earlier:

> Frequent mention has been made, of Corn remaining out in the Fields of the High Peak at Christmas, indeed I saw myself, Oats standing in the Shock, and covered by Snow, on the 25th November, 1808, between Buxton and Hartington; but it occurred to me, from the great number of fields which had long been cleared in similar situations, that it must have been the effect of neglect and mismanagement on the part of the Farmer; and such was the opinion, on this and every similar instance, which became the subject of remark, in the many enquiries which I made on this subject, except in particularly late and wet seasons, like that of 1799, when Corn here is much damaged, as indeed it is in more favoured situations.[26]

4

The Wonder of Wonders

Unlike other counties Derbyshire was not blessed with an early historian. Topographers and antiquaries were not drawn to write about it. The early Tudor topographer, John Leland, barely visited or wrote on the county,[1] whilst Philip Kinder, a native of the Peak, compiled a bizarre manuscript entitled *The Historie of Derbyshire* (c.1663) which tells us almost nothing.[2] The first printed historical observations on the county, which served as a model for most subsequent attempts, were by William Camden, Clarenceux King of Arms. Writing in Latin, he was also the first to attempt to list the Wonders of the Peak:

> Miro alto Pecco tria sunt, barathrum, specus, antrum;
> Commoda tot, plumbum, gramen, ovile pecus.
> Tota speciosa simul sunt, Castrum, Balnea, Chatsworth;
> Plura sed occurrunt qua spetiosa minus.[3]

(In the High Peak are three wonders, a chasm, a cavern and a grotto. There are as many bounties of lead, pasture and sheep folds. As many again are the beauties, a castle, a bath and Chatsworth. More numerous still are the lesser splendours that abound.)

However, Camden's verse lists five – Eldon Hole, Peak Cavern, Poole's Cavern and Chatsworth – of what were soon to become the established Seven Wonders. He includes Peverels castle at Castleton, but excludes Mam Tor and the Ebbing and Flowing Well at Tideswell. Most importantly he included Bess of Hardwick's newly completed Chatsworth House.

Seven had been a mystic or sacred number since time immemorial and certainly had special significance among the Ancient Greeks. The Pythagoreans esteemed the number seven and considered its components of four and three as lucky numbers and so began septimal associations of spiritual abstractions, people, objects or places. Among the last was the set known as The Seven Wonders of the Ancient World, whose earliest origin is in an epigram of Antipater of Sidon of about the mid-second century B.C. The list is varied by subsequent writers but came to be accepted as the Pyramids of Egypt, the Hanging Gardens of Babylon, the statue of Zeus at Olympia, the Temple of

Artemis at Ephesus, the Mausoleum of Halicarnassus, the Colossus of Rhodes and the Pharos of Alexandria. All had one feature in common – they were masterpieces of human creation.

Renaissance writers in Europe were well versed in descriptions of these seven *stupores mundi*, though by the 16th century the pyramids alone survived. Attempts were made to establish a modern set, which included wonders as far apart as the Great Wall of China and the circle at Stonehenge. It was by this process that various writers after Camden began to refine the lesser topographical curiosities of the Peak which, initially, were all natural marvels. Michael Drayton, the Warwickshire poet, who had travelled England almost as much as John Leland, published his *Poly-Olbion* in 1622. This contains some 3,000 lines of rhyming couplets crammed with his knowledge of England and Wales; of these 160 lines are devoted to Derbyshire and principally to the Peak.[4] Drayton borrowed books from various antiquaries, including Camden, and accompanied his description of the Wonders of the Peak with a strange map which would have been of little use to the contemporary traveller (see p.10). It is a poet's map populated with the nymphs and muses of rivers, hills and natural features. The Peak itself is represented by a stooping hag described in the poem thus:

> But to th' unwearied Muse the Peak appears the while,
> A withered beldam long, with bleared waterish eyes,
> With many a bleake storme dimd, which often to the skies
> Shee cast, and oft thearth bowd downe her aged head
> Her meagre wrinkled face, being sullyed still with lead.

Although influenced by Camden's work, Drayton refined the Seven Wonders a little further. He included Mam Tor and the Ebbing and Flowing Well but excluded Chatsworth. Instead he included Peak Forest, 'whose hills do serve for brakes, the rocks for shrubs and trees'. Chatsworth, an artificial creation, had less qualification for the poet than the seven natural marvels.

Drayton, in turn, influenced Thomas Hobbes (1588-1679), better known to posterity as a political philosopher than a poet. The young, impecunious Hobbes, newly out of Magdalen Hall, Oxford, was recommended as tutor to William Cavendish of Chatsworth in the Peak, son of the 1st Earl of Devonshire. The classical scholar and the dilettante, wastrel aristocrat, who was only two years younger, struck up a strange friendship which provided matter for the gossipy John Aubrey.[5] About 1636, a year after William had become the second Earl, Hobbes presented him with his famous poem, *De Mirabilibus Pecci*, as a birthday present. This took the form of a topographical estate poem based on a tour of the Peak on horseback by the two friends. It was composed in hexameters, was much influenced by Virgil's *Bucolics* and had a tutor's didactic intent.

Hobbes, aping Camden, finally standardised the Seven Wonders in this order:

> Alti censentur septem miracula Pecci,
> Aedes, mons, Barathrum, binus fons, antraque bina

Hobbes's poem was translated into what is still the standard English text, and the order of the above lines was altered to fit the rhyming couplets:

> Of the High Peak are seven wonders writ,
> Two fonts, two caves, one palace, mount and pit.

Hobbes had, in fact, placed Chatsworth (*aedes*) first in his list and made, in his eyes, the 'Palace of the Peak' the supreme glory among country seats. Here he lived out his life as tutor and secretary to the 3rd Earl, finally dying in 1679, aged 91, at the Earl's second Derbyshire seat, Hardwick Hall.

Charles Cotton, in his own *Wonders of the Peak*, written three years after Hobbes's death, maintained the latter's selected seven though in different order and emphasis. He chose to conclude, rather than begin, his poem with Chatsworth and the house of Cavendish, though he is hardly less fulsome than Hobbes in his praise of both.

17 *Devil's Arse in the Peak. Sketch by Sir James Thornhill, c.1699. Tourists are about to enter the inhabited cave accompanied by a guide.*

18 *Castleton's Norman castle from the village. Sketch by Sir James Thornhill, c.1699. The remains of the castle were more extensive then.*

None of the poetry of Camden, Drayton, Hobbes or Cotton is great, yet collectively it constitutes the earliest tourist literature of the Peak and it had an influence on the literate traveller well into the 18th century. Thus we find the 1720 edition of Camden's *Britannia* liberally dosed with extracts from Hobbes and Cotton. Archives contain numerous unpublished manuscript accounts in Latin and English. One example of the former is an anonymous, undated poem in Virgilian style[6] which mentions Hobbes and endeavours to extend his eulogy upon Chatsworth; the latter is interestingly typified by schoolboy verse, in the style of Cotton by Richard Poultny who travelled to see the Wonders in 1746.[7]

Not all, having seen the Wonders, were uncritical of the praise heaped upon them. Defoe, as we have seen, had little time for Cotton as a poet and even less for the Wonders he described. He sums up his own tour of them by dismissing five as wonderless and accepting only Eldon Hole and Chatsworth – 'one a wonder of nature, the other of art'.[8]

But Chatsworth was, as we shall see, a passing wonder, a man-made marvel, subject to the human foibles of fashion and taste. For a century and a half,

THE WONDER OF WONDERS / 35

from the time of Bess of Hardwick and Camden to the days of Boswell and
Johnson, it was regarded as a national wonder. However, as the neo-classical
style gripped the country in the second half of the 18th century, the house
and gardens looked jaded and archaic and had only a passing interest for the
poets and painters of the romantic era. Chatsworth's renaissance had to wait
until the mid-19th century when the 6th Duke of Devonshire and his friend
and head gardener, Sir Joseph Paxton, had transformed the house and grounds
and enabled them again to eclipse their rivals.

The first and most ancient Wonder of the Peak was Peak Cavern, known
as the Devils Arse or, in jest, Nick's Fundament. Those too embarrassed to
use such terms disguised its name in Latin as *Puteus Pecci, Arx Diaboli* or *Anus
Plutonis*.

We have seen the earliest reference to it in Domesday Book; it first appears
on a map of about 1250 by Matthew Paris, who represents the High Peak with
a rectangle enclosing the word PEC. Around this he notes *eol[iorum] put[eus]
ventoru[m]* (the pit of the aeolian winds) and *fontes* (springs).[9] Paris notes nothing
further for Derbyshire, thus indicating the importance of Castleton's cave to the
medieval scholar. Gough's map, drawn about a century later, names the rivers
and some half a dozen towns in the county, each of which is designated by a
single-bayed, gabled house. Most interestingly, Castleton is represented by two
pictograms more prominent than the others (see plate 2, p.3). The first represents
battlements with a central gate and is labelled *Castrum* (castle); the second is
in the form of two concentric circles entitled *Puteus Pek* (Peak's Hole).[10]

The Gough Map, then, presents us with a double wonder – a huge cave
with the famous castle of the Peverels standing on a sheer cliff's edge 250
feet above it. William Peverel, who had fought at Hastings, was granted much
land in Derbyshire and he and his family erected fortifications at Bolsover,
Wingfield and possibly Nether Haddon. His castle in the Peak, which gave
Castleton its name, was standing by 1086 when it is recorded in Domesday
Book. It performed a function like the old Roman forts at nearby Brough
and Melandra, namely to protect the lucrative mineral veins in the region.
In addition it sat within the rocky hunting park known as Peak Forest and
in general served as the administrative capital of the High Peak. Henry II
confiscated the lands of the Peverels who rebelled against him and strengthened
his newly acquired castle by adding a small but elegant stone keep. Although
thereafter it remained the property of the Crown and the Duchy of Lancaster,
its decline was marked by the end of the 14th century and by 1480 it was said
to be greatly decayed.[11] Records of the castle's history are sparse and it may
have seen only short military action when its constable held it briefly against

King John in the barons' revolt at the end of his reign.[12] The truth is that the
depredations of the townsfolk and the ravages of time rendered the castle the
picturesque ruin it had become when Sir James Thornhill first sketched it at
the turn of the 17th century (see plate 18, p.34). Like the Peak Forest around
it the castle was a wreck from the past.

The Cavern, however, remained almost timeless. In the late 16th and early
17th centuries a growing band of tourists was prepared to tackle a journey in
summer to see this Chamber of Horrors (see plate 17, p.33). It was hailed as a
natural and unpredictable phenomenon created by Satan. Some came for thrills
and an opportunity to look into the very bowels of the earth; others with a
scientific mind came to ponder the geology and structure of the planet.

The courts of Elizabeth I and James I were fascinated by the Cavern. Sir
Philip Sidney had written verses on it at the same time as Camden.[13] The latter
taught Ben Jonson at Westminster School and Jonson in turn was a friend of
Drayton and the two Derbyshire poets Sir Aston Cockayne and Charles Cotton.
Not surprisingly Jonson, the famed writer of court masques, who had visited
Derbyshire, used Peak Cavern as the setting for *The Gypsies Metamorphosed* which
was performed for James I and was commissioned by his favourite, the Duke of
Buckingham, in 1621. It was printed in 1640, appropriately after the death of
both of them. Jonson, drawing on the old gypsy associations with the Devil's
Arse, uses the location to make coded references to the homosexual relationship
between King James and his favourite. The latter, as the Gypsy Captain, tells the
King's fortune during the revelries there and sings a ballad about his forebear
Cock Lorel,[14] the prince of rogues, who entertained the devil to dinner at the
Devil's Arse. The Cock becomes Cook and served such specialities as poached
Puritan, userer stewed in his own marrow, Justice of the Peak trussed with a
brace of clerks, lawyer's head in green sauce, two roast sheriffs and Lord Mayor
stuffed with pudding of maintenance. The Devil gobbles up these urban middle
class delights with relish and reduces them to excrement:

> All of which he blewe away with a fart,
> From whence it [the cavern] was called the Devil's arse

When the young Thomas Hobbes and his companion William Cavendish
came to see the cavern, about 1635 or earlier, they rode their horses inside it
and stopped short at the strange sight before them. Here in the cave's mouth
was not a gypsy encampment but 'houses within and haycocks mounted
high'[15] – a small village with byres and stables on which neither the sun
shone nor the rain fell. Cotton commented on the smell of the place which
'can only fume from Satan's fundament'.[16] Charles Leigh, in 1700, gives us

the earliest engraved view inside the cavern where he almost diagrammatically depicts the smoking cottages with grass-thatched roofs arranged on either side of the cavern. Beyond are the 'three waters' which the intrepid traveller must cross.[17]

The cavern's entrance, which is 100 feet wide, slopes to the left in the form of six large steps. On these ledges, or rope walks, for more than three hundred years the inhabitants, and especially their children, were involved in the manufacture of ropes, pack-thread and twine. Some of the crude poles, pulleys and winding gear still survive in the cave (see p.156).

The families in the cave depended also for their livelihood on the seasonal income from the curious who came hesitantly to gaze into this inhabited abyss. No sooner were they within the threshold than the troglodytes rushed to greet them and drag any

19 *The Devil's Arse. Engraving from Dr Charles Leigh's* The Natural History of Lancashire, Cheshire and the Peak of Derbyshire, *1700.*

claustrophobic waverers into the inner reaches of the cavern. One visitor considered that the number of people attending 'with lights made an entrance into this romantic cavern not unlike the descent into hell as represented by the poets'.[18]

Indeed, the classically educated tourist used the metaphors of Ovid, Horace and Virgil to differentiate parts of the cavern. The first water to be negotiated was named the Styx and it is not difficult to see why. To pass beyond, it was necessary, until the mid-19th century, to lie prostrate in a straw-lined boat, candle in hand, and be pushed by one of the cave dwellers who stooped in the water. This part of the journey was only some fourteen yards, but the hanging rock above closed down to within a few inches of the floating tourist's nose. One intrepid visitor declared 'what with the boat and the horror of the place, the candle showed a scene that to me suggested the bark of Charon'.[19]

When the young Byron made this journey the wanderings of his imagination took, as we might have expected, quite a different turn. He was 15 years old, on summer vacation from Harrow and accompanied by his vivacious cousin Mary Chaworth, two years his senior. Byron snuggled down in the straw with his candle and tells us 'the companion of my transit was M.A.C. with whom I had long been in love, and never told it, though she had discovered it without. I recollect my sensations but cannot describe them, and it is as well'.[20]

Beyond the Styx, according to Cotton's hyperbole, one passed through a classical arch with Tuscan columns and entablature. Further in the crashing sound of a cataract brought to his imagination a subterranean smithy where Brontes, one of the three Cyclops, was forging thunderbolts for Jupiter. Such were the metaphors of Cotton and his contemporaries who viewed the Cavern in terms of primitive vulcanology.

By the time of Byron romantic and gothick allusions were in vogue. One of the vaults which distilled showers upon those passing beneath was dubbed Roger Raine's House. The vaster, gloomy chambers, which the flicker of candles and torches could barely illuminate, seemed like lofty vaulted cathedrals. Thus one feature was named the Chancel and the unsuspecting visitor was suitably awed when a choir of troglodytes, waiting in readiness on a ledge, struck up some ecclesiastical chant that made the vault resound. Pistol reports and exploding charges of gunpowder heightened the sense of horror. Suggestions

20 *Peak Cavern (Roger Raine's House). Engraving by T. Noble after Edward Dayes, 1804.*

21 *Passing through the supposed siphon in Peak Cavern. Lithograph by R.M. Archer, c.1890.*

of a tolling bell were derived from a great dome-like void in the roof which was hailed as Great Tom of Lincoln (see plate 11). Nor were Lucifer and all his medieval associations with the Cavern forgotten; one chamber was designated the Devil's Cellar or Hall. Presumably this was the place, according to legend, where Cock Lorel supped with the Prince of Darkness.

Until the beginning of the 19th century the tourists at the cavern, as at the other attractions in the Peak, were genteel or scholarly travellers. The former often lorded it over the rough menials who acted as guides or custodians and expected freedom of access and no distribution of *pourboires*.

The Dekin family, who acted as guides, had their own way of dealing with such ingrates. About 1770 a certain baronet who had paid one of the Dekins 'very sordidly for his trouble' came again to visit the cavern and the old man recognised him and dealt with him as follows:

> Dekin, however, endeavoured to persuade him to desist from entering it [the Cavern], as the waters were out above, and the stream likely to overflow below. But … the noble baronet … insisted on being taken in. More wise than his companion, Dekin planted a man at the little river over which the visitor is ferried, with orders for him to discharge a pistol when he perceived the waters begin to rise. The duet had reached the extremity of the Cavern, and were now returning when the report of the pistol was heard. 'What is that?' exclaimed the baronet, astonished at the reverberated sound. Dekin informed him, and at the same time contrived, as if by accident, to extinguish the tapers in his hand. In this dreadful situation 'every man for himself' seemed to be the obvious rule of action; and Dekin, with many expressions of alarm, slipped from the side of his companion. Nothing could now equal his horror; he prayed and entreated not to be left in this desperate situation, and made offers of the most liberal reward, if the guide would return and re-conduct him into day. Dekin supported the farce with great

address; and making a merit of disregarding his own preservation for the sake of the baronet, took him under his direction; feeding his terrors by occasional doubts whether he should be able to discover the intricacies of the caverns (though every inch of them was as familiar to him as his own threshold) and thus brought him to the ferry just in time to save their passage before the stream met the rock. The adventure, by which justice was satisfied and revenge indulged, served the old man for a laugh as long as he lived.[21]

Such was the humour of the peakrils! However, punishing the tight-fisted was time consuming and not likely to work repetitively. By the end of the 18th century the Dekins had become more businesslike in their endeavours to cope with the increasing flow of tourists. The following information was posted in the town:

TO BE PAID THE GUIDE FOR SHOWING
THE CAVERN AT CASTLETON

	For showing		candles		Total	
	s	d	s	d	s	d
One person	2	6	1	0	3	6
Two persons	4	0	1	0	5	0
Three persons	4	6	2	0	6	6
Four persons	6	0	2	0	8	0
Five persons	7	6	2	6	10	0
Six persons	8	0	3	6	11	6
Every person above six	1	0	0	6	1	6

Servants attending a party One Shilling each

BLASTS 2s 6d each[22]

These admission fees were not cheap but were well within the reach of the wealthy, whilst serving as a strong deterrent to the poor.

5

A Pit, a Mount and a Well

Originally, Castleton was a small town of very humble houses principally inhabited by leadminers. By the late 18th century it had become a tourist centre with a few small hostelries catering for those who came to see its Norman castle and parish church and, above all, its Cavern (see plate 87, p.165). The *Castle Inn* was its best hotel, noted for its excellent larder, good wine and good accommodation.

The first guide book to the town, published in 1805, described it as 'one of the most healthful and interesting villages in the kingdom; its fertility so much surpasses the neighbourhood, its produce of every necessary of life so abundant, and its air so pure and wholesome that it may be truly called the Garden of the Peak.'[1] Apart from its small market there were a few tourist shops selling trinkets made from the local minerals. Indeed, trading was so brisk that in 1793 Dr Plumptre was scandalised to find that the shops remained open on Sundays.

Short excursions were made on foot or horseback to see three further Wonders within the old bounds of the vanished Peak Forest – Eldon Hole, Mam Tor and the Ebbing and Flowing Well at Tideswell.

Camden and Defoe had surprisingly opposed views on Eldon Hole when one considers that a century or more divided their visits. The former was faint in his praise and considered there was 'nothing to be wondered at, but that is of an huge widenesse, exceeding steepe and of a mervailous depth'. Conversely, Defoe acclaimed it as the only true natural Wonder of the Peak 'and what the like of is not to be found in the world, that I have heard or believe'. For once Defoe is prepared to accept Cotton's statement, which perhaps in turn is borrowed from Drayton, that he let down 800 fathoms of line and still did not plumb the bottom. Defoe therefore concluded that this great chasm 'goes directly down perpendicular into the earth, and perhaps to the centre'. He would have been much nearer the truth had he paid more attention to Cotton's tale of the goose that was thrown down Eldon Hole and emerged without its feathers in Peak Cavern, two miles away.

A possible journey to the centre of the earth has long taxed man's imagination, but in days before potholing became a sport or speleology a science, there were no volunteers to descend into Eldon Hole. Hobbes tells us of the first attempt when the Earl of Leicester, who was a guest of the Earl of Shrewsbury and his wife, Bess of Hardwick, at Chatsworth, lowered one of his reluctant servants into the black abyss on a rope. This luckless explorer was equipped with a pole to push himself away from the jagged sides and a basket of stones to cast beneath him in an effort to sound the bottom. Having been lowered, we are told, to the rope's limit of 200 yards the man was hauled out a gibbering wreck. His inability to speak left the impatient Leicester in the belief that the poor wretch, who died eight days later in a frenzy, had gazed upon Hell itself.

Such tales drew travellers from far and wide, rich and poor, to gape into the earth and to dismantle the local dry stone walls in order to make their own soundings. Cattle and sheep occasionally fell in and tourists neared the brink at their peril. Cotton, as has been mentioned, tells of murderers who hurled their victim's body into this vast pit.[2]

When Celia Fiennes came at the end of the 17th century attempts had been made to place a fence around the mouth of the Hole but visitors smashed it down and hurled it hellwards. By 1735, when John Loveday visited,[3] a stone wall had been erected and by 1793 a gate and padlock were in place together with a custodian. However, stones were still cast with a high trajectory over the wall by those who declined to pay an entry fee.

The mystery and magic of the great Hole were finally dispelled when one Lloyd was lowered down about 1761. He reached the floor of the first cave only 62 yards from the mouth, at which point he found sufficient daylight to read a book. He then proceeded to explore a lower, lateral cave system. Lloyd published his findings in the *Philosophical Transactions*[4] and these were summarised in the new guidebooks and histories of the county by writers like Davies, Britton and Brayley.[5] Thereafter the number of visitors to Eldon Hole declined and many made their way to the new underground wonder, Treak Cavern, below Mam Tor (see pp.195-6).

The very words Mam Tor aroused curiosity as to their etymology. Hobbes considered them a corruption of Maimed Tor which originally described the great scree scar on the side of the mountain. Cotton toyed even more unconvincingly with the meaning of Mam as mother. Such speculations are of no value and today it is suggested that Mam is a Celtic hill-name.[6]

To most tourists the ancient belief that the mountain continually wastes itself but never diminishes was what lured them to see what Cotton called

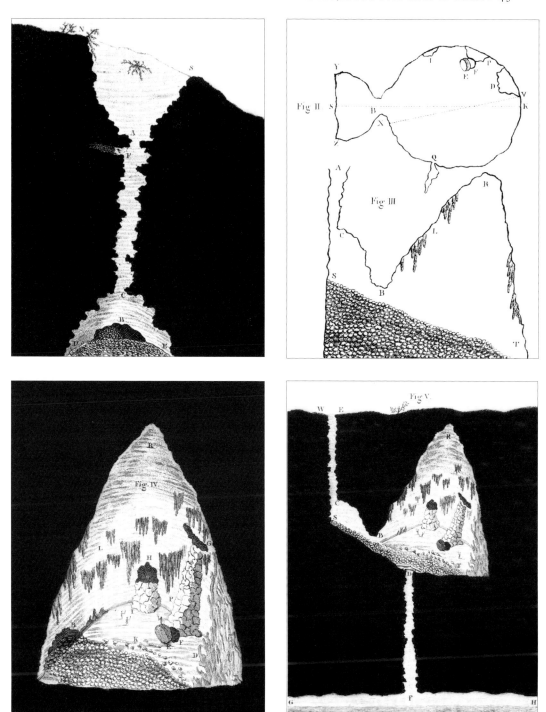

22 *Sections and plans of Eldon Hole, 1761. Published in* Philosophical Transactions, *vol. LXI.*

23 *Mam Tor from Castleton. Sketch by Sir James Thornhill, who is seated in the foreground, c.1699.*

the 'Phoenix of the Peak'. To this day, following a heavy downpour of rain or a protracted frost, the slippage of shale down its eastern face can still be seen. Hence it was known as the 'Shivering Mountain'. But no serious spectator believed that it never diminished. Most tourists stayed at the foot of the scree and grubbed in the shale for those fragments of quartz called 'Derbyshire diamonds'; others were interested in entering the nearby Odin leadmine or, like numerous artists from Thornhill to Constable, sketching it (see p.23).

The more energetic traveller, who took the track towards the Wynnats Pass and then the footpath to the top of Mam Tor, was doubly rewarded by greater wonders. The first was the Iron-Age fort – the largest in Derbyshire – which occupies its summit; the second is still one of the best views in the Peak looking beyond Castleton along the Hope Valley towards Hathersage and over the hills towards Tideswell.

In this last direction lay the smallest and least significant of the Wonders, the Weedon or Ebbing and Flowing Well. A number of these curious springs existed on the limestone and, instead of making a constant flow, debouched water at intervals of minutes or hours. Drayton maintained this well was a greater marvel than some he had heard of in Wales because it was furthest from the sea, whose tides governed its ebbing and flowing. But how could it be linked to the sea when its movements did not coincide with the lunar tides and its water was not saline?

Travellers looking for this self-effacing phenomenon – even Cotton felt it looked contemptible – could easily pass it by. It was often camouflaged in summer with weeds around its man-made basin and by cattle gathering to drink. Indeed, in hot summers when water levels in the limestone were low there was no semblance of a spring for weeks together.

It had long been assumed that Tideswell obtained its name from its tidal stream but Camden could not corroborate this etymology[7] and Hobbes, whom Cotton praised for his scientific knowledge, was one of the first to ridicule the tidal theory and consider a siphonic solution. A gentleman from Oxford in the 18th century suggested a double siphon to account for the reflux that, after an interval, drew the water back into the rocks.[8]

24 *The Ebbing and Flowing Well. Anonymous engraving for the* New Buxton Guide, *1842.*

Defoe had little patience with these theories and declaimed that 'all this wonder is owing only to the situation of the place, which is a mere accident in nature, so that if any person were to dig into the place and give vent to the air, which fills the contracted space within, would soon see Tideswell turned into an ordinary running stream, and a very little one too.' This time Defoe was right. A century later Farey tells us that a Mr Goodman of Eccles, in Chapel-en-le-Frith had made such an artificial spring in his garden![9]

By the beginning of the 19th century the wonder of the Ebbing and Flowing Well had also vanished. Jewitt, who thought highly of this marvel and described its functions at length, considered it 'the shame of the county in general, and to the proprietor of the land in particular, this well ... is now only a dirty pool, where the water has no other receptacle than what is generally seen in the most rude pastures for the accommodation of cattle'.[10]

6

The Wells and the Cavern at Buxton

Buxton, England's highest and bleakest town, stands 1,000 feet above sea level. Its warm and cold springs were known to the Romans who had a settlement here called *Aquae Arnemetiae* – 'the waters of Arnemetia'.[1] This site had even older significance since Arnemetia was a goddess of the 'sacred grove' whose name appears elsewhere in Celtic Britain and Europe.

The numerous finds of Roman votive offerings in the form of trinkets and coins, the latter representing every Emperor during the Roman occupation of Britain, attest to the soothing and salubrious properties of the waters. This place of rain and winds, mists and snow must have seemed a miraculous haven of recuperation to the Mediterranean legionary stationed in the Peak, or the lead merchant shivering with his pig-laden pack-horses among these harrowing hills. Archaeology is yet to make clear what other buildings and settlements clustered around the baths. A fort, for instance, is thought to have existed on the site of the present market place, and at Staden, to the south, the remains of agricultural buildings and field enclosures have been revealed. However, insufficient is known to give a clear indication of the extent and prosperity of a small provincial settlement established during the last quarter of the first century A.D.[2]

Buxton was always small until it was launched by the Dukes of Devonshire as an important national spa in the late 18th and early 19th centuries (see plate 26, p.51). Its fate following the departure of the Romans is quite unclear. Farming and lead-mining continued but bathing almost certainly ceased; libations and douches were of little concern to the barbarians.

The name Buxton is Anglo-Saxon, but it does not appear in Domesday Book. It is met for the first time, by chance, as part of the grant of lands by one of the William Peverels of Castleton in the foundation charter (*c.*1100–08) of the Priory of Lenton near Nottingham. Here it appears as 'Buchstanes' which may derive from 'bug-stan' meaning 'rocking-stone', a phenomenon of Ice-Age erosion not uncommon on the gritstone outcrops of the Peak.

25   *Buxton. Pen and wash sketch by Sir James Thornhill, c.1699. The market-place is on the left, the* Talbot Inn *is in the centre behind the Grove, and the Wye flows past St Anne's chapel in the foreground.*

Alternatively the origin of the name could be 'buck stones', a reference to the rocky regions where deer roamed within the royal Peak Forest. In 1366 the place was called 'Kyngesbucstones'[3] within the Duchy of Lancaster and was divided ecclesiastically between the parishes of Bakewell, Hope and Hartington.

During this period of the Middle Ages, however, there are no references to the famous springs nor any suggestion that this place was a wonder. It is not until the late 15th century that a spring at Buxton is mentioned as a holy well where miracles were performed by the waters. William of Worcester (1415-82) was a chronicler who travelled England and left detailed accounts of his journeys. He delighted in tracing rivers from their source and writes,

> Memorandum quod Holywell, principium aquae de Wye, in comitatu Derby … facit plura miracula faciendo infermos sanos, et in hieme est calida velut lac mulsum. Flumen Weya vocata Holywelle, incipit in villa de Buxton … [4]
>
> (Note that the Holywell, the source of the Wye waters in the county of Derbyshire, … works miracles by restoring the sick to health and in winter is as warm as sweetened milk. The River Wye called the Holywell, rises in the town of Buxton.)

He is wrong in claiming the Holywell as the source of the Wye whose origins are now traced to the Wye Head Springs, outside Buxton, which are fed from a number of swallets on Axe Edge and Stanley Moor.[5] His memorandum is interesting in suggesting that people were once more making pilgrimages to Buxton. The warmth of the water, a constant 81.5°F, was like the temperature of milk fresh from the cow.

By the early 16th century a chapel and a shrine to St Anne had been erected and the warm bath attracted infirm pilgrims from the Midlands and the North. The association with St Anne was fictitious and may have derived from a misreading of the fragmentary Latin dedication to Arnemetia. The Chapel was ablaze with candles, prayers requested the intercession of St Anne, the apocryphal mother of the Virgin Mary, and valuable offerings of money, trinkets and jewels were left at her shrine.

The new fame of Buxton's wells and the wonders wrought at the shrine of St Anne were halted abruptly in August 1538 when Sir William Basset, acting on behalf of Thomas Cromwell, Henry VIII's Secretary, came to Buxton with his agents. They moved swiftly and ruthlessly within the day so that Basset could write with all speed and obsequiousness:

> Right Honourable and my Inespecial Good Lord,
>
> According to my bounden duty and the tenor of your Lordship's letters lately to me directed, I have sent your Lordship … the image of St Ann of Buckston … which image I did take from the place where it did stand, and brought it to my house within forty eight hours after the contemplation of your Lordship's said letters, in as sober a manner as my little and rude will would serve me. And for that there should be no more idolatry and superstition there used, I did not only deface the tabernacle and the place where it did stand, but did take away crutches, shirts and shifts with wax offered, being things that allure and entice the ignorant to the said offering; also giving the keeper orders that no more offerings should be made till the King's pleasure and your Lordship's be further known in that behalf. My Lord, I have locked up and sealed the Baths and Wells at Buckston that none shall enter to wash there till your Lordship's pleasure be further known. Whereof I beseech your good Lordship that I may be ascertained again at your pleasure, and I shall not fail to execute your Lordship's commandments to the utmost of my little wit and power … written at Langley with the rude and simple hand of your assured and faithful orator as one and ever at your Commandment, next unto the King's to the utmost of his little power.
>
> William Bassett, Knight.[6]

By Queen Mary's reign the wells and the chapel were in use again under the control of the Cotrell family, local landowners, who seem to have been the first to exploit the commercial advantages of the site. However, Roger Cotrell could not control bath-time hooliganism and was bound over for £100 at Derby Assizes in 1553 to maintain good order at the wells and to prevent 'youthful persons to wash and bathe them in the wall called Saint Anne's well, not only to get tipple and drink within the said chapel on the Sundays and holydays, but most irreverently also to pipe, dance, hop and sing within the same to the great disturbance of the inhabitants of Buxton'.[7]

It was the Elizabethan aristocracy that restored Buxton's fortunes, established order and decorum, made the town the principal tourist centre of the Peak and its wells one of the Seven Wonders. George Talbot, 6th Earl of Shrewsbury, one of the greatest landowners in the North and among the wealthiest men in England, saw the financial potential of the wells and bought them from the Cotrells in 1572.[8] Beside the Bath and St Anne's Well he built the famous tower house known as New Hall, to distinguish it from the Old Hall, until then the town's principal inn. It was unlike Derbyshire's other tower houses; they were country houses whilst this was an hotel for the wealthy. Indeed, it may have been built specifically for its most celebrated occupant, Mary Queen of Scots. Mary, a state prisoner, was entrusted by Elizabeth I to the custody of the reluctant Earl of Shrewsbury who carefully changed her places of confinement from Coventry to Ashby-de-le-Zouch and Tutbury Castle, to Wingfield Manor, Sheffield Manor and Chatsworth. The damp quarters of the older medieval buildings, especially at Tutbury, exacerbated her rheumatism and arthritis. Her requests to be allowed to take the waters at Buxton were eventually and cautiously allowed by Elizabeth I. In 1573 she took up residence at the New Hall for the first of five known visits.

The inset at the base of John Speed's map of Derbyshire (1610) is the earliest illustration of New Hall, or the Sign of the Talbot (see plate 76, p.146). It is a four-storeyed tower with mullioned and leaded casement windows on the upper two floors. It has a battlemented parapet, behind which the chimney stacks are half concealed, along with a gabled stair-head. A battlemented wall surrounds it on three sides – an added security perhaps for the visits of the Scots Queen – whilst around it are St Anne's Well and the chapel. The Bath is incorporated in the wall and courtyard.

Dr John Jones describes the Hall as follows:

> joining to the chief spring, between the river and the Bath is a very goodly house, four square, four stories high, so well compact, with houses of office beneath and above, roundabout with a great chamber, and other goodly lodgings, to the number of thirty.[9]

Jones is also our only source for some understanding of how the interior of the building was arranged. He describes two galleries in the building where guests could walk when confined by bad weather. Ladies and gentlemen and their servants could exercise in one and the infirm in another. The former could use their gallery to play indoor games such as 'Trule in Madame'. Jones tells us that 'in the end of a bench eleven holes are made in which to trowle

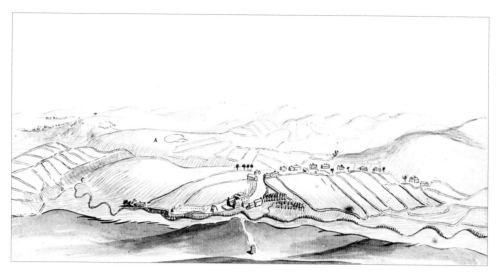

26 *Prospect of Buxton. Pencil and wash sketch by William Stukeley, July 1725.*

pumments or bowls of lead, by little or mean, or also of copper, tin wood, either violent or soft'. Did Mary Queen of Scots relieve her boredom by playing this game, which seems rather like modern bagatelle?

Jones does not deal with the drinking of the waters in Buxton's cold well but the habits of the Elizabethan aristocracy indicate the importance they attached to imbibing. In 1559 the Earl of Pembroke had such faith in the water's health-giving contents that, having left Buxton for Belvoir Castle in Leicestershire, he had barrels of the water sent to him there. Likewise the Earl of Leicester visited Buxton Bath a number of times and his physician recommended that, to cure his gout, 'he must drink and use Buxton's water twenty days together'. Leicester, in turn, extolled its virtues to Elizabeth I and arranged for it to be sent in hogsheads to the Court. When he visited Buxton the Earl of Sussex began his treatment by drinking three pints of water a day and increased this by a pint a day until he was consuming a gallon. Thereafter he reversed the dosage. Lord Burghley consumed similar amounts over a ten-day cycle, declaring that 'mixed with sugar I find it potable with pleasure, even as whey'.[10]

The poor flocked to the wells in many cases to beg from the wealthy. Queen Mary herself had been approached by a poor cripple – much to Shrewsbury's and Elizabeth's consternation. Dr Jones expressed his concern for the poor invalids who had trekked to Buxton and could only afford treatment if they were successful mendicants. He recommended charges for the wealthy ranging from £5 for an Archbishop and £3 10s. for a Duke to 12d. for a yeoman and advocated that half these receipts should be contributed to a charitable fund for poor invalids and the other half to the maintenance of a resident physician.

However, in 1572, the year Jones wrote, an Act of Parliament dealing with vagrancy and the relief of the poor specifically dealt with the congregation of the poor beggars at Buxton. They were now required to obtain a licence from two JPs in their county of origin which would entitle them to seek relief in each parish through which they passed. Such legislation must have been prohibitive to the majority of sick paupers, especially those from afar.

Mary Queen of Scots and Dr Jones were Buxton's best advertisements. The latter, by means of his book, gave the impression that the magical waters in the bath were the panacea for almost every ill. The following are some which the waters help:

> Women that by reason of overmuch moisture or contrary temperature be unapt to
>   conceave.
> Also all such as have their whisker too abundant and overwatry.
> For weak men that be unfruitful.
> Likewise for all that have Priapismus and that be perboyled in Venus Gulf.
> Profitable for such as have consumption of the lungs.
> Very good for inflammation of the liver.
> Excellent for overmuch heat and stopping of veins.
> Beneficial for such as vomit blood.
> Good for continued desire to make water and unordinary desire to going to stoole,
>   doing nothing or very little with great pain.
> The haemmorroids and pyles it soon mendeth.
> Against the overflowing of women's months it much availeth.
> Overmuch vomiting it cureth.
> It openeth the obstructions of the milt and liver.
> For them that be short winded, it much availeth.
> The green sickness perfectly it cureth and the morphaw soon it expelleth.[11]

The numbers coming to Buxton put a strain on accommodation. By 1577 there were two inns, the New Hall and the Old Hall, and eight ale houses around the market place. The latter had little accommodation. As the Old Hall was closed so it was replaced by the Eagle and Child but visitors constantly complained (see plate III).

Whilst the poet Drayton enjoyed 'strong ale and good cheer' there in 1605, Lady Arabella Stuart took the precaution of having her ale brought in from Tideswell. In 1652 Edwarde Browne declared 'our entertainment was oatcakes and mutton, which we fancied to taste like dog, our lodging [was] in a low rafty room ...'.[12] We have seen that matters had not improved when Celia Fiennes stayed at the Hall in 1697.

The fact is that following the last visit to the New Hall of Mary Queen of Scots in 1583 its standards gradually deteriorated, especially after the Earl of Shrewsbury's death in 1590. The Hall and the bath seem to have passed into other hands until they were reunited in the ownership of the Cavendish family.

The Hall itself was damaged by fire in 1670 and partially rebuilt; later the lantern on the roof was repaired. Thus a century after Buxton's late Tudor and early Jacobean claim to fame, it had declined again. As both Sir James Thornhill and William Stukeley sketched it, it remained little more than a village high in the folds of the Pennines, dominated by the now outmoded and run-down Hall.

There was little outdoor amusement for those staying there. As at Castleton a trinket shop or two sold souvenirs made from local minerals. The town's market was small and did not receive a charter until 1813. There was no parish church; those seeking Sunday workshop attended the Well chapel or rode up to Fairfield. What did one do apart from taking exercise on foot or horseback or playing bowls on the new green laid out beside the Hall in 1696?[13]

27   *Buxton Bath, Derbyshire, July 1712. Pen and wash sketch by William Stukeley.*

28 *St Anne's Well at Buxton, July 1712. Pen and wash sketch by William Stukeley.*

Almost every tourist in Buxton paid a visit to the last of the Seven Wonders, Poole's Cavern, less than a mile from the Bath. Certainly the Elizabethan nobility came to see it and Sir Philip Sidney in his *Sidera* (*c.*1580) says,

> Peak hath a cave whose narrow entrance finds
> Large rooms within where droppes distill amaise
> Till knit with cold though there unknowne
> Deck that poore place with Alabaster remains linde.

Although Sidney uses the word 'alabaster' poetically, as a rich contrast to the bareness of the interior, he mentions the narrow entrance through which one had to enter on all fours and refers to the underworld of stalactites and stalagmites for which the cave is celebrated. Sidney also implies that the formations are set like icicles in the cold, though the temperature throughout the length (1,000 ft or 310 metres) of the cave remains constant at 44°F/7°C – the average temperature of the town of Buxton.

Sidney probably visited Poole's Cavern whilst staying at Chatsworth. Most aristocratic and literary visits to the Wonders had their starting point there. Dr Richard Andrews began his curiously recorded visit to Poole's Cavern from the House. A writer of English and Latin verse, Vice-President of St John's College, Oxford and a Fellow of the Royal Society of Physicians, Andrews was, by the 1620s, a protégé of William Cavendish of Bolsover Castle (created Viscount Mansfield in 1620 and Earl of Newcastle in 1628).[14] He was also patronised by Cavendish's cousin, William, 3rd Earl of Devonshire, about whose seat and family he wrote *The Muse to Chatsworth.*[15] Within this cultured Derbyshire network Andrews was associated with Ben Jonson and Thomas Hobbes, both visitors to, and writers on, the Peak.

Andrews's poem on Poole's cavern, beginning 'Have you not heard of
Derbyshire …', was written in 1627.[16] It is a long rambling burlesque of rhyming couplets, probably intended to be read at a country-house revel. Having
journeyed with six companions from Chatsworth to Buxton, Andrews visits
Poole's Cavern where he is met by six 'lustie fellowes' who act as guides.

> They had their candles in their fist
> And gave to everyone that list.
> Each man his Candle now had lighted,
> The sight would have a man affrighted.
> One it a wedding feast did call,
> Another said a funerall,
> Because at both these solemn rites
> They carry Tapers, or such lights.
> But I did say, and I said well,
> 'Twas like procession down to Hell.
> Well now our forman all on foure
> Did lead the way, close to the flore.
> He did incline, and so went crawling,
> Though I have heard something of hawling
> Them in; with blanketts I doe followe
> In this unholied hell, but hollowe.
> And on my knees, as t' were to pray
> That once again I may see day,
> And like a crab away I past,
> My heeles went first, my head came last.
> One place was straight, I doe remember
> That it did crush me every member.
> And then begining to want breath,
> I thought on those are prest to death.
> But I at last did wriggle out,
> Like to a worme I turn'd about,
> And by the twinkling of my light
> I saw an horrid hideous sight.

Thus Andrewes entered the great void which he likened to Hades. He
slipped and staggered about in the dimly-lit cavern where ominous shapes
reared up and water seeped, dripped and splashed. Resting a while, Andrews
took his knife and, by the flickering light of his candle, scratched the following
graffito on the glistening wall:

> A Melting Rocke, a flowing walke,
> A Marble flood, a dropping chalke,
> A Stony Sea, a Rayneing flint,
> A weepeing Tombe, and I am in't.

29 *Poole's Hole. Engraved for Dr Charles Leigh's* The Natural History of Lancashire, Cheshire and the Peak of Derbyshire, *1700.*

Andrews came out alive! He has left us another story from the underworld by recounting in his poem how the Devil, having dined with Cock Lorel in Peak Cavern, was stricken with strangury and stone and retired to Poole's Cavern. This ailment, it was held, was responsible for the constant dripping of water and the boulder strewn floor in the cave! In describing the grisly concoctions which eventually produced a cure Dr Andrews combined his love of poetry with his knowledge of physic. There is some grotesque similarity with the menus that his friend, Ben Jonson, described at Cock Lorel's feast in Peak Cavern. One can well imagine the Doctor, who was Reader in Rhetoric at his College, declaiming his verse, bawdy in parts, to social gatherings at Chatsworth and Bolsover.

Today archaeology has revealed Poole's Cavern to have been occupied by man from prehistoric down to Roman times and later. To the 16th-century tourist this was unknown. Imaginations were stirred by the tales of outlaws taking refuge there – in this case the robber named Poole, whose name the Cavern bears. Who he was and when he lived is unclear. His name is first associated with the place in the late 15th century. He appears to some to have been a new Robin Hood rather than another Cock Lorel. Ralph Thoresby, the Leeds antiquary, tells us in his diary for 1681 that Poole came from Poole Hall in Staffordshire and was 'a man of great valour who, being outlawed, resided here for his own security'. Hobbes gives a less flattering account of the rogue:

> Poole was a famous thief, and as we're told,
> Equal to Cacus, and perchance as old.
> Shrouded within this darksome hid retrieve
> By spoils of those he robb'd he us'd to live,
> And towards his den poor travellers deceive ...[17]

Did Mary Queen of Scots, who had come to Buxton suffering from rheumatism and whose every move was carefully observed, really crawl into this dank, dark hole? Cotton tells us she did, though this is barely credible. Camden, Andrews and Hobbes say nothing about such a royal visit and the earliest reference to the Queen's association with the cave occurs in Justinian Paget's notes made in 1630. He refers to the remarkably large, pendant mass of stalactite and calls it 'The Queen of Scotts pillars'.[18] And so they have remained named to this day. Cotton says the Queen penetrated the cave to this point, her 'Non Ultra' ('No Further').

Fact or fantasy, the Queen's name drew visitors to the cave as it did to the Bath. But fantasy did not stop there; the formations in the cave and the candlelights flickering across them presented a range of animals and objects which fill the tourist literature. Here were a flitch of bacon, lions, cats, apes and humans. The guides even pointed out Poole's chair, bed and chamber pot!

The cavern was a place for nervous hallucinations, and one wonders what Dr Charles Leigh had seen! He published the earliest engraving of Poole's Cavern, as of Peak Cavern, which appeared in various subsequent works

30 *Poole's Hole in Derbyshire, 26 July 1725. Sepia sketch by William Stukeley. Compare this with Leigh's diagrammatic view.*

31 *Entrance to Poole's Cavern. Coloured engraving, c.1860. The 6th Duke of Devonshire widened and landscaped the entrance.*

including Moll's *Map of Derbyshire* (1720). It bears little resemblance to the actual cave but was calculated to draw countless curious visitors. The much more realistic rendering of the cave's interior by William Stukeley in 1725 was never engraved and known only to his friends. Many visitors must have been disappointed. Defoe certainly was and scathingly denounces yet another wonderless wonder:

> The wit that has been spent upon this vault or cave … had been well enough to raise the expectation of strangers, and bring fools a great way to creep into it but is ill bestowed on all those that come to the place with a just curiosity, founded upon ancient report; when these go in to see it, they generally go away, acknowledging that they have seen nothing suitable to their great expectation, or to the fame of the place.[19]

Today, however, the cavern is truly one of the Wonders of the Peak, and not for the old mythological reasons. Electric lighting has revealed its marvellous geological formations.

7

The Tourist Invasion

The turnpike roads of the 18th century, established by Acts of Parliament, revolutionised travel and communication throughout the country in a manner not known since Roman times. As usual, London and the Home Counties were the first beneficiaries. Derbyshire, and especially the Peak, was eventually touched by these changes. The High Peak, which Defoe had described as 'perhaps the most desolate, wild and abandoned country in all England', gradually became a region traversed by gigs and chaises, coaches and carts, horsemen and walkers. By the beginning of the 19th century tourism, as well as commerce, was making its mark, literally, on the landscape.

The first turnpike trust was set up in 1663 to improve a notoriously bad stretch of the Great North Road in Hertfordshire and Cambridgeshire. The first road to be turnpiked in the High Peak – the fiftieth in England – was undertaken at the wishes of the merchants of Manchester, not principally to facilitate travel into the Peak, via Chapel-en-le-Frith and Buxton, but rather through it. As their petition to the House of Commons declared, this road was 'the most direct Way from the Town of Manchester to the City of London; and is very deep and … in some parts so bad, that Coaches and Waggons cannot pass through the same with safety'.[1]

Meanwhile, from the south, the Derby, Buxton and Manchester road was being turnpiked in 1720. It began at the Trent crossing at Cavendish Bridge, Shardlow, to the south-east of Derby, and reached Brassington in the Low Peak and stopped. The gap between Brassington and Buxton was not turnpiked until 1749.

However, these early turnpike roads were not necessarily well made. Although the Peak had an abundance of stone for road construction, much of which lay about the landscape, especially at industrial spoil heaps, the road makers do not appear to have graded the stone with much care and surfaces were not smooth. In 1735 John Loveday complained about the stoney unevenness of the roads and noted that where they passed through rocky terrain they were often 'covered thick with stones falling'.[2]

The Manchester to Derby turnpike road followed the old route through Buxton, Brassington and Hognaston that Ogilvy had mapped and that Stukeley, Defoe and their contemporaries had travelled. The new road improved little on its predecessor. Ebenezer Rhodes, who toured on Derbyshire's roads for many years in the late 18th and early 19th centuries, made the following indictment of the Peakland turnpikes following his experience on the road between Glossop and Chapel-en-le-Frith:

> This road, like many others in Derbyshire and elsewhere, has been made in despite of both hill and dale. Hardly any set of people commit greater blunders than the projectors and makers of public roads. If a valley interferes in their line of operations, they show their utter contempt of the accommodation it offers, and their talent at surmounting difficulties, by clambering up and down every hill that nature has interposed between them and the point of their destination.[3]

Rhodes travelled the Peak in a gig and was humorously chided by a local wag, 'That cockling thing yo' ride is no' fit for these roads; and I should no' wonder if yo' were to have a fa' before you get to Wirksworth: an' if he have he'ill no' find it very soft, for the road is a' covered wi' stones and they're no' some on 'em very little ones either … '[4]

Those on horseback did not like these early turnpike surfaces either. Not all types of horse travelled them with equal ease and the Reverend Davies particularly commends the local Peakland horses. He says 'the breed is small, of light and slender make: and shews great agility in ascending and descending the steep mountains, over which they are employed in carrying limestone on their backs. Accustomed to a scanty fare, they are very hard, and able to undergo very great fatigue'.[5] Few visitors had horses like these.

Many tourists would only travel on horseback but did not always calculate the difficulties their mounts would encounter. One such was that indefatigable horseman, John Byng, Viscount Torrington (1742-1813) who toured much of England and has left us a fine account of his travels. He toured the Peak twice, in 1789 and in 1790. He was adamant about riding and declared, 'I do not envy chaise tourists who are to be bumped or jolted along in danger of bad roads and without ever seeing the country to advantage'.[6] He had been a lieutenant-colonel in the Foot Guards and was used to long periods in the saddle at the head of a column. Yet, although he admired its landscape, he had little time for the turnpike roads of the Peak which he described as 'all hills and stones'. He was assiduous in caring for his horse, ensuring it was well shod, fed, watered and stabled, much as a careful motorist today checks his petrol, oil and tyres. Byng carried a spare set of horseshoes with steel tips and was very short with inn-keepers whose stabling was inadequate. In this way

32 *Matlock. Engraving by I. Widnell after a watercolour by J.M.W. Turner, 1794. The bridge, now widened, gave access to Matlock Bath and Cromford.*

he travelled lightly, his laundry and mail sent by coach ahead of him and his servant, Tom Bush, despatched forward each evening to secure their next night's lodgings. The untrustworthy summer weather in the hills did not deter him. He lifted the collar of his greatcoat, lowered the brim of his hat and pressed on. Occasionally he would shelter under a rock or a tree, retire to a cave or ride into a barn, just as Celia Fiennes undoubtedly did a century earlier. Only once did he bemoan inadequate clothing when he complained, 'We hope August will prove fairer than July, else we must buy Lunardi's jackets and go swimming through our tour'.[7]

Despite their roughness the early turnpike roads drew an increasing number of tourists on foot. These were the precursors of the modern ramblers, though they kept to the roads and public tracks in an age when landowners did not tolerate trespassers on their estates. Potholing and rock climbing were not part of their itinerary and they took pot-luck at the inns along the road. There was not, as today, standard walking equipment and even the better off were often suspected of being foreigners, vagabonds, tinkers or even footpads on account of their strange garb.

Byng had remarked that 'the Scotch are always wrap'd up in their plaids as a defence against heat, cold or wet, but they are preventious of speed or activity'. In fact, this mode of dress was commonly adopted by the English tourist whether in the saddle or on foot. James Plumptre and his companion, having been ill clad for a Welsh tour they made in 1792, were well prepared to tackle the Peak in the following year:

> ... we had short blue coats, or rather Jackets, but in other respects made in the fashion; and here, for once, fashion coincided with reason, the large lapelles being convenient to button over in case of cold or rain; our Breeches were nankeen, with gaters of the same, which came up to them; and, to complete our dress, we had Scotch plaids, which in cold or rain wrapped round us, and in fine weather tucked up and hung at our backs without the least inconvenience. Thus was our dress at once handsome, neat and light; yet serving the double purpose of being airy in fine weather, and a safeguard from cold or wet in more intemperate changes. Our former knapsack was covered with goatskin, for the sake of looking handsome, and contained our usual change of raiment.[8]

These young buffs obviously fancied themselves, striding through the hills and dales; but how were they shod? Stout boots were worn by the peakrils; even the ragged poor had some sort of footwear in this terrain. Those coming ill-equipped were soon in difficulties. Carl Philip Moritz, a German tourist who, in 1782, had slogged on foot to Castleton found that, after a tour through Peak Cavern, 'my shoes would hardly cling to my feet, so soaked and torn were they from going through the damp sand and over the hard sharp stones'.[9] The local cobbler expressed his incredulity that Moritz should have come all the way from Germany wearing shoes so badly made. Unable to provide a ready-made pair, he set about repairing Moritz's battered remnants.

Moritz's hat caused quite a surprise in Tideswell where he went for a shave to the barber's shop. The locals took him for a gentleman, on account of the quality of his hat. He had paid a guinea for it in London! At least Moritz was well prepared in other regards and tells us, 'I have an accurate map of England in my pocket, together with an excellent guide book ... entitled *A New and Accurate Description of all the direct and principal Cross-roads in Great Britain*. This book I hope will serve me well in my wanderings'.[10]

There were maps aplenty to be had by this period but hardly any of them marked footpaths. Once off the roads the walker and the rider still encountered difficulties. Byng needed guides to take him through Dovedale in a thunderstorm and found no-one who could understand his enquiries in Alport when he wished to visit Robin Hood's Stride, only a mile and a half along the old Portway; again, he eventually sought and found a guide. He was evidently less happy out of the saddle in rough terrain. Near Buxton, for instance, he declared, 'No fat man can walk in this country as the upright stone stiles are so narrow, as only to admit the passage of a well sized leg'.[11] How Dr Johnson would have agreed!

By 1825 the tourist could consult the best *vade mecum* for those on foot yet printed; this was Dr William Kitchinir's *Traveller's Oracle: or Maxims for Locomotion, containing Precepts for Promoting the Pleasures and Hints for Preserving the Health of Travellers*. In an age which delighted in gadgetry, principally produced in Sheffield or Birmingham, he combined a variety of useful equipment in an attempt to lighten the tourist's load. Improving on Plumptre's pocket knife and fork he advocated a knife, fork and spoon that folded into a large pocket knife and promoted a small lantern which also contained a night light and was capped with a half-pint tin cup. Among other devices were a thermometer that slotted into a toothpick case and a barometer fitted into the head of a walking stick. For rainy weather Kitchinir recommended a light umbrella which doubled as a sword stick to repel footpads.

John Byng always carried clean sheets in his baggage to reduce the ravages of inn lice, but Kitchinir preferred leather sheets which had the additional virtue of coping with damp beds. Whilst travelling, the leather was rolled tight to hold a canteen consisting of a kettle, knives, forks, two saucepans, lamp, stand and spice box all contained in one saucepan!

Plumptre carried a compass and a telescope but the *Traveller's Oracle* preferred an 'invisible opera glass'. And finally every gentleman carried books – for note taking, sketching and reading. In the last category Moritz chose the poetry of Milton and Plumptre that of Cowper.

River crossings had been improving for some years since the Restoration. Bridges like the elegant packhorse crossing over the Wye at Holme between Ashford and Bakewell or the wagon bridge downstream at Haddon Hall are typical of those that replaced wooden structures at fording places (see plate 70, p. 138). The Derwent, wider and swifter than its tributary, the Wye, also had its bridges improved or replaced. This probably began when in 1685 the county mason took down the medieval bridge at Chatsworth and replaced it with a stronger one to reopen the road from Edensor to Beeley and Chesterfield.[12] By 1735 John Loveday, who criticised the roads, praised the Peak's bridges as excellent and fifty years later Erasmus Darwin, writing to Josiah Wedgwood, boasted that 'our new bridges are the eighth wonder of the Peak'.[13]

33 *Scarthin Nick. Anonymous pen and ink drawing, early 19th-century.*

Not so the roads, whose construction improved but slowly. Many tourists still used the old ones rather than pay the turnpike tolls. However, the turnpike roads, despite their charges, at least allowed the easier passage of the broad-wheeled wagons (see plate 89, p.170), especially those of hauliers like Pickfords,[14] whose eight-horse teams were able to haul their loads up the steep sides of the dales. The days of the pack horses were numbered.

Coaches came late to the Peak. Even when the road from Manchester to London was completely turnpiked through Derby and Buxton early coaches still took the old, gentler southern route through Macclesfield and Ashbourne. The earliest recorded through-coach from London came to Buxton from Derby in 1740 and passed on to Warrington and Liverpool. Its progress must have been very slow across the Pennines. By 1768 the *Buxton Flying Machine* was starting from London three times a week, but as late as 1785 the first London to Manchester *Royal Mail* still preferred the swifter route via Macclesfield and Leek.

Buxton became the coaching centre of the Peak and the expansion of the postal system together with the growing numbers of travellers and tourists led to the construction of a better network of turnpike roads which followed the river valleys and avoided the old, natural obstacles. A new breed of road builders, often drawn from the mines and the quarries, was prepared to blast passages through rocky terrain. The line of the present A6 pursued the Derwent upstream from Derby to Matlock, once a gap had been blasted through Scarthin Nick at Cromford. Then it proceeded to Darley and Rowsley where, in 1759, it was switched into the Wye valley and so to Bakewell (see plate IV). More rock excavation took it beneath the overhanging Endcliff and on to Ashford. Here it stopped and travellers had to take the old hill roads to reach Buxton by way of Sheldon and Chelmorton. However, in 1810 the Duke of Devonshire linked his estates in Ashford and Buxton by driving the turnpike road up to Taddington and then along the Wye once more into Buxton. This was a fine achievement and today provides the traveller on the A6 with one of the most scenic routes in England.

By this time the roads in the Peak had excellent surfaces. There was a feeling of exuberance and confidence abroad and road builders considered their surveying and engineering skills had at last equalled, if not surpassed, those of the Romans. Thus in 1791 Sir Philip Gell built a new road from his lead mines and quarries at Hopton to Matlock and called it the *Via Gellia*! The Reverend Richard Warner considered this a quaint affectation but conceded that the new road 'contributes much to the enjoyment of the traveller, conducting him through a shorter, more agreeable and convenient road than the former one', which another tourist described as 'an unpleasant ride over rough ways'.[15] Warner described his seven-mile journey from Tideswell to Buxton as tremendously hilly but comfortable on 'a road as hard as adamant and smooth as a bowling green'.[16]

The secret lay in grading the limestone from the coarse foundations to the fine surface. Rhodes tells us that the road-makers 'understand the best principles of making and repairing roads. They break the limestone to a circular gauge of from two and a half to three inches in diameter, and a forfeit is incurred for every stone that will not pass the ring: the stone when broken is laid upon the road six or eight inches thick, and shortly it becomes so hard and compact that the carriage wheels, as they pass over it, scarcely leave a mark behind them. In the vicinity of Bakewell, Baslow, Calver, Hassop etc. etc. this system of road making has long prevailed, and has been found very beneficial; the roads are not only easy to travel on, but they are very durable and made at little expence.'[17]

White Watson of Bakewell corroborates this description and gives a sketch of the iron rings for grading limestone. He tells us the system was first used at Chelmorton and Flagg in 1806.[18] All these improvements were made a decade and more before the ideas of the great John Macadam.

Now the Peak was alive with fast coaches with splendid names like *The Defiance* which first ran from Ashbourne, through Bakewell to Sheffield in 1807, *The Bruce* and *The Peveril of the Peak* which called at Bakewell on their way from London to Edinburgh in 1818. In one week in that year, Watson tells us, 655 passengers passed through Bakewell by coach.[19]

A brave sight they were, speeding up and down the hills. Rhodes give us a fine description of the Bakewell-Buxton coach high above him, beneath on the banks of the Wye, as it plunged down the new road near Topley Pike:

> I was startled from my reverie by the sound of a coachman's horn, that came gently upon the ear, when I was least prepared to expect such a greeting. Shortly a stage-coach appeared, which seemed actually to issue from the clouds that obscured the higher elevations of this stupendous hill; and I observed it pass rapidly along, where the eye could scarcely discern the trace of a road, and where to all appearance a human foot could with difficulty find a resting place. Had I supposed this vehicle to have contained within it beings like myself, I might have shuddered with apprehension, but the coach from its great height above me looked so like a child's toy, and the sound of the horn was so soft and unobtrusive – so unlike the loud blast of a stage-coachman's bugle – and altogether the place was so unfitted for the intrusion of such an object, that it appeared more like a fairy scene, or a picture of imagination, than any real thing and substantial.[20]

Such romantic sights were the stuff of Georgian prints and today's greetings cards. In the winter, however, coaching was not so romantic for coachmen or passengers and to keep warm spirits were commonly taken at staging posts – occasionally with disastrous results. On New Year's Day, 1830, for instance, the crack Manchester to London coach, *Telegraph*, was pelting down Swinscoe Hill on its approach to Ashbourne. *The Staffordshire Advertiser* reported what happened:

> The coachman was accidentally thrown off his box and pulled a passenger down with him. The horses experiencing liberty, went down the hill at full speed, crossed the bridge at the bottom, and carried the coach with great violence against the corner of the public-house on the opposite side, forcing off one of the wheels. They then galloped towards the toll-bar, where the coach came in contact with the gate-post and was dashed almost to pieces … The guard and coachman, it is feared, were far from being sober, as they had called at many inns on the road to drink, in commemoration of the day.[21]

34 *Ashbourne from the Derby Road. Lithograph by Samuel Rayner, 1830. A road mender is at work and the 'Derby Dilly' enters the town.*

Tourists entering the Peak by coach faced a variety of hazards. The terrain allowed for easy ambush by highwaymen though this was more readily attempted in the misty days and dark evenings of autumn and winter. The winter weather alone could make the roads impassable and it was not unusual for Buxton to be incommunicado for a week or more. Every effort was made to get through with the Royal Mail and large coaching inns, like the *Rutland Arms* at Bakewell, recorded in their *Snow Book* the extra horses required to haul the coaches over the Pennines.[22]

The sturdy horses used on these runs were often headstrong and required a good coachman to control them – winter or summer. In 1835 Sir George Head gives a graphic, Pickwickian account of his journey from Manchester to Buxton:

> We departed at three o'clock in the afternoon, and had proceeded on our way till we arrived in sight of our partner coach, advancing in the opposite direction, when we perceived that the horses were running away as furiously as their clumsy action would allow, for they were apparently (even seen under present advantages) a pair of floundering heavy brutes. Our driver immediately gave them a wide berth, and inasmuch as they preferred the wrong side of the road, he very prudently took up a station on the other. It was well he did so; for on came a coach, rolling and swinging in the track we left, while a stout coachman sat on the box, calling *who-ho* in vain,

and pulling with all his might against a pair of determined hard-mouthed 'uns, both obstinately bearing towards the off side of the road.

The vehicle had no sooner passed us (much closer, by the way, than was agreeable,) than it was evident that a catastrophe was inevitable, as the cattle continued to incline more and more towards the hedge; in the mean time we remained stationary, anxiously waiting the result. Nor were we long in suspense, for some obstacle caused the vehicle suddenly to stop; either a horse fell or ran foul of the bank, or a wheel grazed, or some such casualty happened, we could not see what it was, otherwise than by the effect produced; the coach gave a violent lurch, being all but over, then righted, at the same time flinging out of his seat an unlucky man who sat on the top. I saw him with his heels up, and his head downwards, in figure like the letter X; and in that position he fell, with the joint force of gravity and progressive motion.[23]

Head was extremely concerned about the luckless passenger's fate but his own coach driver whipped up the horses 'in spite of entreaty and remonstrance'. Thus, Head believed, coach accidents were prevented 'from finding their way to the ears of the public'. He completed his journey after the long descent into Buxton on a 'well-kept gravelled road'. The coach drew up in front of the splendid Crescent 'within whose colonnade are the post-office, show-rooms of bijouterie, marble ornaments etc, also the three principal inns – namely the Great Hotel, St Anne's Hotel and The Hall'.

On leaving Buxton for Bakewell and Matlock a few days later, Head gives us a rare and humorous description of his fellow coach passengers – a newly married couple and a plump young mother with her suckling child:

I took my place in a two-horse coach, which departs every day from Buxton, wherein a young lady and her very young bridegroom, for such I took him to be, occupied the opposite seat. Having probably passed their honeymoon at Buxton, they were returning, as they said, to Sheffield. Their looks and behaviour caused me to arrive at the above conclusion, as well as other indications, such as the ring on the lady's finger, and the various frivolous changes she insisted on among parcels carried in the gentleman's pocket; besides, both simpered on the subject of domestic felicity, and declared that the walks, shrubbery, and hermitage at Buxton were quite enchanting. The young gentleman was an arch-looking little being, but certainly an apology for a husband; he had youth on his side, being under twenty, but he was a starveling, very probably an abortion, for the lids of a pair of large eye-balls were imperfectly separated, as in the case of a little dog ten days old. The lady, on the contrary, was at least half-a-dozen years older, of fine features, and a showy figure. On my side was a fat married lady, holding a healthy little child on her lap with remarkably large staring eyes. The bride showed much attention to the child, and, although with a patronizing air, talked very graciously to it, and to the fat lady, its mother, now and then: and, moreover, being laden with ornaments, she at last drew from her wrist a broad golden bracelet, and gave it to the little girl to play with. The child soon grew restless and cried, till other measures having failed, the fat lady, flattered by the attention paid to her infant, very

35 *The steep turnpike road at Topley Pike. Sketch by J.M.W. Turner, 1831.*

reasonably resolved to consider herself as if at home, and in her own nursery, at the same time making preparations that caused the whole party to look different ways. In the first place, the young gentleman looked at the bride, saying something in her ear at the same time that made her frown; the young lady, drawing down a thick, white plaited veil, looked discomposed, and as if she wished to find a way out of the coach; the little child, with open mouth and outstretched arms, looked as if it were ready to devour its mamma; the fat lady, resting her chin upon her throat, looked as if she thought the child's swallow not half big enough; and I looked, as far as I was able, passive, and quite determined to see nothing improper.

On arriving at Bakewell (and by this time the child must have been nearly choked) our party broke up. Here we met the Sheffield coach. The mother, child, bride, and bridegroom, went together to Sheffield, while I proceeded alone to Matlock, and took up my quarters at the old Bath Hotel.[24]

Of course, the number of coaching inns increased as more frequent change of horses cut journey times. At Newhaven, in 1795, the Duke of Devonshire built the splendid *New Inn* as the only coaching stop half way between Buxton and Ashbourne and at the point where the turnpike road crossed from Hartington to Bakewell. Such an inn, where local tradition asserts that George IV stayed and expressed his satisfaction by granting the inn a free and perpetual licence, was an admirable place for tourists to stay. It gave excellent access by way of Hartington to Dove Dale and the Manifold Valley and travellers had less need for a guide and a much more comfortable base than the disreputable *Dog and Partridge* on the way out of the Dale. In the opposite direction, a mile off the road, lay Arbor Low, 'the Stonehenge of the North' and a great tourist attraction.

Towns, too, were springing to life as new coaching inns transformed their day-to-day business. *The Green Man* in Ashbourne was renowned, not least because it was frequented by Dr Johnson and James Boswell who came to stay with Dr Taylor who lived in the town. In 1805 the Duke of Rutland pulled down the old *White Horse* in Bakewell and built the *Rutland Arms* with its elegant coach yard and stables. *The George* at Tideswell, another fine inn, was erected beside the county's most elegant medieval church, within a town that Jewitt described as 'the very reverse of beautiful: its buildings are mean, its streets crooked, contracted, and dirty, its shambles disgusting, and its passages loathsome … The [ebbing and flowing] well is now nearly choaked up with weeds and rubbish'.[25]

Many villages still appeared 'medieval' as the new coaches rattled through them. Tourists did not linger at Taddington, described in 1811 as 'one of the meanest villages in Derbyshire', and 'a dirty, cheerless, inhospitable village, devoid of every kind of beauty, and inhabited by a race of Peakrills, as uncouth and barbarous as a horde of savages'. Taddington's only claim to fame was the longevity of the villagers which was attributed to 'the healthfulness of its situation and the salubrity of its air'.[26]

But Tideswell, Taddington and other once isolated towns were gradually dragged into the 19th century. As their old lead-mining industry declined and their agricultural practices changed, they witnessed the beginnings of the Industrial Revolution which developed along the rivers of the Peak.

The old, low, thatched vernacular villages and towns slowly gave way to the polite architecture of the Georgian period, from the magnificence of the Duke of Devonshire's new Crescent at Buxton and Dr Taylor's grand town house in Ashbourne to Sir Nathaniel Curzon's Palladian and neo-classical mansion at Kedleston. Style and fashion were finally making inroads into the boorish region of mists and hills, rocks and rivers. The grey changeable weather remained constant over the limestone ravines and the black gritstone moors, but as the Romantic Age dawned new tourists with new vision found new wonders at which to marvel. The artist and the writer, the antiquary and the scientist began the 'Grand Tour of Britain' in the Peak along with the growing crowds of simple pleasure-seekers who came to enjoy the social round with its accompanying fripperies and knick-knacks. Thus, in the second half of the 18th century a tourist 'industry' slowly developed to accommodate the travellers' needs.

8

Geology, Commerce and Tourism

From earliest times visitors to the Peak have been fascinated by its mineral formations. Pieces of polished Ashford marble have been found in prehistoric barrows and fluorspar must have been found by the Romans whilst working in the lead mines. Some maintain that the Romans turned vases from fluorspar, though none has been certainly associated with Britain. Even before the dawn of geology as a science at the turn of the 18th century, men were drawn to picking up pieces of sparkling spar or breaking off stalactites and stalagmites as souvenirs or the beginnings of a collection of minerals. They were frequently prepared to pay the local inhabitants to procure for them fossil and mineral curiosities from the caves and the mines. Thus Defoe and his companions, on meeting a lead miner emerging from a shaft laden with galena (lead ore) 'looked on the ore, and got the poor man's leave to bring every one a small piece of it away with us, for which we gave him two small pieces of better metal called shillings … '[1] Such an exchange, or trade, with the natives had two rapid developments by the end of the 18th century; the first was the research into the geology of the Peak; the second was the growth of the tourist trade in fossils and minerals and the artefacts produced from them.

There is always an element of vandalism in tourism. The more enterprising of the visitors to the Peak sought their own treasures from the limestone formations, often obliterating thousands of years of nature's work by smashing off a stalactite or hacking out a fossil or a piece of tufa. Some simply entered caves, like Poole's Cavern, to hurl rocks at icicle-like structures. Others would, by chance, find 'treasure' at their very feet in the form of 'gems' or, as they were known locally, 'Derbyshire diamonds'. White Watson described them in geological terms as 'crystals of quartz … in hexagonal prisms terminating with a hexagonal pyramid at each end, sometimes in macles by two crystals crossing each other, and sometimes in clusters'.[2] Such crystals were, and still are, to be found in a variety of hillsides after heavy rain and Diamond Hill outside Buxton was a popular resort for treasure hunters. An anonymous lady writing from Buxton to her sister in 1810 described how she and her brother, whilst exploring Miller's Dale, 'picked up many specimens of the Derbyshire diamond. After rain they lie sparkling in the road'.[3] These, one would guess, were not the finer specimens described by White Watson but the 'semi transparent grains of quartz' described by Farey.[4]

It was quite possible to stumble on interesting crystals or fossils on the road surfaces which were largely composed of crushed limestone rubble, often from mining spoil heaps. This is what happened when the carver and statuary, Henry Watson of Ashford and Bakewell, was riding with Lord Duncannon in Eyam, or Middleton, Dale in 1743. 'His Lordship's horse stumbled on a piece of water-icle [i.e. stalactite] which lay in the road, which appearing a different nature of stone from what they had generally seen on the road, his Lordship asked Mr Watson if he thought it possible to procure a quantity of it and to make it into ornaments; to which he replied he wished much to try it; upon which his Lordship, in a short time, sent Mr Watson a drawing of an urn he had brought from abroad; when Mr W got a quantity of water-icle and began making the vase in his house in Bakewell.'[5] Henry Watson, together with his assistant, Robert Bradbury, invented a lathe and began again the craft of turning vases. It was Henry Watson who mechanised the marble industry in 1751 by patenting his famous water-powered 'machine'.[6] This enabled slabs of black limestone from the quarries and mines around Ashford-in-the-Water to be cut, ground and polished. It could also turn lathes for making vases and made Ashford famous in the early days of the Industrial Revolution. It drew tourists as an amazing machine, quite apart from the variety of artefacts it produced. The local poet, John Howe, a tallow chandler of Ashford, described the processes carried out in his poem, Monsal Dale, published in 1816.

> And turning to the left, by Cliffend green,
> We first admire the curious machine.
> Here grating saws divide the ponderous blocks,
> (Hewn from the quarries of the neighbouring rocks,)
> And here the engine's retroactive power
> Sweeps the rude marble's rugged surface o'er,
> Till polish, by another process brought,
> Gives elegance, surpassing even thought,
> Fit to adorn the palace and the dome,
> The poor man's grave-stone, or the rich man's tomb.
> Here Stalactites are, by artists' aid,
> Wrought to all forms that fancy e'er pourtrayed;
> And, when thus manufactured, may conduce
> Either to luxury or real use. [7]

Blue John, or amethystine, became the most sought-after Derbyshire mineral by the collector and the tourist. It is the loveliest of the fluorspars, or crystallised fluates of lime with bandings ranging from purple to yellow, and is found at its finest in the Treak Cavern at Castleton. Called Blue John from a corruption of the French, bleu jaune, it had long been known to the lead miners (see plate 40, p.79). Henry Watson appears to have first seen its commercial potential when in 1750 he sold it in Bakewell at two shillings per hundred weight to the Marquess of Rockingham who laid it in the gravel walks of his gardens at Wentworth Woodhouse.[8] Adam tells us that in 1770 John Platts of Rotherham, who had taken over the Ashford marble mill from Henry Watson, 'picked up two

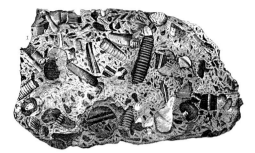
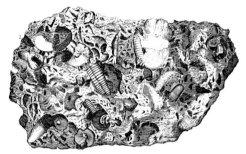

36   *Fluorspar, found in the mines of Derbyshire. Engraving from Dr Charles Leigh's Natural History of Lancashire, Cheshire and the Peak of Derbyshire, 1700.*

or three pieces of the spar in Earl Fitzwilliam's gardens at Wentworth. Being struck with its peculiar character, he formed a pair of salt cellars of considerable beauty, which attracted the attention of Mr Robert Hall of Castleton' (a mineral surveyor and the first practical geologist of the Peak).[9]

White Watson says Hall was 'the first man who procured a quantity of this spar and his neighbours styled him Blue John'.[10] The competition to profit from it became fierce as Platts and Henry Watson began to work large pieces into urns and vases for the aristocracy and into trinkets for the tourists. White Watson, again, gives us an early example of industrial espionage leading to the development of the spar and marble industry outside the Peak:

> When Mr Watson had brought the business to great perfection his man, Jonathan Morton, in whom he placed great confidence and who was the principal man in working it, stole some of the stone and, erecting a lathe at his house in Great Longsdon, carried on the business unknown to his master, – feigning himself ill and neglecting his Master's business. He was connected with Richard Brown, Clerk of All Saints Church, Derby, Stone Mason, who purchased the goods of him. One day he took some to Mr Port's of Ilam Hall who was a great friend of Mr Watson's, and who, suspecting them, detained the goods for a few days, fixing a day for Brown to call again; – in the meantime Mr Port invited Mr Watson to come on that day to Ilam, which he did, and then met Brown, – the

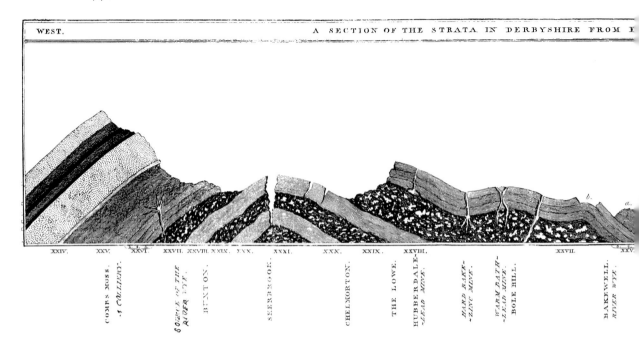

WEST. A SECTION OF THE STRATA IN DERBYSHIRE FROM ...

XXIV. XXV. XXVI. XXVII. XXVIII. XXIX. XXX. XXXI. XXX. XXIX. XXVIII. XXVII. XXV.

COMBS MOSS.
A COLLIERY.

SOURCE OF THE RIVER WYE.
BUXTON.

SEERBROOK.

CHELMORTON.

THE LOWE.
HUBBERDALE – LEAD MINE.

HARD RAKE – ZINC MINE.

WARM BATH – LEAD MINE.
BOLE HILL.

BAKEWELL.
RIVER WYE.

goods were produced, Mr Watson declared that they were made by his man which Brown acknowledged, saying 'he had bought them of Jonathan Morton and paid him for them.' Thus, Brown begun the business – which he still continues in.[11]

Tourist shops, sometimes masquerading under the title of museums, flourished in Castleton, Buxton, Matlock Bath and Bakewell. The Watsons were the pioneers in teaching about, and profiting from the sale of, geological specimens. Henry Watson began the first collection at the Bath House in Bakewell and was among the first practical geologists. He and his brother Samuel, carver and millstone cutter, subscribed to *An Inquiry into the Original State and Formation of the Earth* published in 1778 by the Derby scientist and clockmaker, John Whitehurst (1713-88).[12] Henry Watson discussed geological matters with Whitehurst and both of them were influential on Henry's nephew White Watson and his Delineation of the section of the *Strata of Derbyshire* (published in 1811). In the introduction to this work he says that 'early in life the author was indefatigably engaged for several years in making an extensive collection of the fossils of this county, and particularly of the petrifactions, which he arranged agreeably to their respective strata; this collection he has had the honour of exhibiting with general satisfaction, to many of the virtuosi of this and other nations'.[13] Indeed, White Watson taught geology and mineralogy to the 5th Duke of Devonshire and his wife Georgiana. He sold them mineral

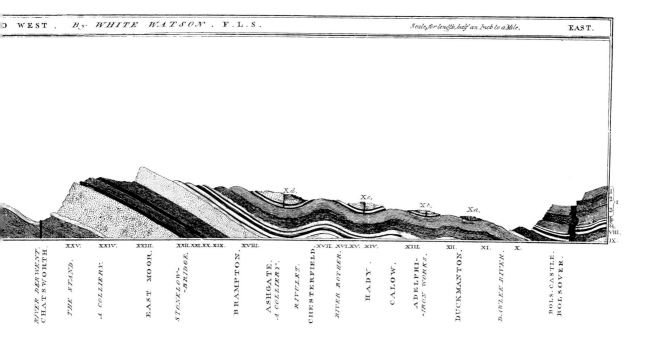

37 *A section of the Strata of Derbyshire from East to West. Engraving by White Watson from his Strata of Derbyshire, 1811.*

cabinets and examples of his strata of Derbyshire using local rock samples, designed a tufa grotto lined with minerals and fossils which the Duchess erected in Chatsworth gardens and was chiefly responsible for inculcating in their son, the 6th Duke, that love of marble and precious stones which is the hallmark of his new building at Chatsworth House.

John Byng was not fascinated by geology. When he arrived in Bakewell 1789 White Watson greeted him as a wealthy tourist and presented him with his card:

BAKEWELL, DERBYSHIRE

WHITE WATSON,

(Nephew and Successor to Mr HENRY WATSON, later of *Bakewell.*)

BEGS leave to acquaint the Nobility, Gentry and others, that he executes Monuments, Chimney Pieces, Tables, Vases and other Ornaments, in all the variety of English and Foreign Marbles, agreeable to the modern Taste and upon the most reasonable Terms.

W WATSON, having attentively collected the Minerals and Fossils of *Derbyshire*, is now in possession of a valuable Assortment ready for the inspection of the Curious, and undertakes to execute orders for the like Productions, properly arranged and described.

Byng described him as 'a collector and seller of all this sort of work and curiosity; but which is to be seen to more perfection in many shops in London. If Mr W hoped for a buyer in me, he was mistaken'.[14]

Yet many tourists were not so grumpy and parsimonious and far more discerning than Byng. Josiah Wedgwood bought fossils from White Watson and in 1790, accompanied by Erasmus Darwin, Francis Mundy and William Strutt, paid a visit to Watson at the Bath House.[15] Through Wedgwood too, the Birmingham manufacturer, Mathew Boulton, enquired about spars, especially Blue John, for embellishing ornaments made at his Soho Works.

Museums of the type set up by the Watsons flourished at Matlock Bath and Castleton, especially after White Watson's death in 1835. The two towns, as well as Ashford, became linked with Derby through the entrepreneurial efforts of the Brown family. Having acquired Henry Watson's secret of turning spars on a lathe, the Derby Spar Works in King Street prospered and eventually eclipsed its rivals in the Peak. The Browns took over the Ashford Marble Works (1824) having brought their own Derby works to the peak of production in 1802 by installing a steam engine.[16]

38 *Ashford marble craftsman's workshop, Buxton Museum.*

39 *Ashford black marble table top inlaid with flowers in the manner of Italian* pietra dura, *c.1851.*

In 1793 Richard Brown had taken into partnership his highly talented former apprentice John Mawe (1766-1829), son of a Derby baker. Within a year he had married Brown's daughter, Sarah. He advertised his business through his book, *The Mineralogy of Derbyshire with a description of the most interesting Mines* (1802) and by means of his *Lessons on Mineralogy* which he subsequently published.[17]

Among Matlock's museums the most famous was the Royal Museum or Mawe's Old Museum, set up by Richard Brown in what was originally the dining room of the *Great Hotel*. Mawe took over the museum. Tourists flocked to buy Egyptian obelisks in spar, paperweights, urns and goblets, mosaic brooches, animal figures and mineral cabinets. John Byng was a little more attracted to Matlock's trinkets than those he saw in Bakewell. He almost confesses to extravagance when he tells us, 'As I pass'd by Matlock Bath, I purchased a sixpenny spar watch for my Frek; and had some foolish thoughts of laying out money for presents in the spar ware; but a sensible wherefore stopt me, especially when I found them as dear as in London'.[18]

One of the great driving forces behind the growing interest in geology was the Birmingham Lunar Society which contained such luminaries as James Watt, Joseph Priestley, Matthew Boulton, Josiah Wedgwood and Erasmus Darwin.

The last had just moved from Lichfield to Derby in 1783 when he wrote to Boulton to announce that 'we have established an infant philosophical society in Derby'.[19] This body, which involved Whitehurst, promoted geological expeditions to the Peak to study the caves and their structure. Darwin again tells us, 'I have lately travel'd two days journey into the bowels of the earth, with three most able philosophers and have seen the Goddess of Minerals naked, as she lay in her inmost bowers'.[20]

Richard Brown certainly collected specimens for both Darwin and Whitehurst and very probably for Wedgwood, who admired Brown's turned Blue John vases. Wedgwood provided at least one jasper-ware plaque for the plinth of one of Brown's vases.[21]

If Chatsworth House was the principal advertisement for Ashford marble then Kedleston Hall was the showplace for Blue John. As early as 1765 Richard Brown had made two 'purple obelisks' for Kedleston [22] and began to make inlaid fireplaces after Robert Adam's designs. By 1768 Boulton also began to create objects from, or incorporating, Blue John. In that year he ordered some 14 tons of the spar from John Platts of Ashford and wrote enthusiastically to Whitehurst:

> The principle [sic] intention of this letter is to tell you that I have found a use for Blew John wch. will consume some quantity of it. I mean that sort which is proper for turning into Vases. I therefore would esteem it as a singular favr. if you would enquire whether the Mine of it has lately been let or when it is to be let again for I wish to take it for a Year and if you find that it is not possible to come at it then please to learn how I can come at any of ye best and largest sort of the produce of it, but above all I beg you will be quite secret as to my intentions and never let M. Boulton and John Blue be named in ye same sentence, when you come to Soho I will shew you what I am about. I am informed that there is one person in Derby that has it. Now if ye mine is not comeatable or if I could not be supply [sic] upon ye same terms as he is but I had rather have the Mine ... [23]

So Boulton and Brown were in competition. Brown's work was certainly the best in Derbyshire and possibly cheaper than Boulton's. Bartholomew Faujas de Saint Fond, a French geologist and correspondent of Whitehurst, wrote of his meeting with Brown:

> ... we went to see Richard Brown. His shop is well stocked with vases of various shapes and sizes, together with other articles in coloured fluor-spar, all much better made and polished than those sold at Castleton and Buxton ... Mr Brown, far from taking advantage of a foreigner, treated us with moderation and courtesy ... The next day we went to see another natural history dealer who makes articles of spar and marble ... but he is dearer and less obliging than Mr Brown. [24]

Soon after 1800 Brown had a London showroom in Covent Garden which subsequently moved to the Strand and by 1816 he had a sales outlet in Castleton itself, thanks to the business drive of John Mawe. Certainly by means of high-class manufacture of articles for the wealthy as well as souvenirs for the tourists, Brown was highly influential in spreading the fame of the Peak and its geological wonders.

As the early Victorian period progressed the craze for Blue John was surpassed by a renewed interest in Ashford marble. Following the success of Henry Watson's venture at Ashford in the mid-18th century and the subsequent success of Richard Brown, new factories were established on the River Wye by John Lomas at Bakewell in 1820 and by George Redfern at the Great Bache works in Ashford as late as 1846. [25] The Ashford factories were patronised by the 6th and 7th Dukes of Devonshire and the one at Bakewell by the Dukes of Rutland. William, 6th Duke of

40 *Turned Blue John vase with applied Wedgwood plaque, c.1785.*

Devonshire, shared his parents' passion for mineralogy and continued to use White Watson as his consultant. Varying shades of the local marble were now added to the black, grey and white – rosewood, birdseye, russet and in 1823 the 'Duke's red'. [26] These can be seen to good effect in the 6th Duke's extension of Chatsworth and, together with Derbyshire alabaster, in the estate church built at Edensor by the 7th Duke.

A hundred years earlier at Ashford and Bakewell Henry Watson had begun to inlay black marble artefacts with other coloured pieces of marble or spar. These were principally for the tourist market. His nephew, White, inlaid frames of black marble to form geological sections of the Peak. Samples of the strata concerned were depicted as anticlines and synclines beneath a white sky

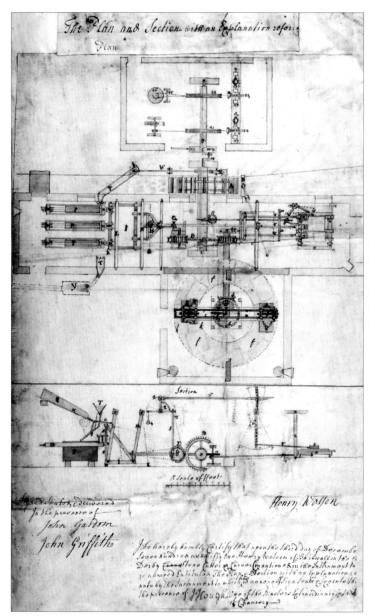

41 *Drawing for the patent of Henry Watson's machine for sawing and polishing black marble and for turning vases, 1751.*

composed of Carrara marble. Such 'pictures' were explained with a title and geological notes engraved on the black frame and equipped with a loop behind for hanging. A hundred or so of these geological aids were made by White Watson, of which a quarter can now be traced. They were sold, together with copies of his *Delineation of the Strata of Derbyshire* (1811) and *A Section of the Strata in the Vicinity of Matlock Bath* (1813), to collectors and to museums. [27]

Mosaic pattern and scrapwork inlays were the chief forms of decoration for trinkets in the late 18th and early 19th centuries. As the early Victorian era dawned the predilection for black, especially after Prince Albert's death, strengthened the vogue for articles of Ashford black marble and Whitby jet. Jewellery in these materials was particularly popular but a vast range of additional items ranging from candlesticks, obelisks and paperweights to thermometer mounts, clock cases and crucifixes found their way into middle-class households throughout Britain and beyond.[28]

It was William Adam, author of *The Gem of the Peak* who, whilst working in Mawe's shop in Matlock Bath, introduced the contemporary Florentine type of inlay, or pietra dura, to Derbyshire. Table tops especially were now inlaid with curvilinear patterns and effusions of flowers, leaves and fruit (see plate 39, p.77).[29] Much of this new branch of marble manufacture was a cottage industry and the skill of the Peakland craftsmen was well demonstrated at the Great Exhibition of 1851 where they won four prize medals.[30]

Another form of souvenir, popular with visitors to the Peak, was the etching of favourite views on flat polished black marble slabs, which served as paper weights or tabletop pictures. Henry Moore (1776-1848), a Derby drawing master, was the first to produce such work for Richard Brown at Derby. Engraving with a diamond was said by William Adam to have been invented in the 1830s by the daughter of Ebenezer Rhodes of Sheffield.[31] By this method moonlight scenes, much favoured in the romantic period, could be produced in a manner like that of working on modern scraper board. Samuel Rayner, the artist and engraver, who published *Sketches of Derbyshire Scenery* (1830) and *The History and Antiquities of Haddon Hall* (1836), was the foremost exponent of this work in which he was assisted by his wife, Anne.[32]

42 *Henry Watson's monument by White Watson in Holy Trinity Church, Ashford-in-the-Water. It is made of Derbyshire marbles with a Blue John inlay, 1786.*

Finally, some mention is required of the most curious tourist 'knick-knacks' produced in the Peak – 'petrifactions'. These were most readily obtained at Matlock Bath where the hot springs had created the extensive Tufa Terrace. Here strange objects were received from far and wide to be placed in the petrifying wells and be coated with limestone precipitates from the water as it rapidly evaporated. Birds' nests with eggs were a popular subject, as were wigs and wicker basketry. Parties of tourists were eager to see the process at work and Adam described the three wells:

> We shall take them as they occur, and first we find Mr Joseph Pearson's (the Royal Well), visited by the princess Victoria in October 1832, on the road side, just under the way leading to the Old Bath. Mr Peter Smedley's, under his spar shops, still further on, where a piece of a cable of a man of war (the Victory) is now being petrified; and Mr Boden's, by the Post office, near Saxtons Green, where the head and antlers still are, of the deer killed at Chatsworth, on the arrival of the princess Victoria. All these three wells are literally filled with all sorts of things, being petrified, which *must* be shifted every now and then to prevent them sticking to each other, or to the bottom.
>
> Recently, Mr Walker, at the Boats, has made a large one by the side of the river, to which he politely ferries all parties if they wish it.[33]

9

Antiquaries, Barrow Openers and Ecclesiologists

Haddon Hall, one of England's foremost domestic antiquities, was a late 'discovery' of the romantic age. Camden had simply mentioned it as a seat of the Vernon and then the Manners families. In the early 18th century Stukeley gave the place scant attention. However, it was he who heightened the interest in the antiquities of Derbyshire in general. His two visits, recorded in *Itinerarium Curiosum*, are as interesting for what he saw as for what he missed. Roman remains were his principal preoccupation, especially those of the Roman camp at Little Chester (Derventio) near Derby; at Buxton (Aquae Arnemetiae) the site of the Roman baths delighted him and he sketched them, used them and found them less harmful to over-indulgence than those at Bath (see plate 27, p.53).

However, Stukeley's reputation as an antiquary subsequently rested on his theories about Druidism, which he considered the 'aboriginal patriarchal religion' of Britain. He developed his hypothesis in *Stonehenge*, a study of the famous stone circle, which he published in 1740. This was 16 years after his visits to Derbyshire were in print and he had reported on neither Arbor Low, the Bronze-Age stone circle near Youlgreave, nor on the Nine Ladies Circle on Stanton Moor. In truth, his ideas on Druidism were not so advanced at that stage, though he did make references to 'Druids' houses' when describing a prominent earthwork set among barrows at Staden, near Buxton.

Stukeley's fascination with caves and their occupants led him to give the earliest descriptions of two in particular. He discovered the first among the ruins of Dale Abbey, beside the Derwent near Derby, and entered the 'little oratory called the hermitage cut as a cell in the adjacent rock face'. The solitary, contemplative life of hermits intrigued him and he travelled north from Dale Abbey to view a more natural cave near Birchover. Here he made the earliest known description and sketch of the hermitage hidden among the rocks and trees where the old Portway climbs between two large outcrops of gritstone, Robin Hood's Stride and Cratcliff Tor. Having ascended the slopes of the latter, Stukeley tells us:

43 *Arbor Low in December. Etching by S. Hartley, 1985.*

I took pains to clamber on hands and knees almost to the top, and I enter'd another hermit's cell, who had a mind if possible to get quite out of the world; 'tis hewn in the rock with a most dreary prospect before it. On one end is a crucifix and a little niche where I suppose the mistaken zeal of the starv'd anchorite plac'd his saint or such trinket.[1]

Stukeley eventually left the Peak and returned to his house at Stamford where he created one of the first 'hermitages', based on the two he had seen in Derbyshire, in an English garden.[2] He inspired his friends and fellow antiquaries to follow his footsteps into the Peak and was instrumental in beginning the 18th-century vogue of establishing 'hermitages' in parks and gardens as part of gothick taste. Nevertheless, 60 years later the poor approach tracks and its concealment among rocks and trees still kept the cave at Cratcliff Tor a secret. Even the local antiquary, Samuel Pegge, rector of Whittington, near Chesterfield, did not know of it. He wrote to his friend and fellow antiquary, Major Hayman Rooke of Mansfield Woodhouse, on 23 December 1783:

I have lately been informed that there is a cavern at Matlock with a crucifix in it, and consequently a hermitage, it being a very private and sequestered spot. It is among the rocks and not easily to be found, but I hope ye will take the opportunity when the days are longer and the weather warmer to go and view it. If you will enquire for Mr William Wolley jnr., a young attorney (who is my informer), he will attend you and show you the place.[3]

Hayman Rooke had already visited it and published an illustration of the carved crucifixion in *Archaeologia*.[4] Gradually the secret location was a secret no longer and in the 19th century it was necessary to place an iron grid across the entrance to the cave to save the carving from mutilation.

Rooke continued in the footsteps of Stukeley, whose earlier visit appears to have been unknown to him or Pegge, and crossed the valley to view another prominent outcrop of rocks over a small warren of caves. These were Rowtor Rocks on the edge of Birchover village. Stukeley had not named the site but described it for what it was, a natural outcrop of gritstone adapted as a rock garden and mount with a fine prospect over the Wye valley. This was the work of the Reverend Thomas Eyre[5] whose vicarage lay at the foot of the rocks. 'There is,' said Stukeley, 'an easy ascent up to it by steps hewn out of the rock and abundance of alcoves, grotts, summer houses, cellars, pinnacles, dials, balustrades, urns etc. All of the same materials; earth is carried to the top with greens planted along this hanging terrace whence you have a free view over many a craggy mountain. I was highly pleased with so elegant a composure, where art and industry had so well plaid its part against rugged nature.'

When Rooke visited the site the garden had fallen into disrepair and had lost its shape and detail. Ironically what Stukeley, the reviver, with John Aubrey[6] of druidical studies, immediately saw as a garden, Rooke believed to be the site of a druidical grove.[7] Rooke and his contemporaries had no conception of the Ice Age and the effect of glaciation in forming rocky landscapes. The skill of the Reverend Eyre's rock cutters was not acknowledged but was classed, along with the natural shapes, as a work of the Druids. Following Dr Borlace

44   *'The Crucifix* [inset] *at the East End of the Hermitage at* [Cratcliff] *Torr in Derbyshire.' Pen and wash sketch by William Stukeley, c.1727. Photograph c.1890.*

45 *A Chantry in Bakewell Churchyard. Engraving by Richard Godfrey, c.1780. Pegge (with Rooke on the left) points to an inscription.*

46 *Rowtor Rocks. Engraving by J. Saddler after Thomas Allom, c.1839.*

in his *Antiquities of Cornwall*, Rooke believed that certain huge boulders that rocked at a push of the hand were druidical deities; others indented randomly with smooth concave bowls he considered were basins worked by hand for some mystical purpose.

On the adjacent Stanton Moor he pronounced the Nine Ladies Circle a druidical temple, as he did the six remaining monoliths in Nine Stone Close on Hartle Moor.[8] Following Borlace again, he interpreted one of the flat-topped, perched blocks on Stanton Moor as a high platform for issuing decrees and a neighbouring stone as an idol. 'The Druids,' he wrote,

> undoubtedly had a power (unknown to us) of moving very large stones … by the number of Druidical remains on Stanton Moor, we may reasonably suppose this place to have been inhabited by the Druids. Here are temples, caves, rock basons, rocking stones, gorfed daus [high stones], rock idols and cairns. Their sacred groves have long since given way to cultivation; but their more durable monuments have stood the ravages of time and remain as helps to illustrate their history.

It was Rooke who made Rowtor Rocks, Stanton Moor and Hartle Moor attractions for more than antiquaries. Coach loads of sightseers came, increasing in numbers as the 19th century wore on. At Rowtor the ravages of thousands of feet wore down the steps and removed the last vestiges of a garden so that Victorian commentators moved far beyond the suppositions of Rooke by identifying sacrificial stones, 'rock basons' as blood containers and Eyre's early 18th-century rock chairs as thrones for Druids and Arch Druids. Thomas Allom's engraving of 1838 shows young and old strolling on the terraces and discovering the rocky labyrinths.[9]

As early as 1793 Plumptre noted that the rocks had been fenced in and visitors were escorted by a resident from a cottage at the foot of the rocks.[10] The local landowner, William Thornhill of Stanton Hall, had, by 1845, repaired and enlarged the old cottage and converted it into an inn to provide accommodation for visitors, a 'desideratum long wanted here in case of foul weather or any needful refreshment'.[11] Its name, of course, was, and still is, *The Druids*.

Rivalling Rowtor Rocks and Stanton Moore in druidical interest was the county's largest and most complete henge, Arbor Low.[12] Though small by comparison with Stonehenge or Avebury, it became a lure to the tourist in the late 18th century. It lies almost five miles west of Bakewell and nine miles from Buxton between the villages of Youlgreave and Hartington. The site is 1,230 feet above sea-level near the summit of the watershed dividing the rivers Bradford and Lathkill, one of the highest and most exposed limestone ridges in the Peak. At a similar altitude and ten miles to the west, near Dove Holes, is the lesser known, but once equally impressive, henge known as Bull Ring.[13]

Arbor Low is 250 feet in diameter with two opposed entrances; of the stone circle which once stood erect within its perimeter ditch, 47 outer and three central stones, all now lying flat, survive. Although the monument was known to local antiquaries such as James Mander[14] of Bakewell, who showed it to Pegge on 10 June 1761, national attention was first roused when Pegge read a paper to the Society of Antiquaries of London on 29 May 1783 and published it, together with a plan, in the same year.[15] Shortly after, as we have seen, access to travellers was made easier when the Duke of Devonshire built the *New Haven Inn* at the Ashbourne-Buxton and Hartington-Youlgreave crossroads.

Pegge and Rooke drew attention to a number of sites and monuments in north Derbyshire (see plate 45, p.86). They were puzzled about Roman lead-mining sites and, as at Rowtor Rocks, were undecided as to what were the works of Nature or of human endeavour. George Gough was quite forthright in giving his views to Hayman Rooke:

> I shall be glad to hear your tour into Derbyshire answered your expectation – I have been in the Peak and admire the wonders of it – and I will tell you what I think of them. Those wonders of the Peak, which have the credit of being natural curiosities, are the work of art – that is, they are the remains of the great works of the Romans in their search after gold and other precious metals.[16]

What Pegge and Rooke thought of this explanation is not clear. Indefatigable, they visited sites of every period, from Roman and Druidical remains to Peak and Bolsover Castles and Beauchief Abbey, which Pegge's ancestor had restored and maintained as a place of worship.[17] Neither Pegge nor Rooke was a grave robber or a barrow opener, though they were well aware that a number of their contemporaries, local gentlemen or curious souvenir hunters like Byng, were tampering with national monuments. The 'discovery' of a Bronze-Age urn or a piece of Saxon jewellery whetted the appetite of collectors who were assembling private museums throughout Britain. White Watson's museum in the Bakewell Bath House was not simply comprised of mineral specimens. Among the many curious relics of antiquity Glover noted a basaltic axe-head found on Stanton Moor. From the same location were an entire urn of baked earth found in a barrow in 1799 with an arrow and spear heads of flint. In another urn was a small lamp. A basaltic celt was found near Haddon Hall in 1795 and a glass 'lachrymatory' from the same location in 1801. Particularly interesting was a square tile with the letters of the alphabet impressed in Saxon characters.[18]

A close friend of Watson's who provided him with archaeological specimens was William Bateman FSA of Middleton by Youlgreave, an assiduous collector of antiquities, who published in *Archaeologia* and who died in the same year as Watson, 1835. It was William's son, Thomas Bateman (1821-61) who is today regarded as the best known archaeologist of the Peak and described himself as an 'opener of barrows'.[19] He used his considerable wealth to indulge his passion for digging and opened over 200 barrows in his life-time, often by methods that make today's archaeologists cringe. For instance, he 'rabbited' into the side of Gib Hill, a large mound on the edge of the Arbor Low henge, and brought down in ruin the cist he was seeking. Unabashed, he took the stones away and re-erected them in his garden at nearby Lomberdale Hall. Here, within his house he amassed by excavation, purchase and other means what his friend and fellow antiquary, Llewellyn Jewitt, described as 'such a collection of Celtic remains as no other museum, public or private, has, or even can attain'.[20] He readily made it available to all.

47 *Bakewell Church. Pencil drawing by Thomas Hearne, 1801.*

The growing curiosity about gothic architecture and monuments in the 18th century was late in making an impact in Derbyshire. True, there was some interest in the gothic 'survival' of Beauchief Abbey, which was described by Pegge and painted by Paul Sandby.[21] The gothick style, promoted by Horace Walpole and his circle, was not readily espoused in the churches and country houses of the Peak; the only noteworthy exception was the introduction of Strawberry Hill taste to Jacobean Tissington Hall by William Fitzherbert in the 1750s.

Antiquarianism was becoming fashionable and an increasing reason for travel. Francis Grose, FSA, was abreast of the times. In 1775 he issued the *Antiquarian Repertory*, a bi-monthly journal aimed at a growing, non-specialist readership. The Advertisement dismissed the old view of antiquarianism as 'the idle amusement of a few humdrum, plodding fellows, who wanting genius for nobler studies, busied themselves in heaping up illegible Manuscripts, mutilated Statues, obliterated Coins, and broken Pipkins'. The first volume of the *Antiquarian Repertory* now declared that 'without a competent fund of Antiquarian learning, no one will ever make a respectable figure, either as a Divine, a Lawyer, Statesman, Soldier, or even a private Gentleman … it is the *sine qua non* of several of the more liberal professions, as well as many trades'.

Richard Gough, Director of the Society of Antiquaries and a prominent late 18th-century 'goth', did the antiquarian traveller in Britain a singular service. His *British Topographical Antiquities of Great Britain and Ireland* (1780) dealt with the whole country by county and gave the best bibliography yet printed for the history and antiquities of Derbyshire. However, it is noticeably thin on ecclesiastical matters. Ecclesiology came late in a county with few monastic remains, no cathedral and not noted for its parish churches but rather for its locally sculpted alabaster monuments.

To antiquaries the most interesting church in the Peak was that of All Saints at Bakewell. It was the oldest – of Saxon origins – and contained all the medieval styles from romanesque to perpendicular. Its fine range of monuments, dating from the 14th to the 17th centuries, together with its intriguing tub font carved with figures in low relief, were especially fascinating. Bakewell parish covered much of the Peak; the Dean and Chapter of Lichfield held the advowson and the Dukes of Rutland and Devonshire were its chief benefactors.

Richard Gough was friendly with William Bray, a fellow of the Society of Antiquaries, in 1771 who was to become the Society's Treasurer in 1803. Gough encouraged Bray in his topographical writings and, when the latter sought an illustrator for his *Sketch of a Tour into Derbyshire and Yorkshire*, Gough recommended the artist who was to become the most celebrated draughtsman of the Society of antiquaries and one of the great driving forces of the early gothic revival – John Carter. Carter drew and James Basire engraved Bakewell church's romanesque west door, its Saxon cross, font and monuments. Carter saw himself as a 'Pilgrim of antiquity' and declared:

> I come not … to seek acquaintance, pay compliments, or beg dinners. I come … to seek antiquities, pay my bills at inns, and beg leave of the keepers of the keys of churches for admittance … my sole aim is to make the most of my time in the professional labours of my pencil.[22]

J.C. Buckler FSA, another fine draughtsman and friend of Carter – whom he dubbed 'Antiquity's most resolute friend' – came to Bakewell in July 1812 and made 16 drawings of the church and at least four sepia wash studies.[23]

Were these intended to be the epitaph of a doomed building? It was known that the ecclesiastical wonder of the Peak was in a parlous state. Its elegant 14th-century octagon and spire on an early English tower, whose foundations comprised Norman and Saxon remains, rested uneasily on the steep shale and limestone slope above the town. The new peal of eight bells, installed in 1796, and the zeal of the ringers were sounding the death knell of this celebrated landmark.

Following adverse reports from three architects, the Dean and Chapter of Lichfield reluctantly closed the church, had the spire and octagon taken down and the crossing capped.[24] In this sad state, like a dismasted ship, it was sketched thrice by Turner, painted by J.L. Petit and lithographed by Douglas Morison.[25] There were those who advocated a total demolition and rebuild but the Dean and Chapter and the vicar, the Revd K. Cornish, persevered with their intention of 'restoration'. In his appeal for funds the latter made the following statement on 24 October 1840:

> The Town of Bakewell holds so important a situation in the Hundred of the High Peak of Derbyshire, and is so well known to travellers and tourists, that it needs only to be named in order that it may be at once brought to their recollection, with all the beauty and interest of the neighbourhood.
>
> To such visitors the following appeal is made as well as to all others who have the cause of true religion at heart. It is an appeal in behalf of the Parish Church, which forms so picturesque a feature in the scenery; but which, from its dilapidated and dangerous state, requires that immediate attention should be drawn to it.[26]

48 *Bakewell. Pencil sketch by J.M.W. Turner, 1831. The town is shown bereft of its chief architectural glory.*

49 *Bakewell Church. Lithograph by Douglas Morison, 1840.*

The Duke of Rutland contributed £1,000, the Duke of Devonshire £500 and the requisite £5,960 was raised. A little known architect, William Flockton of Sheffield, was commissioned to rebuild the shattered church. He began by removing the transepts and excavating the foundations of the old crossing in order to lay a new base on which to re-erect a tower, octagon and spire. In doing so he unearthed a wealth of Saxon, Norman and later sepulchral stones, some of which were spirited away into Thomas Bateman's museum.[27] Flockton also opened the Vernon and Manners tombs to give a fleeting view of Dorothy Vernon's cadaver before it collapsed in a pile of dust.[28]

Before 1850 the church had been rebuilt – with a spire 16 feet shorter than its predecessor – and its monuments reinstated. Its nave and chancel were restored in 1852 and 1879 respectively.[29]

Bakewell church's traumatic story drew attention to the other fine peakland churches at Ashbourne, Tideswell and Wirksworth. By the beginning of the 19th century these, too, were established as part of the ecclesiologists' tour.

10

The Satanic Mills and their Secrets

Derbyshire, along with other counties whose rivers coursed out of the Pennines, was at the forefront of early water-powered technology, long before the Industrial Revolution. The cutlers of Hallamshire were renowned for their hammering, slitting and grinding machines from the late medieval period. At Ashford-in-the-Water black marble was being quarried, cut and polished for use on fireplaces and church monuments by the 16th century. A marble-panelled chamber had been produced for Bess of Hardwick's house at Chatsworth and when she began to build Hardwick Hall she had a craftsman, Thomas Accres, who was responsible for 'making of an engyne for the saweing of blackstone'. Accres, whose 'engine' was on the Wye at Ashford in the 1590s, was one of a number of ingenious millwrights who were to be known by the late 18th century as engineers.

Entrepreneurs, technicians and tourists journeyed from London and the South to see these early mechanical wonders. Foreigners from Europe and colonists from North America also came, some to poach ideas to take home. Even antiquarians like Byng could be just as excited by a factory as a castle; the one a many-windowed block, humming with human and mechanical noise, the other a ragged silhouette, the silent world of the owl, the bat and the spider. Yet in the increasingly romantic outlook of the 18th century these structures shared a common context – their isolated rural settings, often sublime and mysterious. Many travellers who were initially drawn by the hills and streams found themselves enthralled by the channelling of water, by the whirr of wheels and belts, the hiss of the grindstone or the metronomic beat of the trip hammer. These new rural centres, ominously noisy and often dirty, posed a threat for the future whilst at the same time they represented a prosperous commercial combination of the arts and sciences in union with nature.

This union culminated most notably at Cromford, where in 1771, Richard Arkwright built his first cotton mill. Set amid picturesque rocks beside the River Derwent where it is joined by Bonsall Brook and Cromford Sough,

50 *Richard Arkwright's Cotton Mill. Watercolour by William Day, c.1789. This is one of the earliest views of Arkwright's first mill at Cromford of 1771. To the rear is just visible the second mill of 1776 and to the left the 'barracks' in use by 1789 to house unmarried workers. On the right is Cromford Sough which flows into the mill by a cast-iron aqueduct over the road.*

the two sources of the mill's water power, it impressed itself on the mind of the traveller. Along with its accompanying new village it became the greatest wonder of the new industrial age. Eventually Cromford was hailed as 'the cradle of the Industrial Revolution' and today is a World Heritage Site.

However, some 16 miles downstream, on an island in the Derwent, was an earlier and larger factory. This was Derby's famous silk mill.[1] It was erected in 1719 by George Sorocold, 'one of the earliest millwrights to become a great engineer … It was his most important achievement [and] was … the first large manufactory in England.'[2] Built for John and Thomas Lombe, it drew countless visitors and challenges the premier claims subsequently made for Arkwright's Cromford mills.[3]

Defoe was astounded by Lombe's silk mill and wrote in 1748:

Here is a Curiosity of a very extraordinary Nature, and the only one of the Kind in England; I mean those Mills on the Derwent, which work the three capital Italian Engines for making Organzine or Thrown silk, which, before these Mills were erected, was purchased by the *English* Merchants with ready Money in *Italy*; by which Invention one Hand will twist as much Silk, as before could be done by fifty, and that in a much truer and better Manner. This Engine contains 26,586 Wheels, and 96,746 Movements, which work 73,726 Yards of Silk-thread, every time the Water-wheel goes round, which is three times in one Minute, and 318,504,960 Yards in one Day and Night. One Water-wheel gives Motion to all the rest of the Wheels and Movements, of which any one may be stopt separately. One Fire-engine, likewise, conveys warm Air to every individual Part of the Machine, and the whole Work is govern'd by one Regulator. The House which contains this Engine is of a vast Bulk, and Five or Six Stories high.[4]

What Defoe extolled in English prose, the Reverend James Gatt, minister of Gretna, applauded in Latin verse in 1748. Whether Gatt had actually visited the mill is uncertain. He might simply have sat in his manse and read the 4th edition of Defoe's *Tour* which was published in 1748. Indeed, Gatt's lengthy title is almost a word-for-word translation of Defoe's passage above. Whilst marvelling at man's genius in constructing such vast and productive machines, his hexameters conclude by measuring these achievements against the inconceivable creations of the Almighty. What begins as a factual statement concludes as a sermon in praise of God.[5]

Certainly Lombe's mill became an early industrial icon. Engravings of it appeared in numerous 18th-century magazines – always external views. Naturally, detailed views of the interior and its machinery were not allowed. Yet the mill was not closed to visitors. Even foreigners were allowed access by the Lombes and their successors, like Richard Wilson and one Mr Swift, 'a very rich merchant'.[6] It was during Swift's ownership that the La Rochefoucauld brothers paid a visit at the start of their tour into the Peak. They had already visited the Crown Derby Porcelain Factory and, surprisingly, encountered no obstacle to visiting the silk mill. They tell us:

> We entered without asking anyone's permission. We were brought by the servant from our inn. We found the [manager?] of works and, without the least difficulty, he took us into the workshops … This mill is built on the lines of those I have seen in France, except that it is on a rather bigger scale.[7]

Having viewed Swift's silk mill they asked permission to see his adjacent cotton mill. At first they were refused on account of the proprietor's absence but his sudden arrival produced the following interesting dialogue:

> Mr de Lazowski asked his permission. He replied that, seeing that we were foreigners, he asked nothing better than that we should satisfy our curiosity, though he certainly would not admit an Englishman; and we entered by an iron door double-bolted.
>
> I report at length the courteous and hospitable behaviour of this manufacturer only to offset what I should probably have to write of the jealousy of the majority of manufacturers, who refuse all entry to strangers. At least, I've been assured that I shall come across plenty of examples in the course of my journey. I find that it is very courteous of them to show their processes to strangers who can do no harm to their business; or at least very little harm, and a long time in the future, by establishing these processes at home. It is very natural that they should want to exclude their compatriots who, in appropriating an idea not already established, might do them real, immediate and serious damage.[8]

Further north on the fast flowing streams of the Peak, water power was used for grinding and sharpening. The millstone grit edges provided the best

51 *Richard Arkwright's second Cromford mill. Anonymous watercolour, c.1780, for use by the Derby China Manufactory.*

grindstones in the country. Here Samuel Watson of Heanor and Baslow, son of the more famous Samuel, carver at Chatsworth, was quarrying and cutting millstones from Booth Edge, near Hathersage, and was exporting them around the country and to Europe. In 1774 he patented his own portable milling machine.[9]

The more important patent of 1751 was that of his older brother, Henry, who set up his famous machine for cutting and polishing marble and for turning vases from spar (see plate 41, p.80). The site of his factory at Ashford-in-the-Water may well have been on or near the site where Accres's 'engine' had operated in the late Elizabethan period. Henry Watson's invention, as we have seen, was the techno-logical wonder of the Peak and was extolled alike in prose and verse. Visitors were allowed to view it and it became an early target of industrial espionage whereby its secrets were transmitted to rivals in Derby.

Yet Sorocold, the Lombes and the Watsons could not compare in stature with Richard Arkwright, who stands, with Matthew Boulton and Josiah Wedgwood, as one of the giants of the early Industrial Revolution – whether or not he invented the water frame or stole, as some maintained, another's idea. He came to Cromford and found it an incommodious place in a rocky landscape, a wretched leadminers' hamlet of hovels huddled under the pall of the smelters. He left it on his funeral carriage, drawn along the crowd-thronged road to St Giles's church in Matlock for burial in 1792.[10] He had given Cromford its famous cotton mills, its new village with some of the first planned industrial housing in England, a market, a school, a chapel, good roads and a canal. For himself, a knighted factory owner, he employed the London architect, William Thomas, to build his fanciful gothick-classic house, Willersley Castle (see plate IV).

John Byng visited the house whilst it was being built during his tour of 1789 and wrote quite scathingly of an industrial parvenu's taste:

Below Matlock a new creation of Sr Rd Arkwright's is started up, which has crouded the village of Cromford with cottages, supported by his three magnificent cotton mills. There is so much water, so much rock, so much population, and so much wood, that it looks like a Chinese town. At our inn (the Black Dog) T. Bush having gone forward, had prepared (as he knows well to do) our beds, and our stables. – We took a meand'ring walk around these little mills, bridges, and cascades; and went to where Sir R: A[rkwright] is building for himself a grand house [Wensley Castle] in the same castellated stile as one sees at Clapham; and *really* he has made a *happy* choice of ground, for by sticking it up on an unsafe bank, he contrives to overlook, not see, the beauties of the river, and the surrounding scenery. It is the house of an overseer surveying the works, not of a gentleman wishing for retirement and quiet. But light come, light go, Sr Rd has honourably made his great fortune; and so let him still live in a great cotton mill! But his greatful country must adore his inventions, which have already so prosper'd our commerce; and may lead to yet wonderful improvements.[11]

In the following year Byng stayed in Cromford again and went to see how the house was progressing. He was hardly less snooty:

I took a short walk to look at the weather, and at Sr Rd A[rkwright]'s new house (of which I spoke last year). The inside is now finishing; and it is really, within, and without, an effort of inconvenient ill taste; built so high as to overlook every beauty, and to catch every wind; the approach is dangerous; the ceilings are of gew-gaw fret work; the small circullar stair-case, like some in the new built houses of Marybone, is so dark and narrow, that people cannot pass each other; I ask'd a workman if there was a library? – Yes, answer'd he, at the foot of the stairs. Its dimensions are 15 feet square; (a small counting house;) and having the perpendicular lime stone rock within 4 yards, it is too dark to read or write in without a candle! There is likewise a music room; this is upstairs, is 18 feet square, and will have a large organ in it: what a scheme! What confinement! At Clapham they can produce nothing equal to this, where ground is sold by the yard.[12]

The de la Rochefoucauld brothers passed quickly through Cromford and made only passing reference to the cotton mills. (Arkwright had built a second, larger mill in 1776 and a third in 1783.) They must have seen no point in delaying to request Arkwright's permission to view the mills. The response would certainly have been that which François recorded a week later in Manchester:

I would have been glad to see over one [mill] to check the observations I had made at Derby. I asked if I could, but was told it wasn't possible. The merchants are afraid to let strangers in because they have had several of their inventions stolen: among others M. de Crillon went through all these factories some years ago, and made off with several good designs.[13]

England was not yet at war with France again but commercial hostility was strong. The distinguished French geologist Benjamin Faujas de Saint Fond, who was touring England in 1784, was also refused entry to the cotton mills.

Erasmus Darwin had no such difficulty. Quite apart from being English, he was a respected physician, a member of the Lunar Society and no stranger to Arkwright. He appeared with James Watt as a witness to support Arkwright's defence of his patent in court. Darwin described what he saw in the mill in neither scientific prose nor Latin hexameters, but in Augustan heroic couplets in imitation of Pope, a fusion of romantic feeling and classical imagery. Here is an example of what Klingender called one of Darwin's 'cameos' within his poem *The Botanic Garden*:

> So now, where Derwent guides his dusky floods
> Through vaulted mountains, and a night of woods,
> The Nymph, Gossypia, treads the velvet sod,
> And warms with rosy smiles the watery God;
> His ponderous oars to slender spindles turns,
> And pours o'er massy wheels his foamy urns;
> With playful charms her hoary lover wins,
> And wields his trident, – while the Monarch spins.
> – First with nice eye emerging cull
> From leathery pods the vegetable wool;
> With wiry teeth *revolving cards* release
> The tangled knots, and smooth the ravell'd fleece;
> Next moves the *iron-hand* with fingers fine,
> Combs the wide card, and foams the eternal line;
> Slow, with soft lips, the *whirling Can* acquires
> The tender skeins, and wraps in rising spires;
> With quicken'd pace *successive rollers* move,
> And these retain, and those extend the *rove*;
> then fly the spo[o]les, the rapid axles glow;–
> And slowly circumvolves the labouring wheel below.[14]

As for the romantic setting of the mills, this was captured by a number of artists who came to paint the new features in Cromford including Arkwright's 'castle' and his village. William Day painted the first two mills in 1781 and again in 1789. Christopher Machell painted them in 1785 and they appeared in a number of general views, even among landscapes painted on Crown Derby porcelain services. Most famously they were the subject of at least three studies by the brilliant local artist, Joseph Wright of Derby.[15] Wright had painted portraits of Arkwright and Erasmus Darwin but his mill studies were not portraits in the sense of an historical record. Wright was more interested in their location and the effects of light upon and from within them. He was enthralled by the night shift and the way the oil or candle light shone through the factory windows to contrast with the light of the moon.

In 1790 John Byng mused that 'these cotton mills, seven stories high and fill'd with inhabitants, remind me of a first rate man of war; and when they are lighted up on a dark night, look luminously beautiful'.[16] He liked the new village and its inn, the *Black Dog*, which he much preferred to the *White Horse* at Bakewell, a town of 'dirt and dullness'. He admired Arkwright's business acumen and the new market he had established, though he was already sounding an early note of alarm concerning the adverse effect that industrial sites were having on the landscape.

52   *Masson Mill. Watercolour by George Robertson, late 1790s. Arkwright's third mill on the Derwent, near Cromford.*

The cotton industry was steadily spreading into the Peak to places like Wirksworth where water was not abundant or to villages like Great Longstone where there were no streams. Here James Longsdon of Little Longstone and John Morewood of nearby Thornbridge Hall set up a cotton manufactory with links in Manchester to trade with St Petersburg. A small mill operated carding machines powered by a horse capstan, whilst manually operated spinning jennies produced the thread. Weaving was carried out in local cottages.[17] Tideswell, Castleton and Brough also had small manufactories but the larger water mills on the Wye at Bakewell, Cressbrook and Litton and on the Derwent at Calver were more important and have left more considerable archaeological remains.

Sir Richard Arkwright's cotton mill at Lumford, between Bakewell and Ashford-in-the-Water, again drew the inquisitive Byng in 1790. Having dined at the *White Horse* he took an evening stroll to Arkwright's new factory, built in 1777. He was denied entrance 'for this (no doubt right) reason, however odd, "That I should disturb the girls"!' [18]

Some of these girls, who were lodged in the town, came from as far afield as Scotland. Indeed, whilst the bulk of the workforce operating the Peak's mills came from the neighbouring towns and villages, a good number, of necessity, came from the wider county and beyond. So the Peak's population grew as the new industries replaced the ancient one of lead mining.

Rhodes indicated how, following the construction of the Cressbrook and Litton mills, the old lead mining town of Tideswell had changed:

53 *Arkwright's cotton mill at Lumford, Bakewell. Pencil drawing by John Price Halton, FRCS, 1827. Built on the Wye in 1777, the mill was destroyed by fire in 1868.*

We observed a great portion of its inhabitants employed in spinning and weaving cotton – a business that since the introduction into this little place has almost excluded every other. Nearly one-half of the present population are now engaged in some branch or other of this widely-spreading manufacture. I was surprised to find that the moral-murdering system of congregating a great number of boys and girls together in the same factory had ramified so extensively into this part of the Peak of Derbyshire: it is no doubt a source of wealth: but may not the riches thus acquired be obtained at the expence of public morals.[19]

A similar effect could be seen at Bakewell where the Arkwrights had built new cottages for factory workers in the town and had leased and then purchased and converted the Tudor Parsonage House from Sir Philip Gell. The Arkwrights considered themselves humane factory employers, though by 1833 the report of inspectors were only moderately good. Richard Arkwright, when pressed on the long hours children worked, replied: 'I never saw the children affected at all by the work; and it is very extraordinary, from my house [i.e. Willersley Castle, Cromford] I see the children playing in groups in the summer time till it is dark'.

The doctor involved in the 1833 inspection found that of the 46 girls under 18 employed at Bakewell 18 enjoyed good health, 19 middling health and nine bad health. Bronchocele, or Derbyshire neck, a disease already referred to in the limestone settlements of the Peak, was 'a very common disease', according to the doctor, 'at Bakewell, Matlock [i.e. Cromford] and Cressbrook Dale (see plate 11, p.22). I found numerous examples of it amongst the factory children of those places'.[20] Conditions in the mill run by the Gardoms at Calver may have been somewhat better since it was located on the Derwent at the foot of the gritstone edge at Curbar.[21]

The Cressbrook and Litton mills, locked away in the gorge cut by the Wye and guarded by walls and gates, were among the sad secrets of the Peak. Here not only were the technical secrets of the mills closed to prying eyes but also the attitudes towards the infant workforce. There were those commentators, amazed by the romantic settings of these mills, who considered that they must have been wonderful places in which orphans from London and other cities and towns could escape into a Rousseauesque elysium.[22]

Rhodes found the mill and the dale somewhat incongruous. He enthused that

> the scenery about Cressbrook mill is strikingly picturesque: the buildings are backed with rock, and wood and lofty hills, and the water plays delightfully about them; yet they seem strangely out of place. The residence of the 'Peak Minstrel', the sequestered beauties of Monsal-dale, and the murmurs of the river Wye, are combinations that do not harmonise with the rattling of the various machinery and the noise and bustle of a cotton mill … The margin of the river between Litton Mill and Cressbrook is but rarely visited by human footsteps; sometimes a solitary angler … will penetrate the dell … and occasionally a solitary tourist, in search of the hidden beauties of the Wye, will pass through it. This, however, seldom occurs, as the attempt is arduous, and cannot be accomplished without some difficulty and, perhaps, danger. The river here flows through a deep cleft of perpendicular rocks, which to the man who transverses their base, have the appearance of impending masses, that threaten all below with destruction.[23]

The Peak Minstrel who lived in this remarkable place was one William Newton who was born in the nearby hamlet of Abney in 1750. He followed his father's profession as a carpenter, became a skilled framesmith and so found employment in constructing the machinery of the new cotton mills of the Peak. In due course he rose to be manager of Cressbrook Mill. Self-educated through addictive reading he showed an early aptitude for writing verse. In a romantic age which delighted in vernacular or peasant literature, Newton's humble origins and poetry appealed to his more lettered neighbours. Just as Scott discovered the Ettrick Shepherd so the Reverend Peter Cunninghame, curate of Eyam and himself a minor Derbyshire poet, came upon Newton who describes the occasion in a letter written from Monsal Dale: 'Last week Mr Cunninhame found me in this lovely valley surrounded by wheels, springs and various mechanical operations; to his creative fancy they appeared as the effect of magic, and he called me "Prospero".'[24]

Cunninghame introduced Newton's work to his friend, the poetess Anna Seward, the 'Swan of Lichfield', who became his patroness and who introduced him to her literary friends such as Erasmus Darwin, Thomas Day and William Hayley. It was Hayley who, when considering the poetry of Robert Burns, went so far to say, 'I admire the Scotch peasant but I do not think him superior to your poetical carpenter'.[25] To many who came to seek out Newton in his house at Cressbrook he appeared the poetic and philanthropic genius of the place. Mary Sterndale in her *Vignettes of Derbyshire* (1824) was unctuously fulsome in his praise and Sir Francis Chantrey, to whom she dedicated her work, sketched the only known likeness of Newton.

Whilst Newton's verse, like that of Cunninghame and Seward, commands little admiration today his other reputation as a kindly employer has aroused far more interest.

Rhodes, who tempered the euphoric judgement of Newton as a poet, did not question his caring nature with the young waifs and orphans in his employ even though, as we have seen, Rhodes abhorred the idea of child labour. In his passage on Cressbrook and Monsal Dale, Rhodes describes the cotton mill

which finds employment for a great number of exotics of both sexes, who are periodically imported from their native soil to fade or flourish among the hills of the Peak. Mr William Newton ... resides near this factory and, if I am not mistaken, has the superintendence of those children who are incarcerated from the world within it. Once when passing down this dale, I heard him remark that he had that day a considerable increase to his family – upwards of thirty boys and girls from London. What a train of ideas did this observation create! Thirty boys and girls, deserted by their natural protectors and thrown, like waifs, upon the world's wide waste, without a single being to show them kindness – not one to love or be beloved by them; no parent to pat them on the cheek and pray 'God bless them'. One pleasant consideration, however, mingled itself with my reflections; I felt assured that these friendless children were confided to the care of an indulgent master, who would take an interest in softening the rigour of their situation, by kindness and attention.[26]

Newton was buried at Tideswell in 1830, mourned by his contemporaries. However, the posthumous indictment of him by some of those who were abused whilst in his care has led to a reassessment of his conduct as an 'indulgent master'. Recent historians have now sullied his reputation along with that of Ellis Needham of Litton Mill, where Newton was once his partner.[27]

True, the abuse of children in the Peakland cotton mills did not compare with the excesses of brutality and heartlessness of, say, Manchester. Nevertheless, it was one of the dark secrets of the Peak which has only recently been exposed. Fortunately, the public philanthropy of powerful

54 *William Newton, the 'Peak Minstrel'. Pencil sketch by L. Jewitt after Sir Francis Chantrey, RA.*

men like Lord Shaftesbury and the improvements brought about by the Factory Acts which it inspired meant that these injustices were steadily dealt with. Moreover, the decline of the cotton mills of the Peak by the post-Napoleonic period was in part due to the decline of the method of spinning cotton which Sir Richard Arkwright had introduced. Steam power eventually saw the rise of the new more prosperous mills across the Pennines near the Lancashire coalfields.

For less than a century the factories had prospered in the Peak. Their lasting legacy was an increased population of men, women and children from the four corners of the kingdom – a population that was more fluid in its movement and employment and not rigidly tied to the old industries; a population that was to grow and change even more with the coming of the railways.

II

Gateway to the Spas

In July 1755 an anonymous London gentleman and his companion rashly journeyed to Buxton in a chaise. They found the roads hazardous for their light vehicle and better suited 'to the vast number of pack horses travelling over the hills of which we counted sixty in a drove'. The chaise was damaged on three occasions, the last accounting for four spokes in one wheel. The two travellers had taken the waters at Buxton but found little by way of distraction in the town's leisure amenities. No doubt they were thinking of Bath when one of them wrote disparagingly,

> The walks are adjoining the well [i.e. St Anne's Well] and are contained in a field of about an acre, almost circular; bounded on one side by a pretty river; on the other, by the aforesaid dirty lane: the walks are not of grass or gravel, but of pure natural earth, strew'd over with fine ashes to prevent the soil from sticking to the ladies' shoes: on the side next the river, stands a large temple, dedicated to the goddess Aoacina; in the middle a mount is cast up and planted with trees and shrubs; and to enliven the scene, a number of tame rabbits run scutting about, hiding themselves among bushes and nettles, to the high amusement and entertainment of the company. Finding but few ladies on the walks (six or eight at most), we returned back to our inn, disappointed in our expectation of finding Buxton a grand and brilliant place.[1]

They had heard of the growing attraction of a new bath at Matlock which was rapidly becoming Buxton's rival. They set off along the newly turnpiked road to Ashbourne as far as Newhaven and then turned east to Pike Hall where they dined. The roads from Newhaven were unturnpiked and they trundled via Bonsall and Cromford into Matlock Bath which 'made sufficient amends for the disappointments we suffered at Buxton'.

Matlock Bath on the River Derwent was the last of a string of small settlements which, as one progressed upstream, included Matlock Dale, Matlock Bank, Matlock Bridge, Matlock Green and lastly Old Matlock or Matlock Town. The Matlocks were linked by a four-arched, 13th-century bridge; by this means the local lead miners could pass through the narrow gorge which, until the early 18th century, had never seen the wheel.

55 *Matlock Bath. Anonymous engraving after John Boydell, c.1760.*

Warm springs were known in Matlock Dale in the Middle Ages. The name Haliwelker (Holywell) occurs in 1374 but little is known about it and, as we have seen at the better known St Anne's Well at Buxton, any sacred association could not have survived the Reformation.

The Wolley family of nearby Riber had used the springs cascading on to the tufa-clad rocks beside the Derwent for some years before they constructed a small bath there in the late 17th century. However, it fell to two freeholders of Matlock manor to realise the commercial potential of the springs and about 1698 they dug a little bath on the river bank at the foot of Masson Hill. The ownership passed to another freeholder, George Wragg, who enlarged the bath and erected outbuildings to accommodate bathers. Wragg made large profits and about 1727 he sold the lease to Messrs Smith and Pennell of Nottingham for £1,000.[2]

It was about this time that Daniel Defoe arrived in Matlock Bath, enjoyed the waters and gave the following description of a place on the verge of development.

> There are several warm springs; lately one of these being secured by a stone wall on every side, by which the water is brought to rise to a due height, is made into a very convenient bath; with a house built over it, and room within the building to walk round the water or bath, and so by steps go down gradually into it …
>
> This bath would be much more frequented than it is, if two things did not hinder; namely a base, stony, mountainous road to it, and no good accommodation when you are there. They are intending, as they tell us, to build a good house to entertain persons of quality, or such who would spend their money at it; but it was not so far

concluded or directed when I was there, as to be anywhere begun. The bath is milk, or
rather blood warm, very pleasant to go into, and very sanative, especially for rheumatic
pains, bruises, etc.[3]

Smith and Pennell provided the amenities Defoe had found wanting. They
improved and extended the small complex of buildings known as the Old Bath
by adding a large assembly room and private rooms where visitors could play
cards, billiards or simply read. They also upgraded the old track from Matlock
Bridge (see plate 32, p.61), blasted a road through Scarthin rocks which blocked
the southern end of the gorge and so laid the line of the subsequent turnpike
road and the present A6 (see plate IV).

So began Matlock's prosperity. A second bath was soon opened and visitors
were offered excellent accommodation at the *Old Bath* and the *New Bath* hotels.
When the two Londoners rattled into the spa in July 1755 they felt they had
reached a new elysium. Their account of the place and how visitors amused
themselves amid the waters and precipices of this isolated gorge is a charming
passage in the literature of tourism and should be read with Boydell's engraving
of Matlock Bath in 1749 as a visual accompaniment:

> Matlock-Bath is indeed a most beautiful place; happy in its situation, for those who
> love a peaceful solitude, or would divide their time betwixt that and agreeable society:
> It seems calculated in the due medium between the gay flutter and extravagance of
> Bath and Tunbridge, and the dull, dirty, lifeless aspect of Buxton and Epsom; abounding
> with every thing that tends to health and rational pleasure: Further than this it has not
> to boast; and beyond this, happiness is sought for in vain.
>
> Matlock Bath consists of one uniform range of buildings; except an out-house
> of handsome lodging-rooms, nearly adjoining, and the stables, which are out of sight
> of the house. In the first part of the building are two baths; one for gentlemen, the
> other for ladies; the entrance and dressing rooms are quite distinct; the ladies' bath
> is arch'd with stone about ten feet above the surface of the water, which makes the
> place cool, and renders it impervious to every eye but their own: over the baths are
> the lodging-rooms, for the convenience of those who most constantly bathe. Beyond
> the bath, on the ground floor, is a range of rooms, each capable of entertaining a
> dozen people; at the further end is a large kitchen and servants' hall. In the middle
> of the building is the grand stair case, fronting the top of which is the music room,
> which is large and commodious, having a passage out on the side of the hill, which
> rises to a great height, and shelters the pack part of the house. As the company who
> come to this place, are, for the time being, one family, they breakfast, dine and sup
> together in this room. On the left hand of the music room are bed chambers, and
> others on the floor above.
>
> Before the front of the house runs a spacious terras; from whence a few steps bring
> you down to a level grass plot, convenient for the company to walk or play at bowls
> on, as they like best; and at the end of the green is built a dwarf-wall, beyond which
> descends a rocky shelf to the River Darwent, which is here very wide and rapid, and

runs with a murmuring noise, greatly increased by the repercussion of the sound from the high rocks that over-hang it; the highest of them called Matlock Torr, a person near the place told me had had plumb'd and found the perpendicular 123 yards, being 10 yards higher than the top of St Paul's. On one side of the house is a grove of lofty trees, on the other a delightful shady lawn, called The Lovers Walk: in short, the whole place is surrounded with agreeable landscapes, fine woods, pleasant walks, high rocks, steep hills, and romantic views; which, together with the constant rolling of the Darwent Streams, render it a perfect Paradise.

Towards evening we strolled by the river side, about a mile to a pretty house at the foot of a rock, call'd The Boat-house; we found the landlord a facetious fellow; who, after drinking to better acquaintance, grew very sociable, shewed us his garden, the wall of which, he told us, is one solid block of marble, and, for ought he knew, was a mile thick: We found it, on enquiry, to be a vein of grey marble, such as we had seen at Ashford, and that at some distance is a quarry from whence it is hewn: he afterwards shewed us his house, and a neat assembly-room where company from the bath frequently come to drink tea, and have a concert; there being a handsome orchestra furnished with a harpsichord and divers other instruments: sometimes the company go in the pleasure-boat on the river, and have a concert of French horns etc, which must make fine harmony among these rocks. He told us his company of performers was at present but thin but that, if we liked music, his daughter and himself would endeavour to entertain us; accordingly, she on the harpsichord and he on the violin play'd us half a dozen pieces in a very agreeable manner.

About seven we return'd back to the Bath where we found sufficient amusement till supper-time by observing the different employments of the company. Some were loitering on the terras, some frolicking on the green, some sauntering in the grove, and some amusing themselves in the lovers walk. In the great room some ladies were employ'd at their needle, while others were as busy at cards: I observed this difference, those who were at work had the happiest flow of spirits, and were the chearfullest of the company. About a quarter before eight, a servant rang a great hand-bell on the terras, which we found was notice to the company that supper was ready; about ten minutes after he rang again, which was to inform them supper was serving up. We sat together at one table, and supped by daylight. The company consisted of about two dozen of ladies, and two thirds of a dozen gentlemen. When grace was said, and the company seated, a band of music play'd for some time: the supper, which was plain, and plentiful, being ended, the bell was a third time rung, on which the company arose, and being dismissed by their chaplain, formed themselves into parties, some to cards and some to country-dancing. As neither of these suited my companion or me, we retired to a private room, chatted over the pleasures of the day, smoak'd a pipe, drank a pint, discharged our reckoning, and went to bed.

What makes Matlock Bath still more agreeable is, that besides the place being pleasant, and the people who resort to it polite, there are no extravagant charges annexed; the company pay nothing for lodging or bathing, let them stay ever so long or short a time, and the ordinary expenses are three shillings a-day for meals, including tea in the afternoon: and tho' there is neither master nor mistress of the house, there is found the most courteous and complaisant behaviour from the attendants, and the whole business

56 *Matlock Church. Engraved by John and Letitia Byrne after a drawing by Joseph Farington R.A., 1817*

is conducted with the utmost politeness, decency and economy. The reason of its being thus managed, by servants, we were informed is, that the bath rooms, house etc. being new erections and render'd so compleat at a great expence, by the subscription of divers gentlemen round the country, who are now the proprietors; at first they could not let it at any rate, nor since at the rate they set upon it; for having tasted the profits, and finding their dividends amount to more *per ann*. Than by any rent that had been offered, they chuse to continue it to themselves in the manner it is.

I hope you will excuse my dwelling so long on the description of this place: I admire it greatly and my companion left it with great reluctance.[4]

Roads continued to improve. In 1759 the Wye and Derwent valley road from Longstone via Bakewell to Rowsley and Matlock was turnpiked and continued to Cromford and then via Black Rocks to Wirksworth. Although the Derwent valley road from Cromford to Belper was not turnpiked until 1817, tourists to the Matlocks increased considerably. Many used Matlock as a new gateway into the Peak, entering from Chesterfield on the road that was turnpiked in 1760.[5] The *Temple* and other comfortable hotels were built in Matlock Bath and accommodation for some 500 visitors was available by the late 18th century, including one hundred at the *Old Bath* and fifty at the *New*.

All this was a source of concern to the proprietors of the baths and hotels in Buxton. True, the waters at Buxton were warmer and considered more beneficial, but Matlock Bath was a cheaper resort in which to stay and, on account of its lower altitude, its season began earlier and continued from the end of April until November.[6] Furthermore, as tourists became increasingly beguiled by rocky landscapes, Matlock's setting was considered unsurpassed. It provided gentle terrace or riverside promenades or a frightening climb to look down on the gorge from the precipitous heights of High Tor, some 350 feet above the Derwent. On the opposite side of the river rises Masson Hill whose summit, the Heights of Abraham, took its name from the site of General Wolfe's victory in Canada in 1759. From the Boat House the continuous curtain of crags could be explored by pleasure craft, whilst outings by carriage to Haddon Hall and Chatsworth or to Sir Richard Arkwright's new factory and village at Cromford were popular attractions.

Visitor after visitor extolled the beauties of the Matlocks. Warner declared, on first viewing it, 'Here a scene burst upon us at once, impossible to be described – too extensive to be called picturesque, too diversified to be sublime, and too stupendous to be beautiful; but at the same time blending together all the constituent principles of these different qualities.'[7] Against this must be set the more down to earth judgment of the itinerant agricultural correspondent, Arthur Young, who set the scene comparatively within natural landscape wonders of England:

> Matlock on the whole cannot fail answering greatly to whoever views it. It is different from all the places in the kingdom. Several exceed it in particular circumstances: the rocks at Keswick are infinitely bolder, the water there and at Winander Mere [Windermere], far superior: the beauty that results from decoration is met with every day in a much finer style; for here is nothing but nature. But the natural terrass, on the edge of the precipices, with the variety of views commanded from it, is in the style exceeded by nothing I have seen.[8]

Finally, the most elegant assessment of Matlock Bath as a spa in the late 18th century was penned by George Lipscomb of Birmingham in his *Description of Matlock Bath*. He held that:

> Matlock must be allowed to possess superior advantages to the generality of watering places. It has gaiety without dissipation, activity without noise, and facility of communication with other parts of the country undisturbed by the bustle of a public road. It is tranquil without dulness, elegant without pomp, and splendid without extravagance. In it the man of fashion may at all times find amusement, the man of rank may meet with society by which he will not be disgraced, and the philosopher a source of infinite gratification; while they who travel in search of health will find here a silver clue that leads to her abode.[9]

Matlock was the first of the new wonders of the Peak and lay outside the hundred of High Peak and within the wapentake of Wirksworth, or the Low Peak. As the population of England rose dramatically as the 18th century progressed so more travelled to see this increasingly accessible novelty. Spas in general flourished and not least the queen of them all, Bath.

Buxton, since the early 17th century, had lacked the entrepreneurial vision from which Matlock Bath had profited. It possessed, however, a lord far more powerful and wealthy than did the Matlocks in the person of William Cavendish (1748-1811), 5th Duke of Devonshire. It was he who had the perspicacity to invest in the town, reshape and modernise it and gradually restore and increase its former prosperity.

The Duke was well aware of the new buildings rising in Bath where, between 1767 and 1777, John Wood the younger had completed the new Assembly Rooms, the new Hot Baths and the Royal Crescent. He puzzled how the difficult location of Buxton's baths could be improved and embellished, but clearly saw that heavy financial investment would bring long-standing returns. A rich source of income came on tap at just the right moment in the form of profits from his copper mine at Ecton in the Peak. This mine on Ecton Hill in north Staffordshire was almost unique in the limestone Peak, being richer in copper than lead.[10] As such, it became another wonder of the Peak much visited by tourists. The Swedish visitor, Eric Geisler, who came here in 1772, described the mine's interior where 'such a horrid gloom, such rattling of waggons, noise of workmen boring of rocks under your feet, such explosions in blasting and such a dreadful gulph to descend, present a scene of terror, that few people not versed in mining, care to pass through'.[11] Reckoned to be the deepest mine in Britain in the late 18th century, Ecton is calculated to have provided the Dukes of Devonshire with returns of over a third of a million pounds between 1760 and 1818.

The 5th Duke called in the respected architect John Carr (1723-1807) of York to help him plan the new developments at Buxton.[12] Carr had been successfully employed by Devonshire's brother-in-law, the Duke of Portland, and was well acquainted with Buxton. As one who endured acute rheumatism and staggered with the aid of a stick, he came to Buxton for a cure. The bath he used had been reconstructed and covered with a stone vault by the local mason, John Barker of Rowsley, in 1712 and this was followed by another refurbishment in 1750, when the bath was incorporated in the Old Hall. Carr was not impressed (see plate 27, p.53).

He was first commissioned to remodel and extend the Baths and his sketch for a colonnaded scheme was significantly discovered in his copy of the design

57 *Carr's Crescent at Buxton, after a drawing by Edward Dayes. The Old Hall and Bath are on the left, St Anne's Well is opposite.*

by Woods for the new Hot Bath at Bath. Carr's scheme for Buxton was never executed.

Instead, the Duke switched his attention to the accommodation and entertainment of visitors and considered a bold scheme which would centralise Buxton's amenities and compensate for the scattered lodgings and stables in the town's inadequate hotels. This new development had three main features. The first was the erection of a large crescent on the site of the rabbit-ridden pleasure ground known as The Grove. Whilst no doubt inspired by Wood's semi-eliptical Royal Crescent at Bath, its semi-circular curve was to some extent dictated at that point by that of the River Wye. The west end of the new Crescent, nearest St Anne's Well, was the first part to open as an hotel in 1790. In Jewitt's time, twenty years later, the western half of the Crescent was divided into three hotels – the *Great*, *St Anne's* and *Centre*. Some private accommodation was incorporated in the Crescent, together with shops and coffee, dining and card rooms. Its great glory was its ballroom which Carr embellished with elegant Corinthian columns and pilasters and a coved ceiling with superb plaster work by James Henderson of York in the Adam style. All these amenities in one building were linked by a paved, covered and arcaded walk at ground level. The ingenious Crescent had a three-storeyed inner curve of 240 feet and a

58 *St Anne's Well, Buxton. Drawn and engraved 1796 by William Martin, a resident geologist, drawing master and actor. The Bath is in the background.*

four-storeyed outer one of 300 feet. Although its inner, fair face is somewhat obscured at the foot of a steep slope, it is an architectural masterpiece which cost the Duke £38,600. Matlock Bath had nothing to compare.

The Duke compensated visitors to Buxton for the loss of what Jewitt called 'a rich and beautiful Grove'. New walks were laid out with trees on the slope above the Crescent, though Byng felt it could have been 'planted and decked out to much better advantage'.

At the foot of the slope on the western side of the Crescent Carr designed a pretty square pavilion for the new site of St Anne's Well. Lined with marble and distilling water from a new marble basin, its shallow original roof was graced with a four-handled vase and cover.

To the rear of the Crescent Carr erected another amazing building, the Great Stables (see plate 59, p.119), an essential accompaniment since the Crescent lacked accommodation for horses, carriages and grooms. Six coach houses were built in an adjacent block and the stabling was housed within a large square building with chamfered corners. The interior comprised a huge circus of Doric columns with stalls for 88 horses radiating to the perimeter wall and a circular ride beneath the covered interior of the colonnade. It was a unique masterpiece erected in local stone from Buxton, Bakewell Edge, Matlock, Youlgreave and Chelmorton by local masons, Robert Smith and William Booth of Stoney Middleton, who had also built the Crescent.[13]

The Great Stables were set well back from the Crescent to avoid any noise and smell and some found this a little inconvenient. The carping Byng, ever mindful of the safety and comfort of his horse, recorded in June 1790:

> Up early to find my Cavalry; who are lodged in a most ill-contrived, magnificent mews, where all things are common, and where they and their furniture must be hourly watched, nothing like a quiet stable to be called your own – snug lodging houses, with adjoining small stables were more necessary and comfortable, than useless, ill contrived grandeurs; but the Duke, I suppose was made prey of by some architect, as having some genius and no fortune![14]

In the last five years of his life the 5th Duke considered further improvements for his spa. Carr had retired to Yorkshire and died in 1807 and so the Duke turned again to his brother-in-law, the Duke of Portland, and employed his surveyor John White (c.1747-1813). The idea was to extend the hotels on the northern rear of the Crescent, refurbish the baths, construct a square of private houses and erect a private chapel close by to provide a convenient place of Sunday worship. Jewitt tells us that before 1811 the Assembly Room was 'fitted up in a temporary manner as a chapel every Sunday throughout the season'.

Of these schemes only White's new chapel, dedicated to St John the Baptist, was completed just after the Duke's death in 1811. Built in an eclectic classical style in keeping, to some degree, with the Crescent and the Great Stables, it was hailed as an architectural success. Indeed J.M.W. Turner was sufficiently impressed to make sketches of it whilst staying at Hathersage with his friend (see plate 59, p.119), James Holworthy.[15] The new chapel was consecrated in 1812 and old St Anne's church in Higher Buxton was closed.

Such were the changes which restored Buxton's primacy as the peakland spa, second only to Bath. Nevertheless, some tourists still found Buxton unattractive. No amount of human endeavour could change its climate and the sparkle and vitality of the town depended to a large degree on the occasional presence of the Duke of Devonshire, the Marquis of Hartington or other visiting aristocracy. Robert Arbuthnot, a young Scot, visited Buxton in 1787 and wrote the following account of the spa to his friend and compatriot, Sir Robert Murray Keith, British Envoy to Vienna:

> I have not been long enough at Buxton to judge of the effect of the waters. Their efficacy ought to be very great to draw so much company to a place which in every other respect seems to be highly disagreeable. The climate is extremely bad and rainy and the country round is the most bleak and dreary I ever saw. The new hotels built by the Duke of Devonshire … are very magnificent.
>
>   This place is so dull and affords so little variety that nothing occurs, the relation of which could either interest or amuse you, at the same time we are not without our amusements such as they are. There is dancing almost every night, a set of strolling players are expected tomorrow, and we have already had two conjurers and a Dancing Bear. Lord Bulkeley has been here these last eight days, but he goes away tomorrow. Lady Bulkeley came with him, but not finding the entertainment at Buxton she expected she only remained one day … [16]

John Byng, who stayed at the *Great Hotel*, still considered Buxton 'the vilest of all spots' and could not leave the place quickly enough. He despised the 5th Duke's new scheme and on no account could be tempted to the dances in the Assembly Rooms. 'The Piazzas', he declared, 'are too narrow to defend from sun, or rain, and the shops exhibit no temptation like those of Tunbridge … In yesterday's morning walk I instinctively entered the playhouse … which is a mean, dirty, boarded, thatched house, and can hold but few people.'[17]

Against this must be set the opinions of those who found the spa and its surrounding wonders fascinating. Jewitt gives in full the letter of a lady to her sister, written as a diary for a week in August 1810. She concludes her letter by declaring 'the first week of my residence in Buxton, has been passed in a round of ever-varying amusement; and from the many interesting antiquities, scenes, and curiosities, in the neighbourhood, which yet remain to be examined, I am confident that a longer stay than mine may be passed, not only without the ennui too frequently attendant on public places, but with the greatest entertainment and delight.'[18]

There were plenty of aristocrats who liked Buxton in preference to Bath and were prepared to travel greater distances to enjoy its waters and seek the society of their peers. Lord and Lady Macartney, for instance, enjoyed a brief visit to the wells in July 1789 and June 1790 – the very time when John Byng was there. They travelled by public coach, accompanied by two servants, from London to Derby. From there they continued, via Ashbourne, to the spa. The total cost for the party's journey was £34 14s. 14d. of which £2 1s. 1d. was spent on turnpike tolls. The charges in Buxton were cheaper than those of Bath. Here are her ladyship's accounts:

Hire of lodgings for four days:

Drawing room	0-10-6	
Bedrooms	0-16-0	} £1-18s-0d
Spencer's [a servant] room	0-4-6	
Men's room	0-7-0	
Expenses for our dinner the day we arrived		
Our dinner at the Great Room to July 19th		£1-7s-0d
Our breakfast		£0-8s-0d
Servants' dinner		£0-18s-4d
Our tea		£0-5s-4d
To be added for our wine		£0-3s-0d
Tallow candles		£0-1s-4d
Washing		£0-17s-d
Letters, parcels, etc.		£0-4s-6d

I *Washing Lead at Matlock. Aquatint by P.J. de Loutherbourg.*

II *Peak Cavern. Great Tom of Lincoln. Engraving by I. Smith after Edward Dayes, 1804.*

III *Buxton Market Square. Watercolour by T. Wakeman, c.1840.* The Eagle *is the principal inn in the centre.*

IV *Willersley Castle. Engraved by Thomas Allom, 1837. Arkwright's seat overlooks his achievements. Scarthin Nick is busy with coach traffic.*

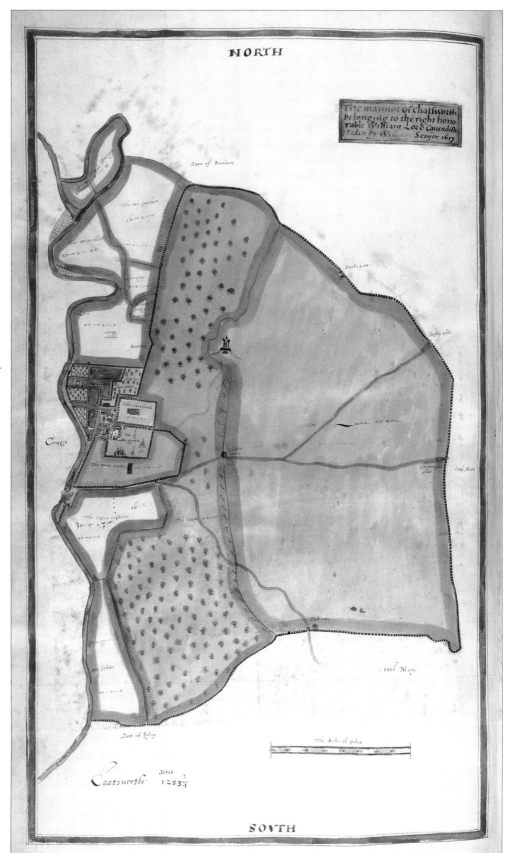

v *'The Mannor of Chatsworth.' Estate map by William Senior, 1617.*

VI Chatsworth. Watercolour by William Cowan, 1828. Wyatville's northern wing and belvedere, added by the 6th Duke. Paine's stables and bridge are on the left.

VII Chatsworth. Oil painting by Peter Tillemans, c.1720.

VIII Haddon Hall. Watercolour by Moses Griffiths, c.1790. Haddon Hall was the manor house for Bakewell, whose church spire is on the left.

The Macartneys paid a half crown subscription to use the bath. He appeared in greater need of its cure; he spent £1 19s. 0d. to her five shillings.

She took their servants to the playhouse, their admission and carriage costing ten and sixpence, and they made two outings, one to Lyme Hall in Cheshire at a cost of two shillings and one to Castleton for which they hired a pair of horses (four shillings) and a hack chaise (one pound two shillings).

Of course, there were the inevitable tips disbursed to the following:

The waiter	£1-1s-0d
The maid	£1-11s-6d
The shoe black	£0-5s-6d
The women at the wells	£0-16s-6d
The helper in the stables	£0-5s-0d
A bather [a poor invalid?]	£0-10s-6d

Finally, they paid 24 shillings for 'petrifactions' to be taken back as souvenirs. In all, their expenses give us an accurate idea of what four days in Buxton could cost two upper-class members of society. Assuming they returned to London, as they came, they had spent some £88.[19]

The intelligentsia were thinner on the ground at Buxton and Dr Johnson felt there was little to be gained there in terms of serious conversation. Canon Seward of Lichfield, father of the fashionable poetess, Anna Seward, thought differently. Anna considered the spa a place where the literati could sparkle and where she could appear as a blue-stocking. She recorded what was probably her last visit there in 1808, the penultimate year of her life. In a letter to her friend, Mary Powys, she snootily describes how she and her companion, Miss Fern, were quite shocked by the activities of the high-spirited, young Regency beaux they encountered:

… in the hope of guarding against the rheumatic suffering of last winter I set out for Buxton on the 15 of August, accompanied by Miss Fern. … My accommodations at Buxton gave to my weak frame every comfort and assistance which my own house afford. We were in the new Centre Hotel of the Crescent, comprised of three houses, once shops with hired Lodgings. This new Hotel is by far the most spacious and commodious of the three; the Great Hotel at which the beautiful Assembly-Room, and Saint Anne's Hotel, to which the Baths adjoin, form the two horns of the half-moon. I had a moderate sized, and very palor [sic], and a large bedchamber adjoining, on the ground floor; in the former a sofa and high-backed, stuff'd arm chair. Miss Fern's sleeping-room was somewhat star-loving, for she had sixty five steps to ascend; in itself spacious and airy and she is stout, nimble and makes petty inconvenience, of every kind, her sport rather than complaint. Buxton was full, and we became acquainted with a few intelligent people, amid a number of commonplaces. On the whole the Society was less endowed by intellect and less adorned by the graces of polished life, than I had ever known it – and men of any age or class were scarce indeed. The young

Marquis of Hartington, with 3 or 4 fine Men in his train, came often from Chatsworth on residences of 3 or 4 days; infesting the Ball-Room with cold-blooded insolence, 'the toss of Quality and high-bred fleer'; once carried by his Lordship so far as to provoke an old Gentleman of the Company to tell him with stentor-lungs that he was a Puppy – The whole room was in a ferment. All the Noblesse, except the young Lord Lowther, who is too rational to flatter and uphold insolence of so much self-danger, as well as public annoyance, siding with the Marquis. Assembly-schism and infringement of the established rules of the Balls ensued; Ill would such behaviour have become any youthful nobleman; least of all Lord Hartington, to whose Father the whole place belongs, affording him immense Revenue. The facility of accommodation at Buxton, now, enables the Aristocracy of the Crescent to abstract themselves from the general Company, and keep their own unwholesome, topsy-turvy hours.[20]

Buxton's raison d'être was its curative waters. Wealthy and healthy aristocrats might grace the place socially but the sick and disabled of all sections of society came here to seek a permanent cure for their ailments. Such finality was rare; temporary relief was the usual benefit. The town displayed in public a whole range of afflictions and the signs of relief following a period of treatment were readily observed by the casual visitor.

Sir George Head gives us a colourful observation of how the halt and the lame arrived in the town unable to move about. Then as the treatment progressed day by day he watched them tackle different levels of the promenades on the slope rising above the Crescent:

I particularly noticed one old gentleman on the first day I arrived; he was remarkable on account of his purple but healthy face, snub nose, and chin projecting over his stomach as if on purpose to balance his body. All disease in his system had evidently flown to his heels, for the lower part of his legs and his ancles were so swollen as to be puffed out over his shoes, till his feet exactly resembled those of an elephant. In this state he was dreadfully lame, and a kind old lady accompanied him in his walks, always holding him tenderly by the point of his elbow. The waters achieved such a surprising effect on this old gentleman (who, by the way, but for this overflowing of the humours, must otherwise have been sound in wind and limb) that, in three days, to use a horse-dealer's expression, 'he pulled out all but right'. I afterwards met him at a distance considerably removed from the old spot, without his old lady, taking his exercise quite alone. He was however, as I imagine, irremediably spavined, or stiff in the joints; for, though he hustled along with great resolution, his pace was a sort of canter, one knee-joint doing double duty, while the other performed only half. As the swelling of his feet subsided, his shoes became too big, and clattered as he dragged them along.[21]

Whilst at the end of the 18th century Matlock, Bath and Buxton vied with one another for the growing tourist trade, another town with wells and springs tried to join in. This was Bakewell, a market town on the Wye almost fourteen miles downstream from Buxton and a similar distance from Matlock Bath. Some 18th-century writers like Bray held that the chalybeate spring here had been a bath in Roman times, an assertion repeated by writers today with no clear evidence to substantiate it. Unlike bleak Buxton and the dale-bound Matlocks, Bakewell was a softer, more pastoral place among green meadows on the flood plain. Here the Wye, leaving the limestone dales, writhes through banks of reed and alder past Haddon Hall and, having collected the River Lathkill, falls within a mile into the Derwent at Rowsley.

This lovely valley had been a hunting park of the Saxon and Norman kings. The wooden keep and palisade of its vanished Norman motte-and-bailey castle once were sentinel to the approaches to the Peak and watched over a prosperous town and church which grew up on the opposite side of the valley. Bakewell had passed from royal hands by the Angevin period and eventually became a manor of the Vernons, from whom it passed by marriage to the Manners family, earls and, after 1703, dukes of Rutland. The latter family, of royal descent by the 16th century, lived over the hill from their wealthier but less ancient neighbours, the Cavendishes of Chatsworth. Their rivalry over the centuries was competitive but peaceful.

In the Haddon Hall household accounts there is mention of making a well to bathe in at Bakewell in 1637. However, it was the 9th Earl and 1st Duke of Rutland who eyed his neighbour's development of Buxton with some interest and not a little envy and in 1697 built a bath house for himself, roofed it in 1705 and invited guests to bathe in the warm (11.6°c) spring at Bakewell. During the second half of the 18th century, as turnpike roads increased and improved and Bakewell became a coaching town, the Dukes of Rutland viewed the injection of new vitality into Buxton with increased interest. Bakewell had certain advantages; it had a milder climate, a very picturesque location, a charter market dating from the 13th century and a place of worship, its ancient church of Saxon foundation, in whose huge parish lay the town of Buxton.

William Eyre-Archer of Holme Hall, Bakewell, loved the Peak and could hardly wait to escape from London to return to his estates there. He was steeped in classical pastoral verse and sought to emulate the *Wonders of the Peak* as described by Hobbes and Cotton. Whereas they had described the ancient wonders culminating in praise of Chatsworth and the Cavendish family, Eyre transposed their treatment of the landscape into the valley of the Wye between Holme and Haddon Halls ending with a eulogy on the 1st Duke of Rutland. An amateur artist, he also took up his brush and sketched very early landscapes of the area (*c*.1720).

He follows the Wye (Wey) from his house as it oxbows through Bakewell's water meadows and is seized by an amusing fit of hyperbole as he rhapsodises upon the town:

> Persue his track ye aged father, leads
> Where pleasant Bakewell lifts its many heads,
> With decent seats and trees so interwove,
> It seems at once a village and a grove:
> As if the plan from trading Belgia came,
> Wey ye canal and it ye Amsterdame
> Not so with different opinions torn
> For all live in that they all was born
> And distant to ye realms of fell despight
> A mutual amity does them unite
> On given faith securely we depend
> None meets his enemy but each his friend
> propounded truths as redily believe
> Unskill'd in fraud and artless to deceave
> But hospitably prone to doing good
> Peace hovers ore ye tranquil neighbourhood.[22]

His poem contains no mention of the bath house which seems to have fallen into disuse. By 1760 it had become the lodging of the sculptor and proprietor of the Ashford marble works, Henry Watson, son of Samuel, the famous carver at Chatsworth. The warm spring still flowed but no one bathed. Moreover, the town lacked adequate accommodation and, like Tideswell, Taddington and other Peakland villages, its squat vernacular buildings, largely of random limestone and grass thatch, were not attractive. Its unpaved streets, alive with running water from its wells and fouled by the horse, sheep and cattle markets, were hardly promenades for the fashionable spa visitors. The shambles, a ramshackle row of shops, stood in the main market street in front of *The White Horse*, the town's principal inn. In 1765 the town was described thus:

> The whole (a very few houses excepted) exhibits a very wretched appearance: consisting for the most part, of low smoaky, mean edifices: the streets are dirty, particularly the principal, where, to increase the narrowness, which is considerable, a whole group of shoemakers' shops, coblers' bulks etc are erected on both sides, and present a rude medley of joysts, rafters and beams, whose craggy projections, by thrusting themselves into the street, incomode the passangers, destroy the vistre and at the same time fill a traveller with fears, lest these ponderous fabrics should tumble about his ears and bury him in their ruins.[23]

The above writer described the market as being 'so mean it does not deserve to be mentioned'; in 1790 Byng referred to 'the dirt & dulness of Bakewell' and in 1797 a gentleman from Oxford described the inn, *The White Horse*, as 'indifferent' and the town itself as 'still more ordinary'.[24]

By this time, of course, Sir Richard Arkwright's new cotton mill on the Wye at Lumford, just outside Bakewell, had helped to increase the town's

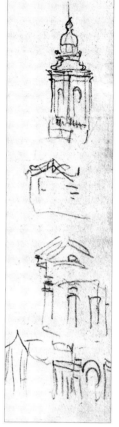

59 *Buxton. The three 'modern' buildings – the Crescent and the Great Stables by John Carr and St John's Chapel by John White. Pencil sketch by J.M.W. Turner, 1831.*

trade, transport and population and from his seat at Belvoir Castle the 5th Duke of Rutland was well aware that Bakewell needed modernising. He had begun to extend the stabling and carriage accommodation once the 1759 turnpike road from Rowsley allowed fast coaches to enter the town. By 1804 he had transformed the centre of the town. First he pulled down *The White Horse* and erected in its place the larger, finer hotel, still known as the *Rutland Arms*, with a splendid coach yard across the road. The days of damp beds and dubious fare were banished as the hotel established an unrivalled reputation in the county under the proprietorship of William and Ann Greaves. The latter provided splendid dinners for local social gatherings and, it is said, was responsible for first serving that world-famous dessert, the Bakewell pudding.

The second part of the scheme was to demolish entirely the shanty town and open up a new market place subsequently known as The Square, in front of the *Rutland Arms Hotel*. This development seems to echo what Sir Richard Arkwright had created with his new market in front of his new inn, the *Black Dog* at Cromford. Thirdly, beside the coach yard and adjacent to the Square the Duke cleared away old barns near the ducal bath house and had gardens with walks laid out between the hotel and the bath – an echo of the 5th Duke of Devonshire's slope above the Crescent and Bath at Buxton.

The administration of the bath and the arrangement of the new grounds were undertaken by the local polymath White Watson who had taken up lodgings with his uncle, Henry Watson, in the bath house about 1774.[25] Following Henry's death in 1786, White and his wife refurbished the bath principally to serve those staying at the *Rutland Arms*. White, a noted plantsman and a Fellow of the Linnaean Society, corresponded with Paxton, Banks, Erasmus Darwin and other gardeners and botanists of his day. He attempted to create a botanical garden by carting tons of black leaf mould on to the alkaline limestone site and tells us that 'trees and plants grow very luxuriantly'. In the garden was a cold spring from which those using the adjacent warm bath could drink. A poem, probably by himself, though he attributes it to 'a gentleman of Bakewell', describes this lost fountain:

> Where Auster sheds his balm from mildest skies
> By Watson grac'd the Fount is seen to rise;
> From latent dark retreat, obscur'd from sight,
> In stony limits bound there greets the light;
> An Antique pile of stones adorns its head,
> By Scient hand in rude disorder laid;
> Here Stalactites, their spiral heads above
> Shoot up and form a pyramidic grove,
> And moss grown stones lie rudely at their base
> Adding a cell-like semblance to the place:
> While flow'ry tendrils, jutting from between,
> Give a wild grace and beauty to the Scene:
> And Cupid too recumbent on a wing,
> Peeps o'er the margin of the silver spring;
> Presiding Genius of this flowing Fount!
> By Watson plac'd to guard the mossy mount!
> Quick rising from beneath, the eye may trace
> The crystal bubbles in their limpid chace;
> Which in a streamlet gently glide along
> His Garden blazon'd in Botanic song.[26]

In addition to a newsroom in the bath house, White Watson also had a very interesting museum of mineralogical specimens and archaeological items from the Peak, backed up by a useful library.[27] Scientists, geologists and botanists came from around Britain and from the continent to see Watson's collections.

This interesting attempt to turn Bakewell into a spa town failed for various reasons. Although the town was much improved, the bath itself was too small and its waters inferior to those of Buxton and Matlock. There was no assembly room, no playhouse and no fashionable shops in what remained an essentially agricultural market town. Tourists came in increasing numbers as the 19th century continued, but not for the waters. Bakewell had established itself as the picturesque jewel of the Peak.

The death of White Watson in 1835 brought the dream of a spa to an end. Bakewell lost an artist, antiquarian, poet, botanist and geologist – easily the most interesting person in the

60   *Martha Norton. Watercolour by C. Orme(?) before 1820. She was 'upwards of 50 years attendant at Buxton Well and died at the age of 90 in 1820. A "well woman" whose clay pipe and ale glass may have contributed, with the Buxton water, to her longevity'!*

Peak in his day. The bath closed, as did his museum; his library and papers were scattered. However, the town still has the lovely Bath Gardens as his memorial where the old bath house still stands.

12

The Rise, Decline and Rise of Chatsworth

As the seventh and only artificial wonder of the Peak, the first of the new Elizabethan country houses in the North and a palace for the Cavendish family, Chatsworth has never ceased to draw visitors for the last four hundred and fifty years. Originally built as a retreat for Sir William Cavendish and his wife, Bess of Hardwick, from the political vicissitudes of mid-Tudor London, in the more settled times of the late Elizabethan period it lured courtiers such as Leicester and Burghley to view a civilised miracle among barren hills. It was and still is the cultural capital of the Peak.

Sir William Cavendish's Derbyshire wife had doubtless chosen the spot where stood an old-fashioned manor house built by her relatives, the Leches. The Cavendishes used this old house as their occasional retreat from London, demolishing it only when their new mansion was habitable. The new Chatsworth, completed by 1585, was almost inaccessible on foot or horseback in bad winters and was only approachable by coach in the late 17th century (see plate 62, p.127). The old road to it from Chesterfield plunged down from the moors, passed alongside the park approaching the medieval bridge and water mill, both relics of the lost medieval hamlet of Chatsworth (see plate v). Queen Elizabeth never visited the house, but reports from her secretaries recommended it as a safe place in which Bess and her fourth husband, George, the 6th Earl of Shrewsbury, could hold the political prisoner, Mary Queen of Scots.

The mansion was not a prospect house like those nearby at Wollaton, Hardwick and Bolsover built shortly after. Instead, it was set below a hill, a quadrangular, keep-like structure with a turreted entrance and turrets at its four corners, all battlemented in a mock military style to conceal its chimney stacks. The apartments rose in three storeys and four in the turrets (see plate 63, p.129). This economy of high-rise space was a great contrast to the sprawling, low double quadrangles of Derbyshire's nearby medieval Haddon Hall and Wingfield Manor and the last Henrician houses of Hampton Court, Whitehall, Cowdray and Nonsuch. The outside of old Chatsworth, built of local gritstone from Bakewell Edge, was somewhat grim in its stark symmetry. The only concessions to exterior decoration appeared between obliquely angled turrets of the entrance – blind balustrading, lion-masked medallions and the escutcheon of Cavendish above that of Hardwick. The windows on all four faces were among the largest yet seen in domestic use, mullioned and transomed to hold casements of leaded, lozenge quarries. The largest, pedimented apertures lit the state rooms, skied on the top storey.

Inside, the fountain court doors gave access to the ground floor and then, by stairs, not in the turrets, to rooms sumptuously fitted with tapestries and fine furnishings – English and continental. The rich stucco was in part, in the early stages, carried out by plasterers from Longleat, the more sophisticated Wiltshire house of Sir William Cavendish's old colleague, Sir John Thynne.

However, the Chatsworth of Bess of Hardwick's day was a private mansion open only to members of the Court and visiting aristocracy who came to take the waters at Buxton and visit the other wonders of the area. Accounts of the house, both inside and in the grounds, do not exist until the general descriptions of Hobbes and the later, more specific, references by Cotton. The latter, of course belong to the time of the 4th Earl and 1st Duke who recreated the house, gardens and park and opened them not only to the aristocracy but to the gentry too. To do this he also improved the roads approaching the house and rebuilt the medieval bridge.

There was much more to see after the team of English and foreign architects and craftsmen had completed the house and gardens of what became known as 'The Palace of the Peak'. The south and east fronts were the masterly designs of William Talman; the north and west by Archer and perhaps the Duke himself. The interiors were painted by Verrio, Laguerre and Thornhill, the carvings in stone, alabaster, marble and wood by Davies, Young, Lobb, Lanscroon, Samuel Watson and Nadauld.[1] Cibber produced statuary for the house and gardens, the latter being the work of English and French designers. London and Wise laid out the south and west parterres, supplying vast numbers of limes, hornbeams, hollies, boxes and junipers from their large nursery at Brompton Park. The French gardeners were responsible for the elaborate water gardens; M. Huet supervised the work between 1687 and 1706 and was assisted by M. Grillet and M. Audias. The fine perspective by Knyff and Kip, executed in 1699, shows a baroque house and gardens unrivalled in England (see plate 64, p.130).

Visitors flocked to see it and access was usually available even if the Duke was not in residence. A lady or gentleman would send their card, or letter of introduction, by a servant and this was received by the steward. He instructed the housekeeper to escort acceptable visitors around the principal rooms before passing them on to the head gardener to view the grounds. Food and wine would be made available for those of some social standing and, occasionally, the Duke would grace the company with his presence. Sir William Dawes, chaplain to Queen Anne and newly consecrated Bishop of Chester, was not so fortunate in 1708. His companion recorded that 'the Duke was in the House but would not see [us], cause hee understood the business was curiosity. A decent repast of wine and tea was sett to refresh the company'.[2]

After the Restoration the increase of Cavendish influence and patronage in the midlands and the north led to a more 'open house' approach by the family. The new bowling green in the gardens added to the pleasure of social gatherings and the Duke of Rutland aped this means of entertainment by constructing his own bowling green and house over the hill at Haddon Hall.[3]

Cotton was among the first visitors to Chatsworth during its metamorphosis from Bess's Elizabethan mansion to the 4th Earl's 'glittering pile' and 'princely house'. Cotton wrote about it slightly earlier than when Knyff and Kip drew it yet the house must have been in the same incomplete state as they saw it with Talman's south and east wings married to Bess's north and west ones. The remarkable metamorphosis was completed in 1707; the new house was erected on the same building lines as the old, to the same height. The rooms bore the names and locations of their predecessors, The Queen of Scots's rooms, the Earl of Leicester's apartments and the state rooms were still skied at the top of the house.[4]

61 Chatsworth House. *Needlework, c.1585. The Cavendish's first house built by Bess of Hardwick.*

Cotton lauded the Earl for his magnificence and his liberality:

> But that which crowns as this and does impart
> A lustre far beyond the pow'r of Art
> Is the Great owner, He, whose noble mind
> For such a Fortune only was design'd.
> Whose bounties as the Oceans' bosom wide,
> How in a constant, unexhausted Tyde
> Of Hospitality and, Free Access,
> Liberal Condescension, Cheerfulness ...[5]

So Chatsworth became one of the earliest of England's great houses to give 'free access' to the genteel tourist. The lower orders of society were firmly excluded, as Cotton tells us when describing the old entrance tower beside the fishing bridge, clearly depicted in the painting of Bess's house by Siberechts and in Senior's plan:

> Over this Pond, opposite to the Gate,
> A Bridge of a queint structure, strength and state,
> Invites you to pass over it, where dry
> You trample may on shoals of wanton Fry,
> With which those breeding waters do abound,
> And better Carps are nowhere to be found.
> A Tower of antick Model the Bridge foot
> From the Peak-rabble does securely shut.[6]

Cotton would easily have gained access as a friend of the resident Thomas Hobbes and one who enjoyed Cavendish patronage, quite apart from his social station as squire of Beresford Hall. Celia Fiennes's aristocratic connections gained her admittance and Daniel Defoe, no doubt, presented a letter of introduction from his patron, Robert Harley, Earl of Oxford. Both these commentators, untrammeled by Latin hexameters or rhyming couplets, as were Hobbes and Cotton, give us the direct reportage of the diarist and the journalist.

When Celia Fiennes arrived in 1698 Chatsworth was still in its state of transition and her description of the exterior of the house and gardens was closer to the Knyff and Kip engraving than Cotton's account. She is the first to give a brief description of the interior of some of the new rooms in the house though 'there was as many roomes on the other side which are not finished, they were just painting the cielings and laying the floores, which are all inlaid; these were the Duke and Duchess's apartments beside which there are a great number of roomes and severall offices'.[7] Moving among workmen she naturally concentrates on the materials, lying around in place, from which the great house was being constructed – stone, Ashford marble, wood carving in the chapel, mirror glass and sash panes. The last as part of Chatsworth's lavish fenestration astounded her as much as it had Cotton. Gone were the old leaded casements of the Elizabethan house to make way for gilded sash frames which contained 'squares of glass … so large and good they cost 10s a pannell'.[8]

The grounds were more complete than the house at the time of her visit and she gives a delightfully succinct portrait of the water gardens as follows:

> …the Duke's house lyes just at the foote of this steepe hill which is like a precipice just at the last, notwithstanding the Duke's house stands on a little riseing ground from the River Derwent which runs all along the front of the house and by a little fall made in the water which makes a pretty murmurring noise; before the gate there is a large Parke and severall fine Gardens one without another with gravell walkes and squairs of grass with stone statues in them and in the middle of each Garden is a large fountaine full of images of Sea Gods and Dolphins and Sea Horses which are full of pipes which spout out water in the bason and spouts all about the gardens; 3 Gardens just round the house; some have gravell walks and square like the other with Statues and Images in the bason, there is one bason in the middle of one Garden thats very large and by sluces besides the Images severall pipes plays out the water, about 30 large and small pipes altogether, some flush it up that it frothes like snow; there is one Garden full of stone and brass statues; so the Gardens lyes one above another which makes the prospect very fine; above these gardens is an ascent of 5 or 6 stepps up to a wilderness and close arbours and shady walks, on each end of one walke stands two piramidies full of pipes spouting water that runns down one of them, runns on brass hollow work which looks like rocks and hollow stones; the other is all flatts stands one above another like salvers so the water rebounds one from another, 5 or 6 one above the other; there is another green walke and about the middle of it by the Grove stands a fine Willow tree, the leves barke and all looks very naturall, the roote is full of rubbish or great stones to appearance, and all on a sudden by turning a sluce it raines from each leafe and from the branches like a shower, it being made of brass and pipes to each leafe but in appearance is exactly like any Willow; beyond this is a bason in which are the branches of two Hartichocks Leaves which weeps at the end of each leafe into the bason – which is placed at the foote of lead steps 30 in number; on a little banck stands blew balls 10 on a side, and between each ball are 4 pipes which by a sluce spouts out water across the stepps to each other like an arbour or arch; while you are thus amused suddenly there runs down a torrent of water out of 2 pitchers in the hands of two large Nimphs cut in stone that lyes in the upper step, which makes a pleaseing prospect, this is designed to be enlarged and steps made up to the top of the hill which is a vast ascent, but from the top of it now they are supply'd with water for all their pipes so it will be the easyer to have such a fall of water even from the top which will add to the Curiositye.[9]

She notes that Grillet's cascade is to be extended and describes it as it appears in Knyff and Kip. Her description of the famous weeping willow fountain is important in that the device was a 'conceit' to ape nature and not, as current garden historians persist in claiming, a 'joco d'aqua', whereby visitors were lured beneath it and drenched at the twist of a tap.

Defoe on his second visit to Chatsworth found the house and gardens 'completely designed and finished'. What astounded him on this occasion was that the Duke had 'removed and perfectly carried away a great mountain that stood in the way, and which interrupted the prospect. This was so entirely gone that, having taken a strict view of the gardens at my first being there, and retaining an idea of them in my mind, I was perfectly confounded at coming there a second time, and not knowing what had been done; for I had lost the hill, and found a new country view, which Chatsworth itself had never seen before'.[10] To do this the Duke had pushed well beyond the bounds of Bess's

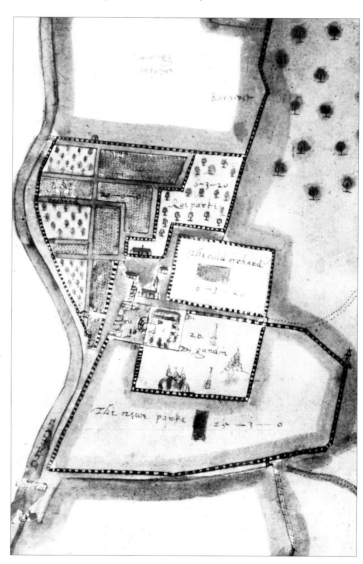

62 *Chatsworth. Detail of the house and gardens, from William Senior's estate map, 1617 (see also plate v).*

south garden, beyond London and Wise's great parterre and across the old Chesterfield road, shown clearly in the foreground of Knyff and Kip's view.

The 1st Duke died in 1707 by which time he had completed almost all his grand designs. All four faces of the house were complete, a canal had been sunk where Defoe had remembered a hill and Grillet's cascade was being extended up the hill to be crowned by Archer's domed cascade house.

Stukeley, the antiquary, saw these elongated water steps and drew them on his visit in 1725. He even projected the steps further up the hill, beyond the cascade house, though this scheme was never implemented, if, indeed, it was ever intended.

The plaudits of Fiennes, Defoe, Stukeley and others represent the brief love-affair of some of the English with the 'excesses' of the baroque. Not everyone liked the new Chatsworth, even before it reached its apogee in the reign of Queen Anne. As early as 1690 one visitor pronounced that Chatsworth's gardens 'have nothing extraordinary but their situation, nothing wonderful but their cost and nothing unusual but their solitariness'.[11] Others wrote pejoratively that the style of both the house and the gardens was 'foreign'. This, of course, meant French, and that in turn meant Versailles and Versailles meant Louis XIV. Together this represented absolutism and tyranny and to many it raised the question of why should England's premier Whig nobleman reflect the taste of her arch enemy.

As the political supremacy of the Whig party endured into the second half of the 18th century, so Chatsworth's ducal triumphalism declined, together with the memory of Louis XIV. The Palladian taste, first made fashionable by Inigo Jones in the early Stuart period, was revived in the early Georgian period by Robert Boyle, 3rd Earl of Burlington, the new leader of Whig taste. Burlington, fresh from his grand tour and surrounded by his artistic disciples, abhorred what Chatsworth represented. The poet Alexander Pope summed this up most wittily and scathingly in *An Epistle to Lord Burlington* (1731) where he describes the villa of the Athenian misanthrope Timon. It has been variously suggested that the passage is an allegory on the Duke of Chandos's Cannons House, Prime Minister Walpole's Houghton Hall or even the Duke of Devonshire's Chatsworth. It is, in all probability, a satire on an imaginary garden incorporating what were considered the worst baroque excesses.

> At *Timon's Villa* let us pass a Day,
> Where all cry out, 'What Sums are thrown away!'
> So proud, so grand, of that stupendous Air,
> *Soft* and *Agreeable* come never there.
> Greatness, with *Timon*, dwells in such a Draught

As brings all *Brobdignag* before your Thought:
To compass this, his Building is a Town,
His Pond an Ocean, his Parterre a Down;
Who but must laugh the Master when he sees?
A puny Insect, shiv'ring at a Breeze!
Lo! What huge Heaps of Littleness around!
Two *Cupids* squirt before: A Lake behind
Improves the keenness of the Northern Wind.
His *Gardens* next your Admiration call,
On ev'ry side you look, behold the Wall!
No pleasing Intricacies intervene,
No artful Wilderness to Perplex the Scene:
Grove nods at Grove, each Ally has a Brother,
And half the Platform just reflects the other.
The suffring Eye inverted Nature sees,
Trees cut to Statues, Statues thick as Trees,
With here a Fountain, never to be play'd,
And there a Summer-house, that knows no Shade.
Here *Amphitrite* sails thro' Myrtle bow'rs;
Then *Gladiators* fight, or die, in fiow'rs;
Un-water'd see the drooping Sea-horse mourn,
And Swallows roost in *Nilus'* dusty Urn ...

Certainly the 1st Duke had bequeathed to his successor a house and grounds
that were hugely expensive to maintain and were outmoded within less than fifty

63 *Chatsworth House and gardens. Oil painting by Jan Siberechts(?), c.1690, with some 18th-century repainting. This was a last view of the house before the 1st Duke's changes.*

years of their creation. The rest of the 18th and early 19th centuries witnessed
their decline. The family found the house increasingly incommodious for their
needs until the 5th Duke and his wife, Georgiana, decamped to Devonshire
House in London as a more comfortable establishment where they were at
the heart of fashionable society and political intrigue.

Tourists continued to come to Chatsworth but their censure grew louder
as they compared it with the houses of the new taste and gardens which were
beginning to reflect the ideas of the English landscape movement and the work
of Charles Bridgeman and William Kent.

One of the principal complaints about the interior of the house was its
lack of good pictures both by the old masters and by contemporary artists.
The painted walls and ceilings were considered anachronisms. John Loveday
of Caversham, for instance, found the gardens less interesting than the house,
though he was particularly surprised by the lack of paintings of quality in
the house. However, he does notice the work of James Thornhill both on
the ceilings and framed on canvas. The latter, then arranged in the Gallery,
whilst not great art, are important as early examples of the English landscape
school. John Loveday calls them the 'Wonders of Castleton' and once again
they indicated the way the house was, outmodedly, linked with the other
Wonders of the Peak.[12]

Visitors increasingly did not like their reception at the house or at the old
Edensor Inn. At the former they often found the servants, instructed to welcome
and guide them, as grasping as the old women at Poole's Cavern; at the latter
they found the accommodation, the food and the service unpleasant. In 1766
Dr Johnson dismissed it as 'a bad inn'. Four years later Arthur Young thought
it 'not improper to warn the traveller against depending on the Inn at Edensor,
as a quarter from when to view Chatsworth. He will there find nothing but

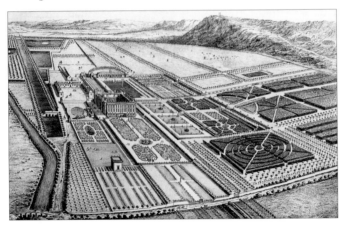

64 *Chatsworth. Engraved
by Jan Kip after Leonard
Knyff, c.1699. The 1st
Duke's half-completed
house is set in the famous
Franco-Dutch gardens.*

dirt and impertinence. If he passes a night there, these attendants will more than balance the viewing a much finer place than that seat'.[13]

Dr Johnson enjoyed his visits to Chatsworth. Perhaps its outmoded style did not offend his Tory taste. Or was it that he enjoyed the food and the flattery offered by the Duke? When Duchess Georgiana met him in 1784 she found his conversation much more appealing than his table manners, commenting in a letter that 'he dined here and does not shine quite so much in eating as conversing, for he ate much and nastily'.[14]

The Duke used to hoist a flag when open house was kept at Chatsworth. The story is told that once when Garrick, Johnson and Boswell were being entertained there Thomas Grove, the vicar of Bakewell, called

65 *Castleton. Oil painting by (Sir) James Thornhill, c.1707, now fixed to the ceiling of the theatre at Chatsworth.*

with the intention of staying for dinner. However, on hearing Garrick ask the Duke, 'Please, Your Grace, are the natives to be down upon us today?' the vicar left in high dudgeon. Shortly after, the Duke, whilst riding with a party near Edensor, saw Grove and called to him, 'How is it you do not come to Chatsworth as usual?' The vicar replied, 'My Lord Duke, I don't like coming whilst these mountebanks and playfolk are with you'. Whereupon the Duke patted him on the back, said that he had handsomely paid them off and suggested he should resume his visits.[15]

However, the 4th Duke needed to address more basic matters if he were to halt the decline of Chatsworth and its reputation. The park and gardens were his principal concern and he pondered how far their formality could be tempered and 'Nature' allowed in (see plate VII). He decided to straighten the river to the north and to remove the Tudor stewponds and the 1st Duke's canal and its fishing bridge. The old stables, uncomfortably near the house, would be demolished and new ones built in the park. A new bridge would give access to the stables and house and the old bridge and the Chesterfield road which crossed it would be removed together with the ancient corn mill.

66 *'The Devil's Arse in the Peak from ye life, July 22nd, 1707.' Pen and wash drawing by Thornhill on which the oil painting was based. Originally the painting was one of a series entitled 'The Wonders of the Peak', which hung in the house.*

A new road from Edensor, through the park, would provide access to the new bridge and would cross the river downstream. The *Edensor Inn* and the vicarage would be demolished and resited out of view of the house. James Paine was commissioned to build the new stables, bridge and corn mill. 'Capability' Brown was to replan the park and gardens.

Brown had to compromise. The terraces and parterres, some dating from Bess's day, were swept away and given over to green sward. The cascade, the fountain on the south garden, the copper willow and the canal were to remain, whilst the bowling green was removed and its pavilion relocated along with the 1st Duke's greenhouse.

The house was not touched. As all this change was being mooted Horace Walpole caught wind of it and wrote waspishly to George Montague in 1760:

> I never was more disappointed than at Chatsworth, which, ever since I was born, I have condemned. It is a glorious situation; the vale rich in corn and verdure, vast woods hang down the hills, which are green to the top, and the immense rocks only serve to dignify the prospect. The river runs before the door, and serpentises more than you can conceive in the vale. The Duke is widening it, and will make it the middle of his park; but I don't approve an idea they are going to execute, of a fine bridge with statues under a noble cliff. If they will have a bridge (which by the way will crowd the scene), it should be composed of rude fragments, such as the giant of the Peak would step upon, that he might not be wetshod. The expense of the works now carrying on will amount to forty thousand pounds. A heavy quadrangle of stables is part of the plan, is very cumbrous, and standing higher than the house, is ready to overwhelm

it. The principal front of the house is beautiful, and executed with the neatness of wrought plate; the inside is most sumptuous, but did not please me; the heathen gods, goddesses, Christian virtues, and allegoric gentlefolks, are crowded into every room, as if Mrs Holman [i.e. the housekeeper] had been in heaven and invited everybody she saw. The great apartment is first; painted ceilings, inlaid floors, and unpainted wainscots make every room *sombre*. The tapestries are fine, but not fine enough, and there are few portraits. The chapel is charming. The great *jet d'eau* I like, nor would I remove it; whatever is magnificent of the kind in the time it was done, I would retain, else all gardens and houses wear a tiresome resemblance. I except that absurdity of a cascade tumbling down marble steps, which reduces the steps to be of no use at all.[16]

Chatsworth's old glory was passing to a neighbouring rival on the edge of the Peak – Kedleston Hall. As the 4th Duke of Devonshire began to 'improve' Chatsworth in the 1760s, Viscount Scarsdale built anew at Kedleston House to replace the old one and laid out the gardens and park in the contemporary landscape taste. Kedleston Hall was begun in the Palladian style by Matthew Brettingham and James Paine and was finished in the neo-classical style by Robert Adam. It was spacious, elegant and graced with a fine collection of pictures. Its park was adorned with a splendid lake and bridge and an elegant fishing lodge designed by Adam. The cognoscenti heaped paeans of praise upon what Pevsner has called the finest Georgian house in Derbyshire.

Of course, there were those who did not approve and who still preferred the grandeur of Chatsworth. Dr Johnson was pre-eminent among the critics of Kedleston and on his first visit attacked it violently, saying, 'It would do excellently for a town-hall'. He was less offensive on his subsequent visit when Lord Scarsdale was present. Boswell, however, spoke for most tourists and visitors when he declared the house, park and the various buildings 'agitated and distended my mind in a most agreeable manner'. He declared that 'the proprietor of all this *must* be happy', but Johnson replied, 'Nay, Sir, all this excludes but one evil – poverty'.[17]

Walpole changed his tune somewhat when he heard that the task of remodelling the park and gardens at Chatsworth was to be undertaken by his hero, Lancelot Brown. 'Chatsworth', he conceded, 'is much improved by the late Duke, many foolish waterworks being taken away, oaks and rocks taken into the garden, and a magnificent bridge built.'[18] Walpole now mentioned Reynolds's portrait of the Duke of Cumberland as a good picture in the house.

Arthur Young listed Chatsworth's modest paintings in order to give, in his view, the more remarkable collection at Kedleston. The modern views of Matlock by Alexander Cozens, for instance, far surpassed Thornhill's 'dated' local views. The general view of Chatsworth's gardens still filled him with 'indifference' and 'disgust' and were still marred with 'hocus pocus gewgaws'.[19]

John Byng's visit elicited the following damning account:

… we walk'd back to Chatsworth; where the porter was so obliging as to find the gardener, and the housekeeper for us; who are allways ready to attend to strangers. Under the guidance of the first, we had the long temporary cascade in front of the house let loose for us; this, when dry, is a disagreeable sight, and not much better, when cover'd with the dirty water they lower from the hill.

Next some fountains were made to squirt aloft for us; and a leaden tree (worthy only of a tea garden in London) to sport about us. Nor could I refrain from remarking what I suppose all others do, at the ground remaining unsloped to the vale and river; which the gardener said might be completely done for 2000£. As for the river, of clear water, meand'ring thro' the meadows, it is now but a pitiful twine, which, under an owner of spirit would be made equal, if not superior to the Blenheim Water: but here is no taste, no comforts display'd. All is asleep! More money may be lavish'd in follies, or lost at cards, in one year than would render this park a wonder of beauty.

Seeing this little of garden, cost us much money; because we were shewn about by a wou'd-be gentleman, and felt ourselves to be really so. The housekeeper next took us in tow, and shew'd us all the foolish glare, uncomfortable rooms, and frippery French furniture of this vile house. If nothing has been done abroad to beautify, if nothing has been done within for true luxury, yet the Dutchess has made a fine display of French tables, gilt chairs, uneasy sofas, and all what is call'd charming furniture. – To complete the French-hood, the oaken floors of the great apartments are all wax'd, so that ice is rougher, and every step upon them is dangerous.

Of pictures, there are some portraits, and much indecency in the other paintings and the tapestry: a great Hampton Court stair case, and a Sr John Vanbrugh chapel make up the total. Hardwick House a house of grandeur as a house of comfort is worth a dozen Chatsworths.[20]

Ebenezer Rhodes summed up the responses of the tourists by stating that 'few noble mansions have been more lavishly praised and indiscriminately censured than Chatsworth, which was once the pride and boast of Derbyshire, "when", as Gilpin expresses it, "trim parterres and formal water-works were

67 *'The Cascade at Chatsworth, July 26, 1725.' Pen and wash drawing by William Stukeley.*

68 *Chatsworth from the west. Oil painting by Thomas Smith of Derby, c.1740s. By this time the 1st Duke's gardens were out of fashion and show signs of change.*

in fashion"; but now, fallen from its high estate, it has become a butt for every pretender to taste to shoot an arrow at.'[21]

When William George Spencer Cavendish, the 6th Duke, succeeded his father in 1811 Chatsworth had lost its pseudonym of 'the Palace of the Peak'; it was now regarded as an outmoded country house. The new occupant was not happy with this image of his family seat. His grandfather, the 4th Duke, had married the heiress of the architect Earl, Lord Burlington and the 6th Duke inherited not only a vast fortune but a passion for architecture. As the owner of six great country seats and two town houses in London he would be little incommoded by alterations to Chatsworth. He was not in a hurry.

The baroque house was not pulled down, though a number of internal rearrangements were made, including a fine library. Instead, the Duke employed Sir Jeffry Wyatville to add a large extension on the north side to allow him to dine and entertain in the grand manner and to show off his growing collections of books and *objets d'art*. Thus were built the dining room, sculpture gallery, orangery and theatre (see plate VI).

Wyatville also helped to construct the new gardens on the west front and restored what is known as Mary Queen of Scots Bower in the park, an Elizabethan garden and fishing tower which, with the Elizabethan Stand, had been spared by Brown and the 4th Duke in the 1760s.

69   *Chatsworth from the west. Oil painting by William Marlow, c.1760s. The hand of 'Capability' Brown is clearly seen. The cascade was spared. The new bridge and stables are James Paine's work.*

The changes in and extension of the gardens were arguably the Bachelor Duke's greatest achievement at Chatsworth. In this the genius of Sir Joseph Paxton was of paramount importance. Together they created an arboretum and a pineturn, vast rockeries, waterfalls, the magnificent Emperor Fountain, and ranges of revolutionary glasshouses including the lily house and the great stove. Here the famous Amazon lily (*Victoria Regia*) was made to flower for the first time under glass; bananas bore fruit; rare trees flourished; and superb collections of camellias and orchids were grown. In short, the gardens rivalled Kew in cultivating rare and exotic plants.

The Duke also rebuilt his estate village of Edensor as a model village in an eclectic *cottage-ornée* style. The fame of Chatsworth spread. In 1843 Queen Victoria and Prince Albert were entertained splendidly in the house and grounds and visitors flocked to the park, especially after the Midland Railway reached Bakewell in 1862 and then proceeded to Buxton. No longer were visitors carping about the lack of attractions; the Duke's fortune and his taste had enabled him to accumulate one of the world's great picture collections, Kedleston was eclipsed and the Victorian tourist revelled in the eclectic splendours of Chatsworth. Once an ailing wonder it was now a miracle – not just of the Peak but of the world.

13

Haddon Awakes

Though a product of the Romantic period, the new Chatsworth of the 6th Duke, Wyatville and Paxton had never been viewed as a truly romantic house. Chatsworth had no vestiges of a gothic past in terms of the Cavendishes or their architecture; this to some degree accounts for much of the indifference to the house of Walpole, Gray and their fellow goths. The romantic distinction belonged to Chatsworth's venerable neighbour, perched in the adjacent valley of the Wye – Haddon Hall.

Haddon was a vernacular rather than a polite architectural pile; a low complex of two courtyards, each with a corner gate tower; an agglomeration of styles and parts from the 12th to the 17th centuries, it had none of Chatsworth's mellow ashlar. Instead it was a charming mixture of random limestone walls with gritstone quoins and jambs, mullions, transoms and sills. Local oak was used for stud partitions and beams and local lead for its low pitched roofs.

Traditionally built, some believe, first by the Peverels, the house passed to the Avenels, then to the Vernons from whom it came by marriage in the 1560s to its present owners, the Manners family.[1]

Of the house's early history little is known. Although its parapets bristle with battlements which are even repeated in miniature on its chimney stacks, its low position on a limestone shelf, on rising ground above the river, meant it could never be a redoubtable fortress. Until the late 14th century the Hall had been part of the village of Nether Haddon which was, like Chatsworth village, subsequently cleared and emparked.[2]

Haddon Hall played little part in the Civil War though Sir John Gell, the governor of Derby, requested permission from Parliament to destroy it along with Chatsworth House.[3] Its survival was a great relief to the Earl of Rutland whose principal seat, Belvoir Castle in Leicestershire, had been destroyed in the war. The Manners family continued to treat Haddon as its chief residence until Belvoir was rebuilt. The family eventually left Haddon in 1700 and the Earl was elevated to a dukedom in 1703.

70 *Haddon Hall. Engraving by F. Vivares after Thomas Smith, 1744. The house had been left empty for almost 50 years by this time, the gardens were overgrown and the park abandoned.*

Just before the family's departure Celia Fiennes arrived at Haddon following her hazardous ride over the hill from Chatsworth. She was not impressed and described it as 'a good old house, all built of stone on a hill but nothing curious as the mode now is; there is a large park upon a great ascent from the house which is built round a court; the park is one part of some of the highest hills which gives a great prospect over the country'.[4]

Unlike Chatsworth, Haddon had never been considered a wonder, a palace or a tourist attraction. Travellers had a distant view of it from the roads from Bakewell to Youlgreave and Over Haddon or from the road near Stanton in Peak. If one rode out of Bakewell through the fields to the track which had once been the old street of lost Nether Haddon the view of the Hall was much as Smith of Derby painted it and Vivares engraved it in 1744. Its garden terraces had lost their parterres and the topiaried trees had grown wild. The park had been stripped of its ancient oaks for use as props in the local lead mines;[5] the deer had been slaughtered and the park was eventually divided into fields and enclosed with quickset hedges (see plate VIII).[6]

The Hall itself was once again in jeopardy and in 1722 it was rumoured in Bakewell that its demolition was imminent.[7] Perhaps the cost of pulling it down and clearing the site proved prohibitive. It remained an empty storehouse for outmoded furniture not wanted at Belvoir.[8]

When the 1759 Matlock to Bakewell turnpike road was laid down it entered the old park at Rowsley and passed within a hundred and fifty yards of the house. Coach passengers could now see it from their windows.

John Byng came in 1789 and described its mournful state:

> Today, I turned to the left over Rowesley Bridge; and soon came under the wall of Haddon Hall park, now quite dismantled and the timber fell'd. I cross'd over a bridge to the house, of awful, and melancholy look, as if deploring its forlorn state; the river below finds tears …
>
> This poor abandon'd place is totally deserted; (tho' surrounded by an estate of £8,000 pr ann:) and uninhabited, because then not subject to the window tax!
>
> As a place it might be made of greater beauty, by the power of water and a romantick country, than could ever be the nasty stare-about Castle of Belvoir. The walls and roof are all sound and good; so only furniture and fuel are necessary to make it habitable: nor, were I Duke of Rutland, shou'd I visit it for more than 2 summer months; but I could not suffer its decay, and that the gallery and kitchen should not be warm'd. The river is so brilliant that it would form a lake of the utmost magnificence; and, as abundant of trout, of much diversion. – One night's losses at play of the late duke had made this a charming place.[9]

Even Horace Walpole, who had visited Haddon in 1760, was not impressed by the house. He described it as 'an abandoned old castle of the Rutlands, in a romantic situation, but which could never have composed a tolerable dwelling'.[10]

Gradually, however, as history and antiquarianism became essential strands of high romanticism, these pejorative views changed. By the end of the 18th century the passing tourists' curiosity drew them to view a fairy-tale house that had slept among the trees for a century. By the beginning of the 20th century Haddon was an inspiration to architects, antiquarians and landscape gardeners throughout Britain and beyond. So much so that the Marquess of Granby chose to restore it and live there after the First World War.

71 *The Long Gallery, Haddon Hall. Lithograph by Samuel Rayner, 1836.*

72 *The Chapel, Haddon Hall. Lithograph by Samuel Rayner, 1837.*

The first printed account of Haddon Hall was by Edward King in *Archaeologia* in 1782.[11] He, like Walpole, considered it a castle. Yet despite his confused chronology, his limited architectural knowledge and the highly inaccurate engraving of the house which accompanied this article, it had the effect of drawing more explorers to this lost wonder of the Peak. Writers came to savour the medieval atmosphere and to dream of deeds of honour and chivalry within its walls. The poet Gray lingered here[12] and Mrs Radcliffe is said to have experienced its gothick ambience and the sublimity of its setting which she recreated in her *Mysteries of Udolfo*

73 *Haddon Hall. Pencil and wash sketch by John Constable, 1801. This view shows the chapel belfry, the lower garden wall and the fishing bridge, later called 'Dorothy Vernon's Bridge'.*

(1794) and other novels.[13] Likewise, Sir Walter Scott is said to have visited Haddon and the surrounding area before writing *Peveril of the Peak* (1823).[14]

Artists also began to seek out Haddon as the 18th century drew to a close. No-one of great standing had illustrated it after Smith's painting for the Duke and Vivares's fine engraving of the picture. Ralph's view of the Hall was engraved by S. Ryland for *England Illustrated* (1764) and Cordall Powell exhibited a view of it at the Society of Artists in London in 1771. Hayman Rooke, the Nottinghamshire antiquary, had his drawing engraved by R. Godfrey in 1780.

By the beginning of the 19th century, however, Haddon was one of the most sketched, painted and engraved house in England. Constable came in 1801 followed by his teacher Farington and a number of other Royal Academicians including Turner

74 *'Dorothy Vernon's Steps'. A late Victorian souvenir postcard recalling Dorothy Vernon's supposed elopement with John Manners.*

in 1831.[15] Reinagle painted in the park and J.C. Buckler has left a complete sketchbook of 20 detailed views of the Hall's exteriors and interiors, drawn in 1812.[16]

It was Stephen Rayner who really brought Haddon to life in both word and image in his two volume work, *History and Antiquities of Haddon Hall* (1836-37). Its engravings and lithographs faithfully captured the magic of the venerable pile, not least by introducing figures in the costume of the 16th and 17th centuries. As we shall see later, Joseph Nash followed Rayner and de Wint and David Cox captured Haddon in exquisite watercolours at the beginning of Victoria's reign. The last two extended their attention beyond the house and the park; de Wint sketched along the Lathkil to Alport and Youlgrave whilst Cox followed the Wye downstream to Rowsley and its *Peacock Hotel*.[17]

The growing flood of tourists prompted the Duke of Rutland to appoint a custodian and guide. The task fell to William Hage who farmed a few acres

75 *Tourists at Haddon Hall. Lithograph by Newman and Company, London, c.1840s.*

in the park and lived in the old cottage next to the stables, which is now occupied by the gardener (see plate IX). Hage was no ordinary guide. Beneath his portrait, lithographed by Rayner, we are told that this 'celebrated guide to Haddon Hall' was 'the descendant of a family which has served in the house of Manners for upwards of three centuries'.[18] Born in 1754, he had served as a guide for 61 years when Rayner took his portrait.

Like the other predatory guides we have met in the Peak, he was generous with his tales as he was with objects belonging to the house – all for the sake of a fat tip. John Byng met him in 1789 and tells us that 'the farmer, who inhabits the farm near the Gate (part of the old outhouses) most civilly put up my nag and then attended me'. So the tour of the Hall began and Hage's tongue was unleashed. When Byng commented how the old kitchen was woefully damp the guide retorted, 'Aye, 'twaid kill a fly in five minutes in summer! Unlike to former times, Sr, when Sir George Vernon (call'd King of the Peak) treated Prince Arthur (Henry VII's son) here as he always did when he kept open his house for the 12 days of Xmas, as he allways did, and was allways done (even at the beginning of the century) by the Rutlands'.[19]

Byng would have had a less romanticised tour of the house had he been taken there by White Watson. His recorded tour with one Captain Carmichael in 1805,[20] although now incomplete, was probably intended for inclusion in his proposed history of Bakewell. Instead the unhistorical ramblings of Hage governed much of what was to be written about Haddon until recent times.

Sixty-one years as a guide is a good time to concoct the history of a long empty house. If Hage was a romantic 'liar', Byng was little better as an antiquary and a tourist. The man who had gladly taken away a piece of Shakespeare's chair from his house in Stratford deplored the vandalism of 'one of my brethren (antiquaries) (a sad dog!)' who had 'lately cut out 5 of the saints' faces from Haddon chapel's east window.' When Hage offered him a souvenir which he described as a sword hilt and broken blade 'said to be worn by the Vernons in the wars with France', Byng readily appropriated it.[21]

Needless to say, the figments of Hage's vivid imagination, like his portrait, soon appeared in print, including his most famous fabrication, the tale of Dorothy Vernon's elopement with John Manners some time in the early 1560s. The story was picked up by Alan Cunningham, the Scottish romantic writer, as he accompanied Sir Francis Chantrey in a sketching tour in the Peak. Cunningham published it in his collected tales in 1822 and it also appeared as a newspaper story.[22]

Thereafter some half a dozen novels appeared based on the story and an operetta with music by Sir Arthur Sullivan was composed in 1892.[23] One recent writer has even claimed the story to be the inspiration for Shakespeare's play *Romeo and Juliet*.[24]

Tourists still flock to Haddon to walk the path of Dorothy Vernon through Haddon's long gallery, leave by the famous steps into the garden and gaze down the descending terraces to the bridge over the Wye where she was spirited away by John Manners. Unfortunately, all these architectural and garden features were built after Dorothy's death in 1584!

The story is a romance of its times and one wonders if Hage had read Scott's *Lochinvar* or Keats's *St Agnes Eve*. Nevertheless, it gave to Haddon a heroine, an icon which Chatsworth, in its brief flirtation with the captivity of Mary Queen of Scots, could never emulate.

Yet the two houses, so different in character and history, remain linked by their close proximity and the fact that the tourist in Bakewell could visit them both by carriage on a summer's day. Little did most of those coming by train to Bakewell after 1863 know that, upon leaving Rowsley, they almost passed under Haddon Hall in an 860-yard-long tunnel, just to the rear of the house.

14

Early Concepts of Landscape: Drawings, Paintings and Prints

The descriptive literature of the Peak, which had first manifested itself at the end of the 16th century, preceded the work of the artists by a hundred years. English artists, like their literary counterparts, were not much moved to depict the perceived deformities of the Pennine landscape. John Speed's county map of Derbyshire, engraved in 1610, contains an inset of the *Talbot Inn* and St Anne's Well in Buxton which might be considered the first landscape view of the Peak. However, it is the work of a cartographer, not an artist; the buildings are inaccurately portrayed and the background range of hills is suggestive rather than observed. The illustration was certainly a curiosity and, no doubt, attracted visitors to Buxton to try the waters.

We owe the beginnings of true landscape art in England to Wenceslas Hollar, a native of Prague, who came to London with the Earl of Arundel in 1636. Whilst not interested in wild landscape *per se*, he was noted for his accurate portrayal of buildings in their landscape settings and especially for his panoramic views of towns and cities of which London was his most important and spectacular. Particularly significant was the fact that he engraved his studies, thus ensuring their circulation as individual prints or as illustrations in books. Indeed, the slow spread of printmaking in the 17th century was important not only for its dissemination of ideas among artists and patrons, but as an incentive to curious tourists to visit various locations.

Among others, Hollar had an influence on the northern English artist, Francis Place. Vertue tells us that Place 'got acquainted with Hollar, of whom he learnt his manner of etching, he already having a knack of drawing and a genious that way.'[1] This was an invaluable skill to Place who 'was the first English artist whose main preoccupation was landscape'. He 'stands at the head of the English tradition of landscape and, in many respects, prefigures its development.'[2] Place, along with the artist George Lambert and the glasspainter Henry Gyles of York, was a member of the York Virtuosi who met at Gyles's house.[3] He and Lambert travelled throughout England, Wales and into Ireland, drawing and engraving prospects of towns. Place was much interested in wild rocky scenes and his engraving of the *Dropping Well at Knaresborough*[4] is much in the style of Salvator Rosa.

Place came to sketch in the Peak in about 1678, though the reference to his visit by Vertue is confused with his visit to Wales. In Derbyshire or Wales he was briefly arrested and imprisoned as a suspicious traveller at a time when provincial authorities were anxious following the Titus Oates plot.[5] If he did visit the Peak no illustrations from his tour are known to us.

Vertue also tells us of a little known artist, Philip Boul, whose pocket book of Derbyshire sketches he had seen. Boul was a subscriber to Kneller's Academy in 1711 but when he made the sketches and what became of them is not known. Significantly, Vertue says they were 'much in imitation of Salvator's manner'.[6] Clearly, at the end of the 17th century artists were visiting the Peak in the hope of emulating the Alpine scenes they had admired in the prints of Salvator Rosa and other European landscapists.

The earliest surviving illustrations of the Peak were executed to commission by artists from the Netherlands. They had generally had some training in Italy and were quite adept at transferring from the flat horizons of the Low Countries to the widely contrasting hills, rocks, dales and streams of the Peak. They were employed by prospering aristocrats who desired pictorial records of their country seats. In this regard they performed the same service as the 'country house poets', Francis, Hobbes and Cotton.

The Earls and Dukes of Devonshire were among the foremost patrons in the land in employing foreign artists. The 4th Earl secured the services of the principal painter of country seats, Jan Siberechts. Born in Antwerp in 1627, where he was celebrated for his genre paintings of peasant women with their cattle set in watery Flemish landscapes, he was lured to London by the Duke of Buckingham in 1672.[7] He quickly found employment with aristocratic patrons painting country seats such as Longleat and Wollaton Hall.

In 1686 Vertue tells us he was 'making drawings of Chatsworth' at an important juncture in the history of the Cavendish family. The 4th Earl of Devonshire was about to pull down his Elizabethan mansion and remodel it along with the gardens and park. Siberechts was enlisted to make a final record before the changes were implemented. He began his task by making a series of sketches which were to be worked up as oil paintings. Of Siberecht's work at Chatsworth there survive three watercolours and one oil painting.

The watercolour sketches are now scattered in English and European galleries. One signed and dated 1699 is a view from the northern edge of Chatsworth Park. The artist, seated alone with his sketchbook in the foreground,

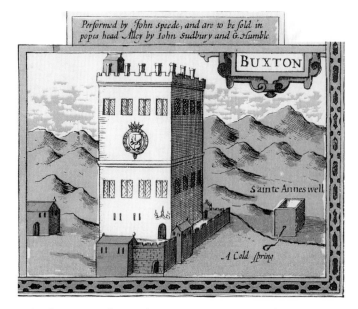

76 *Inset from John Speed's map of Derbyshire, 1610. The Talbot Inn, Bath House and St Ann's Well are set against an inaccurate early landscape.*

is looking up along the gritstone edges of Baslow, Curbar and beyond. It is a sensitive panorama, not given to exaggeration, and can readily be recognised today.[8]

Similarly, another fine watercolour made to the south of the park is autographed 'Bely in darbyshair 22 Augusti 1694 J. Sybrecht f.' On this occasion the artist looks down from Beeley Moor into the Derwent Valley where the river leaves Chatsworth Park on the right and flows towards its confluence with the Wye at Rowsley (see plate 4, p.7). In the foreground a small hunting party comprising a gentleman and lady (the Earl and Countess?) on horseback and two servants with a brace of dogs. Below is the tiny thatched and stone-slated village of Beeley and its small, towered church.[9]

The third view, more a sketch than the others, appears to be of the trees and hills of the park, perhaps taken from near, or on, the Hunting Tower.[10]

A fourth view in oils, traditionally said to depict the estate village of Edensor in the background, is wrongly identified and quite unassociated with Siberecht's work at Chatsworth.[11]

Nevertheless, the first three scenes, taken together, illustrate Siberechts's attraction to the English landscape and how he depicted it most pleasingly. The drawings were certainly done *en plein air*.

As to the oil painting of Chatsworth House, the earliest surviving painting of the building, this still hangs in the house and is the subject of some debate (see plate 63, p.129). The keep-like building and courtyard towers, as shown diagrammatically in William Senior's estate plan of 1617, are central in the

IX *Thomas Hage. Lithograph by Samuel Rayner, 1839. For
61 years a guide at Haddon, he concocted most of the romantic
tales associated with the house in the 19th century.*

X *Chee Tor. Aquatint by P. Scotin after Thomas Smith.
Published by John Boydell, 1769.*

XIII *Returning from the hayfield with a distant view of Haddon Hall. Watercolour by David Cox, c.1838. The ford depicted here was in Bakewell meadows.*

XIV *P.P. Burdett and his wife Hannah. Oil painting by Joseph Wright, 1765. The cartographer holds his telescope and the portrait is set against a Peak landscape.*

xv *The Howden and Derwent Dams.*

XVI *View from the Broad Walk, Buxton. Watercolour by Eugène Lami, post 1870. Buxton's heyday as a fashionable spa.*

picture. The 3rd Earl's refenestration is clearly seen and there is a glimpse of the formal gardens, all set beneath Cotton's 'ignoble jet' – a bare, treeless ridge on which the Hunting Tower stands like a lighthouse. However, the road with figures in the foreground is an inaccurate addition by another hand and the painting of the sky exhibits an 18th-century style and technique which has been attributed to Richard Wilson.[12] In short, the painting appears to be a repair or 'restoration' of a Siberechts original which, nevertheless, gives a prospect of an inimical environment that startled so many visitors. Here is the only man-made Wonder of the Peak that was first extolled by Camden.

It was a valedictory view of Chatsworth in more ways than one. The house was systematically taken down and Siberechts left to take up other commissions. According to Vertue he died in London in 1703.[13] He was not an engraver and his work at Chatsworth was never issued as prints. His patron, the 4th Earl, following his elevation to the Dukedom of Devonshire in 1694, the year Siberechts signed his Beeley sketch, looked for a new artist. This time he commissioned Leonard Knyff, a native of Amsterdam, to portray his new 'Palace of the Peak'.

Born in 1650, Knyff followed his brother Jacob to London in 1673. According to Vertue, he painted 'chiefly fowls, dogs etc.' but by the late 1690s he had embarked on his great scheme to draw and paint one hundred noblemen's and gentlemen's country seats. This endeavour became his memorial in the form of *Britannia Illustrata*, published in 1707 with 80 plates all engraved by Jan Kip. Three of these are of Derbyshire seats; the Duke of Newcastle's Bolsover Castle, the Earl of Chesterfield's Bretby Park and the Duke of Devonshire's Chatsworth. Each subscriber's aim was to acquire multiple copies of the engraving of his seat. Thus Knyff contracts with the Duke of Newcastle in 1698 'for drawing engraving and printing the seats of the said Duke's … the prospect to be regularly taken a mile about ye house'. Knyff also agreed to 'deliver to ye sd Duke four hundred prints of such houses and Seats as ye sd Duke shall chuse, ye sd Duke to pay for ye same Twenty pounds …'[14]

How many prints were ordered by the Duke of Devonshire is not known. Knyff was at Chatsworth in 1699 to draw a half-finished house – the new south and east wings by Talman grafted on to the north and west sides of the old house. The perspective view of the estate, as if taken from a balloon, sets the house and gardens against a background of bare hills. To the north east is the Hunting Tower, a pinnacle on the edge of the moors, whilst further north is almost the same landscape of hills and edges that Siberechts had drawn. Did Knyff have access to this view? The Derwent is seen emerging from trees beside the estate village of Baslow, the spire of whose church is just visible.

This remarkable print is notable for the extent and detail of its accuracy, all superbly engraved in Kip's London studio. It served the Duke as a fine advertisement for the splendour of his taste and style and the striking contrast of the order of his grounds and the wildness of their setting.

How many preparatory sketches Knyff made is not known and only one large oil painting survives, though not at Chatsworth.[15] It is an unsigned and undated view looking over the garden wall to the rear of Grillet's Cascade and down to the house, Edensor village across the Derwent and the hills beyond. Again it shows Talman's completed east and south sides of the house. The date must be between 1703 and 1707, or just after, since the Cascade is now crowned by Archer's Cascade House, begun and finished in those years. Siberechts had died in 1703, so Knyff, who died in 1730, is almost certainly the artist.

It is a vast, varied landscape setting. A pastoral scene is set in the foreground where a coach on the old Chesterfield road descends towards the house. The background, beyond the Derwent, is a fine panorama of the estate extending northwards up the valley. Francis Thompson observed that 'among the objects

77 *Wingfield Manor. Oil painting by Jan Siberechts(?), c.1690.*

78 *Hope. Pen and wash sketch by Sir James Thornhill, c.1699. An early landscape of the Hope Valley and Hope village from the* Black Rabbit *in Pindale.*

still extant may be seen Baslow church and river bridge; beyond them Bubnell Hall; and in the middle distance Hassop Hall. Further to the right appears the smoke from Calver lead mine'.[16]

The first Englishman whose landscapes of the Peak have survived is James Thornhill who succeeded Verrio and Laguerre as a ceiling painter at Chatsworth. Born in Dorset in 1675, he was trained by a relative, Thomas Highmore, who became serjeant painter to William III, Queen Anne and George I. Highmore was painting wainscot and decorative detail at Chatsworth in 1696[17] and about this time, or very soon after, Thornhill joined him. Ten years later he painted the famous Sabine Room ceiling.

However, Thornhill had been active outside the house in the late 1690s and travelled the Peak to make sketches in pencil, pen and wash of some of its Wonders. Some of these survive in his sketchbook, dated 1699 on the fly-leaf.[18] They are the earliest illustrations of the area around Castleton and Bakewell. One is an expansive view into the Hope Valley from the Black Rabbit Cottage in Pindale. The artist has his back to Castleton and looks down towards Hope village and the broached spire of its church. Behind is the ridge stretching from Lose Hill to Win Hill. The steep road into Castleton is on the right and Thornhill looks in the opposite direction to sketch a view of Mam Tor with cottages on the outskirts of Castleton in the middle ground. Like Siberechts,

Thornhill has drawn himself in the foreground, sketching the scene with a companion beside him. The dominant feature is the scree face of Mam Tor (see plate 23, p.44).[19]

There are three figures in the foreground of his sketch of Buxton (see plate 25, p.48). The hill on the left, with the houses of the market place shown, falls steeply down to the *Talbot Inn* (New Hall) and St Anne's Well. The Wye flows by the trees of the old Grove towards St Anne's chapel, whilst the hills in the background are much more accurate than those in Speed's view, almost a century earlier.[20]

At Bakewell the church of All Saints is the central feature with the vicarage beside it, viewed from the Yeld to the south-west. This was a favourite viewpoint for subsequent artists including J.L. Petit and J.M.W. Turner. Thornhill's quick drawing shows the treeless Bakewell Edge in the background up which the pack-horse route to Edensor and Chatsworth snakes its way to the summit of Ball Cross.[21]

Most interesting and most accomplished of his sketches are those of Castleton. Those in his sketch book depict the castle towering over the town and a reverse view of the Castle keep from Cave Dale (see plate 14, p.27). The former shows a straggling group of tourists before the entrance to Peak Cavern whose mouth is crowded with rope-makers' hovels. The latter shows a couple of limestone burners operating a kiln in the foreground (see plate 17, p.33). The artist was fascinated by the disposition of the limestone rock and made three separate studies of rockscapes.[22] There is a further drawing of Castleton by Thornhill in the Bodleian Library, the finest of them all, signed and dated 'July 22nd, 1707'. Here the castle is perched above the gorge and entrance to Peak Cavern (see plate 66, p.132).[23]

This last and most finished study was the basis of Thornhill's oil painting which is still at Chatsworth (see plate 65, p.131). It was one of a series of oil paintings by Thornhill which were on view to visitors to the house. John Loveday, described them as 'Wonders of Castleton'. The view of the cave and castle is dark and glowering with a full moon – an early 18th-century English approach to the sublime manner of Salvator Rosa. However, the landscapes were not particularly admired by visitors who were more impressed by Thornhill's painted ceiling in the Sabine Room.

The 2nd Duke of Devonshire reverted to another artist from the Netherlands to paint portraits of his house and park in the person of Pieter Tillemans. Born in 1684 in Antwerp, as was Siberechts, he came to England in 1718 aspiring to be a sporting artist with a facility for painting horses. He did not continue long in this genre and had more success as a painter of country houses and

79 *Chatsworth* and the *Derwent Valley. Anonymous oil painting by Leonard Knyff(?), c.1710. The village of Edensor can be seen on the left and Baslow on the right.*

topographical views. About 1720 he was commissioned to paint Chatsworth. He completed three views of the house, the finest of which remains there (see plate VII).[24] It is a long horizontal view of the house and gardens across the centre of the picture with the bare gritstone edge and its Hunting Tower on the horizon. A charming foreground – a foretaste of Stubbs – represents a group of mares and foals in a meadow. It was not engraved and with the departure of Tillemans came an end to the Cavendish patronage of landscape artists from the Low Countries.

English practitioners, amateur and professional, were slowly displacing foreigners. William Stukeley, primarily an antiquary, expressed an early 'romantic' predilection for the Peakland scenery in the early 18th century. He made some competent sketches of Poole's Cavern, Buxton and Chatsworth gardens.[25] About the same time John Archer of Holme Hall, Bakewell, aping Hobbes and Cotton, described the Wye Valley between Endcliff and Haddon Hall in rhyming couplets and accompanied it with panoramic sketches. He built a prospect house in his garden in order to view Bakewell's steeple and Haddon Hall's towers beyond. Higher up the Derwent valley he made sketches of his other seat at Highlow Hall with a distant prospect of Hathersage against a backcloth of the prehistoric hill site of Carl Wark and the gritstone moors.[26]

As English interest in and interpretations of landscape began to change, artists widened their horizons beyond portraits of aristocratic estates. The brothers Samuel and Nathaniel Buck were topographical artists and engravers working

80   *Prospect of the River Wye in Monsal Dale. Engraved by F. Vivares after Thomas Smith. First printed in 1742 and reprinted here by John Boydell, 1769.*

in London whose travels in Britain illustrate this width of interest. Among their publications were *Antiquities, or venerable remains of Castles, Monasteries, Palaces etc, in England and Wales with several views of Cities and Chief Towns* (2 vols., London 1730-41) and *Perspective Views of near 100 Cities and Chief Towns in England and Wales* (London 1774). Following a sketching tour in the Peak in 1727 they published *The North West view of Castleton Castle and the Devil's Arse in the Peak* as well as *The South West View of Beauchief Abbey*, the first known illustration of this building.[27]

However, the Bucks were primarily interested in antiquities and their proficiency in perspective compared ill with that of Knyff and Kip. Their prospects made little concession to contemporary picturesque principles and their false sense of scale produced exaggerations in their portrayal of buildings. Nevertheless, their prints proved widely popular and their plates lasted well.

At last Derbyshire produced an artist to reckon with. Thomas Smith, alias Smith of Derby, has left us no information concerning his early life and education. His work has obvious Netherlandish elements. He may have studied in the Low Countries or alternatively may have been associated with artists from there who came to England. An oil painting of Wingfield Manor and its surrounding landscape has been claimed as an early work by Smith but this is questionable. It reveals conventions used by Siberechts and others, such as the cart drawn by four horses in the foreground (see plate 77, p.148). Smith may have been influenced by Peter Tillemans. His painting of Chatsworth (*c*.1740s) was taken from the same viewpoint as the Netherlander's. Apart from featuring a coach and horses in the foreground, instead of Tillemans's mare and foals, it is similar in every way.

About the same time Smith also painted Haddon Hall for the Duke of Rutland. This is the earliest known portrayal of the Hall. There is much landscape in the picture from the Bowling House at the end of a hillside avenue behind the Hall to a pastoral scene of horses, cattle and sheep in the foreground and beyond. The picture illustrates Smith's affection for nature and animals. He even includes a rabbit bolting into its hole, in the immediate foreground of the Haddon painting (see plate 70, p.138).

Both those early oils were engraved by one of the finest printmakers of mid-18th-century England, François Vivares. Born in France in 1709, he spent his adult life in London where he first worked as a tailor. His earliest known work as an engraver dates from 1739.[28] Chiefly a reproductive printmaker, he did engrave some of his own work and he and Smith sketched together in the Yorkshire Dales, the Lake District and Shropshire.[29] So admired were his plates of Chatsworth and Haddon that they were copied and reduced many times later and became available to the tourist in *The Modern Universal British Traveller*, *The Universal Magazine* (1748), *The London Magazine* (1752), *The Complete English Traveller* (1769) and other periodicals.

Here, at last, was the real beginning of the revelation of the Peak's landscape. A new approach to landscape as opposed to topography had begun in the partnership of Smith and Vivares. The latter was important for engraving and disseminating the work of the European landscape masters, Gaspar Poussin, Claude and Rubens. Their work together with that of Nicholas Poussin, Salvator Rosa and the Dutch landscape school had a profound impact on the English artists in the 18th century.

Smith used Vivares and other engravers to produce sets of landscape prints for framing. Glass was reasonably cheap and middle-class patrons, unable to afford paintings often made collections of prints. Some of Smith's engraved works have a charming, if sometimes naïve rococo feel to them, not least when there are rocks, trees and water in close proximity. In 1743, for instance, Smith published a set of eight views comprising Monsal Dale, Chee Tor, Castleton,

81 *Thorpe Cloud. Engraved by I. Mason after Thomas Smith, 1766. The view is taken from the grounds of Ilam Hall.*

Dovedale (two views), Matlock Bath (two views) and the River Manifold at Wetton Mill. These were the earliest published views of the dales.

Smith's drawings and paintings continued to be engraved in later years and even after his death. Some were pirated by print publishers such as John Boydell whose *Forty Views of the Peak* were published in 1760 and as late as 1775 a set after Smith entitled *Twelve Prospects in that part of Derbyshire called the Peak and Moorlands* was produced by a little known engraver called Gouaz.

It was John Boydell, however, who most popularised the views of the dales. His print shop in Cheapside became the most important in the country in the second half of the 18th century and he himself made a fortune and rose to be Lord Mayor of London. His origins were humble. Although born in Dorset, his grandfather was vicar of Ashbourne and rector of Mapleton and he spent some of his youthful years in and around Dovedale. He eventually arrived in London in 1740, at the age of 21, to begin his seven-year apprenticeship as an engraver. In 1748 he tells us of his sketching tour in Chester and North Wales and that 'I likewise made Drawings in the Peak, of Matlock Bath, Crumford [Cromford] and Dove Dale which I engraved on my return to London'.[30]

This popularisation of prints eventually led to their sale in shops in Derby, Chesterfield, Bakewell, Buxton and Ashbourne. Tourists cut them from books or periodicals and pasted them in scrap books and journals or on the very walls of their rooms. Indeed, the English print market, largely dependent on the French market in the first half of the 18th century, was now exporting more engravings than it imported and we are told in 1787 that 'a late order from Madrid to Messrs Boydell exceeded 1,500 pounds sterling'.[31] Prints often served as a record of a journey or a visit, much as the picture postcard does today.

15

A Plethora of Artists

If Thomas Smith of Derby was the first artist to capture the scenic qualities of the Peak, albeit in a rococo manner, Joseph Wright of Derby was the first to do so in the growing romantic mood of the late 18th century. After visiting Italy in 1774, where he was enchanted by the lambent light of the Campagna and the coast of Naples, he experienced the luminosity that he had admired in Claude's landscapes. Re-established in Derby again in 1777, following a brief spell in Bath, he brought his skills as a 'painter of light' to bear on the scenes of Matlock Dale, Chee Dale and Dove Dale.[1] Joseph Farington tells us that Wright painted scenes at four times of day – 'morning – noon (an Italian heated sky) – evening – night'.[2] Whatever the time of day Wright could impart to his landscapes a light that was seldom attainable *en plein air* in Derbyshire. His skies he derived from Claude and his disciple Wilson. Pilkington, writing in 1789, extols the landscapes of Dovedale 'touched by the sweet and magic pencil of Mr Wright of Derby'.[3]

Wright satisfied the contemporary romantic obsession with the crepuscular and the nocturnal, epitomised in the opening lines of Gray's *Elegy*. Thus he could paint the effect of moonlight on Arkwright's busy factory or on the total solitude of Dovedale or Matlock Dale. The last place was especially popular with tourists on clear, moonlit nights. The Thrales were particularly insistent that Dr Johnson should not miss Matlock by moonlight.[4]

The rocks and cliffs of these dales particularly enthralled Wright, as had Vesuvius and the rocky coasts of Italy. He viewed them with awe as monumental excrescences on the earth's surface; his friend John Whitehurst, the celebrated Derby scientist and geologist, strove to reconcile his geological deductions about them with the biblical accounts of the Creation and the Flood. In his *Inquiry into the original state and formation of the Earth* (1778) Whitehurst intended to establish a 'system of Subterraneous Geography' and a link has been demonstrated between Whitehurst's theories and Wright's paintings. Whitehurst, for instance, includes in his *Inquiry* … 'A Section of the Strata at Matlock High Tor'[5] – a rocky eminence much loved by Wright (see plate XII).

82 *View of Peak's Hole. Aquatint by P.J. de Loutherbourg, c.1778. This was used for one of the theatre sets of 'Harlequin of the Peak'.*

There were, however, other influences on Wright's studies of rockscapes and the effect of varying light upon them – in particular the treatises on art by Alexander Cozens. Viscount Curzon of Kedleston was also a subscriber to these publications and two of Cozens's oil paintings, both dated 1756, were listed by Pilkington as hanging at Kedleston. One was 'Matlock High Tor at Dusk'; the other was 'A Vale near Matlock at Sunset'.[6] Alexander Cozens's son, John Robert Cozens, has also been suggested as an influence on Wright. The younger Cozens made a tour of the Matlock area from 23 May to 13 June in 1772 and his sketchbook contains drawings of Bonsall, Cromford, Oker Hill and Wingfield Manor. More importantly, there are 39 studies of Matlock, largely of cliff and rock scenes. Two of them, 'Matlock Bath' and 'Cascade on the Derwent at Matlock Bath', are remarkably similar to Wright's 'Rocks with Waterfall' (*c*.1772) and 'View in Matlock Dale, looking south to Black Rock Escarpment' (*c*.1780–85).[7]

Interestingly, Wright's landscapes were not well known in his own day, beyond the circles of the provincial gentry who purchased them. None appears to have been exhibited at the London societies and although Boydell, John Raphael Smith (son of Thomas Smith of Derby) and others engraved various subjects by Wright, these did not include his Derbyshire landscapes. Nor were any reproduced as aquatints.

However, aquatints, a new medium of engraving, most effectively reproduced watercolours. The first British artist to use this process extensively was Paul Sandby, the Nottingham-born painter.[8] No aquatints of the Peak by Sandby are known, though there are sets by other artists. In 1805, for instance, Thomas Hofland and Thomas Barber published a folio containing four of Dovedale and two of Matlock.[9] The print, as we have seen, was one way of circulating landscape views relatively cheaply. Many were hand-coloured by amateur watercolourists who had usually not studied the scene portrayed and who tinted whole batches, sometimes years after they were printed. Despite careful skills in some cases, the results were often stilted and seldom conveyed light and atmosphere. In the last quarter of the 18th century, Londoners could view the original oil and watercolour paintings in the exhibitions of such newly founded institutions as the Royal Academy of Arts (1768) and the Society of Artists (1754). The promotion of the work of watercolourists received a boost with the foundation of the Old Watercolour Society in 1804. Exhibitions of landscapes at these institutions had the effect of the modern coloured travel brochure on today's prospective tourist.

Collectors purchased works at these exhibitions and in turn created their own private galleries to entertain themselves, their friends and other interested artists. Dr Thomas Monro, a London physician and an amateur draughtsman, was one such connoisseur. He invited many young artists, including Turner, Girtin, Cotman and De Wint, to come to his house to study and copy works by leading landscape artists such as Thomas Hearne, Edward Days and Thomas Malton, all of whom sketched in the Peak.[10] Hearne had first visited it in 1776 on his return from the Lake District in the company of Sir George Beaumont, baronet, of Coleorton in Leicestershire, an avid amateur painter. Dayes and Malton had certainly first visited the Peak separately in the early 1790s.

One could, of course, acquire coloured Peakland landscapes for display by purchasing porcelain plates, vases and dinner services made at various manufacturies in late 18th- and early 19th-century England. In Derbyshire itself two factories provided such suites – Derby and Pinxton. At the former, landscape painting, including moonlight scenes and country houses, came into vogue by about 1780. The fusible nature of the Derby glaze 'readily accepted enamel colours and was particularly sympathetic to the landscape painters working in the style of the English water-colourists, the colours melting to a large extent into the glaze'.[11]

The first known landscape painter on Derby porcelain was Zachariah Boreman who came to Derby on the closure of the Chelsea factory in 1784 and has been hailed as 'the father of landscape painting on china'. From Chelsea also came his colleague and successor at Derby, Thomas 'Jockey' Hill. His work was particularly delicate, with a Gilpinesque flavour, often executed on pieces with the famous canary yellow ground. His two 'Views near Matlock, Derbyshire' on a chocolate-cup cover and stand are an excellent example of his work.[12]

The factory artists derived most of their views from prints and watercolours and as a result Peakland views were not restricted to the painters from Derbyshire factories. A service with views of Haddon Hall, for instance, was painted at the Sunderland factory and the famous 944 piece 'Frog Service', painted in sepia by the Wedgwood factory for Catherine II of Russia in 1773-4, contained a number of Derbyshire scenes.

Paul Sandby had visited Derbyshire earlier than that. He had exhibited a watercolour, 'South-west View of Chatsworth' at the Society of Artists in 1764. An engraving of this, together with one of Beauchief Abbey was included in Francis Grose's *Antiquities of England and Wales*.[13] He also sketched at Kedleston and Castleton but his largest work was the splendid park landscape he executed in distemper on the alcove wall of the painted room at Drakelow Hall, Derbyshire in 1793 – a scene likely to have been inspired by London theatre sets.[14]

Sandby was among the first to produce drawings and paintings of country houses which, with accompanying text, were published in George Kearsley's *Copperplate Magazine* and in John Boydell's *Collection of One Hundred and Fifty Select Views in England, Wales, Scotland and Ireland*. From these sources some of Sandby's scenes were reproduced on Wedgwood's Frog Service made for Catherine the Great.

The demand for book illustrations grew. By the end of the 18th century, as the Grand Tour declined and the war with France precluded travel to Italy, more and more artists – amateur and professional – visited Derbyshire, Yorkshire and the Lakes. Even the best travel writers conceded the need for pictures to complement their words. Rhodes himself, the finest romantic travel writer on the Peak, expressed the inevitable shortcomings of any writer:

> He who undertakes in passing through a country, to describe the scenes he admires, and who hopes to excite a correspondent picture in the minds of his readers, will often have to lament the inefficiency of the means he is under the necessity of employing. The pencil, by an accurate delineation of forms, may speak to the eye, and the canvass may glow with the vivid tints of nature; but it is not through the medium of words, with whatever felicity they may be selected and combined, that an adequate idea of the finest features of a landscape can be communicated. The language of description is likewise so very confused, and its phrases so extremely few, that similar appearances will often suggest a similarity of expression; hence the choicest terms become tiresome from repetition, and the impression they produce faint and imperfect.[15]

Yet Rhodes's *Peak Scenery* was not quite blessed with the illustrations it deserved. Sir Francis Chantrey, RA, Rhodes's friend, was one of the leading sculptors of his day but his illustrations for *Peak Scenery*, even in the hands of capable engravers, were not of the highest rank (see plate 13, p.25).

How different were the early essays of the young J.M.W. Turner who first visited the Peak in 1794. The 19-year-old, who had been well versed in the

83 *Church Rock in Dovedale. Engraving by F.E. May after Joseph Farington, RA, 1817.*

topographical drawings, paintings and prints of the best artists of his day, was commissioned by John Walker to submit topographical views for his *Copper-Plate Magazine*. Two of Turner's watercolours were selected for engraving on copper; the first, 'Matlock', was engraved by John Storer in 1795; the second, 'Sheffield, taken from Derbyshire Lane', was engraved by Walker himself in 1798.[16]

The steady increase in books about the history, topography and landscape of the English counties, drew an increasing number of artists, such as the young J.M.W. Turner, to accept commissions as illustrators. *The Beauties of England and Wales or Delineations Topographical Historical and Descriptive of each county, embellished with engravings* was published by John Britten and Edward Wedlake Brayley. The third volume, printed in 1802, contains a description of Derbyshire. This draws heavily on Pilkington's *A View of the present State of Derbyshire* (1789) and although it is generously illustrated with 22 engravings, the bulk are after the somewhat prosaic drawing master, Henry Moore of Derby (see frontispiece).[17] There are, however, some better examples after the work of the young William Delamotte and especially after Edward Dayes (see plate 57, p.111).

Dayes helped to keep alive the interest in the caves, especially the Peak Cavern, by including three interior studies entitled 'View from the Interior

84 *Rocks in Middleton Dale. Engraving by M.S. Barenger after Joseph Farington, RA, 1817.*

of the Great Arch', 'Roger Raine's House' and 'Great Tom of Lincoln'. These were remarkable because they were taken well inside the cave and the last two depended for their meagre illumination on the candles of the guides and their parties (see plate 11). Such fascination with cave exploration gripped artists into the early Victorian era, when Thomas Allom FRIBA captured similar theatricality in the candle-lit interior of the Rutland Cavern, near Matlock.

Joseph Farington was among the leading illustrators for the new spate of county histories. A devoted pupil of Richard Wilson and a native of Lancashire, he first came to sketch in the Peak in 1776 and again in 1791.[18] A prominent member of the Royal Academy, he was instrumental in giving encouragement and directions to his colleagues on their tours into Derbyshire. More than likely it was he who gave Turner details of the track approaching High Tor[19] and he prompted his pupil John Constable to make a sketching tour in the Peak in 1801 where, by design or accident, the two met whilst drawing in Dovedale.[20]

Having published views of the Lake District and English cities, Farington was approached by Samuel Lysons to make 31 drawings to accompany volume V ('Derbyshire') of his *Magna Britannia*. These drawings were reproduced by various engravers to form part VI of *Britannia Depicta*, published by Lysons in

1818. The scenes were of the usual popular places though Farington's friend, Thomas Hearne, did contribute an unusual view of Bakewell church (see plate 47, p.89) and Farington included a view of Wirksworth, a town little favoured by the tourist and the artist.

However, it was a foreign artist who really transformed the Wonders of the Peak into theatre. James Philip de Loutherbourg was born in Strasbourg and studied painting in Paris where he became a member of the Academie Royale. He arrived in England in 1771 and was introduced to David Garrick at Drury Lane Theatre.[21] De Loutherbourg worked for almost ten years as a theatre designer at Drury Lane until he was elected a Royal Academician. In that period he established himself as the greatest designer of sets for the London theatre. His melodramatic interpretation of landscape transcended the picturesque and evoked sensations of awe and horror (see plate XI).

He exhibited the Wonders of the Peak in a way never before experienced – as a series of backcloths to a pantomime entitled *The Wonders of Derbyshire; or Harlequin in the Peak*. This was not, of course, a pantomime in the modern sense. The entertainment, derived from the Italian *comedia dell'arte*, was not governed by a conventional plot but depended on the burlesque antics of traditional characters like Harlequin and Colombine.

This particular pantomime was conceived by Richard Brinsley Sheridan and de Loutherbourg. Its preparation was long and costly. Never before had the sets for a British stage production concentrated almost exclusively on actual topographical landscapes. De Loutherbourg came to Derbyshire a year in advance of the production to make drawings and paintings; from those he made maquettes and then began to paint his scenery. He abandoned the traditional illusions based on wings, flats and borders. He created a new sense of depth and distance by unifying these parts to create a sweeping oval curve. His ingenious lighting effects enabled him to simulate sunrise, sunset and moonlight in the Peak as well as to add mystery and horror within Peak and Poole's Caverns.

The opening scenes depicted Matlock at sunset and Dovedale by moonlight. Here began Harlequin's dashing pursuit of a comic Frenchman who was betrothed to Columbine. By the end of the first act they appear before Chatsworth House and its gardens. The pursuit continues in the second act, taking in Mam Tor, Peak Cavern and the Ebbing and Flowing Well. Finally, all appear in Poole's Cavern for the grand finale.

Critics were ecstatic about the scenic effects. The *Westminster Gazette* reported: 'As an exhibition of scenes this surpasses anything we have ever seen: as a pantomime we think it is the most contemptible'.[22]

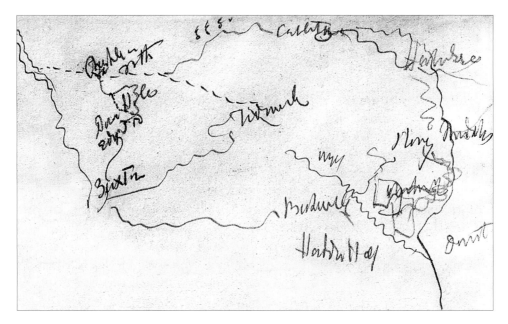

85   *J.M.W. Turner's sketch map of his tour of the Peak, 1831.*

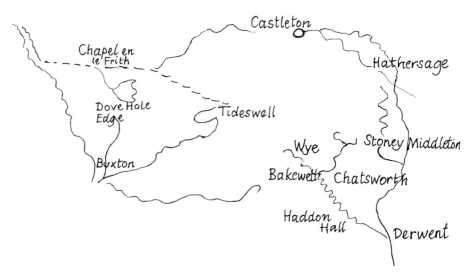

The stage performance soon faded from the memory, but not the artist's brilliant sets and lighting effects. Derby Theatre fleetingly revived the pantomime for one night on 8 March 1789, under the title *The Rape of Proserpine; or Harlequin in the Peak*. The sets were painted, unmemorably, by Mr Gamble, a local artist.[23] There were no ecstatic reviews and the pantomime plunged into oblivion.

However, de Loutherbourg had enjoyed double success; he had revolutionised stage design and had given many their first pictorial experience of the Peak. Some of his theatre maquettes survive in the Victoria and Albert Museum [24] and his original paintings were among those he exhibited at the Royal Academy. He published a folio of 18 of his views of England as aquatints entitled *The Romantic and Picturesque Views of England and Wales*. Prominent among these is a view looking into the mouth of Peak Cavern, as used in the pantomime (see plate 82, p.156). The folio's title is important in art-historical terms as the first printed work to contain the words 'romantic' and 'picturesque'.

De Loutherbourg, like Wright, is also remembered for his portrayal of industrial scenes. Lead-mining in particular intrigued him and he exhibited at the Royal Academy *An engine to draw water out of a leadmine near Matlock Bath* and an associated scene, *A view near Matlock – washing lead ore* was published as an aquatint (see plate 1). Constable, too, more accustomed to depicting agricultural scenes, sketched the Odin Mine at Mam Tor and the millstone quarries near Grindleford on his 1801 tour (see plate 16, p.30).[25] Turner was also fascinated by such scenes and sketched the High Tor mine and probably visited the Ecton copper mine in 1794.[26] The ancient industries of the Peak, quite apart from its modern factories, continued to attract the artist and the writer.

Sadly, Turner's greatest work in the Peak is lost. The oil painting he exhibited at the Royal Academy in 1827 was entitled *Scene in Derbyshire* and accompanied with the quotation: 'When first the sun with beacon red'. It has disappeared since originally exhibited and all we are left with are paeans of praise in the *Morning Post* and the *New Monthly Magazine*.[27] Equally mysterious is the date when Turner made the sketch for this picture. He is not known to have entered Derbyshire in the 1820s, his previously recorded visits being in 1794 and between 1807 and 1809.

However, he did make a final tour in 1831, primarily to visit his old friend, the watercolourist, James Holworthy. Having married Joseph Wright's niece, Ann, Holworthy moved to the Peak and purchased Brookfield House and the adjacent North Lees Hall, near Hathersage.[28] Turner had given the Holworthys a couple of drawings as a wedding present and in return he was continually invited to visit his old friend.[29] Holworthy knew of Turner's passion for angling and temptingly described the fine trout to be had in the local streams and rivers.

Eventually Turner succumbed and made what was probably his final visit to the Peak on his way to or from Scotland in 1831. Obligingly, he left us a quick sketch map of the places he visited whilst he fished the Wye and the Derwent. His undying love of architecture is reflected in the rapid drawings he made of Castleton, Chatsworth, Haddon Hall, North Lees and Brookfield together with the churches of Bakewell, Hope, Hathersage and the newly built St John's chapel at Buxton.

His obsession was with the distant prospect and the mass of the buildings which could be dramatised as he might choose with variations of light and colour. He was not interested in recreating and populating the interiors of the houses as they might have looked in 'the olden times'. This contemporary genre of history painting had its roots in the romantic novels of Scott and drew some artists to portray Britain's ancient halls and castles in their imagined chivalric splendour and baronial hospitality. In Derbyshire two houses inspired such visions of the past – Hardwick Hall and Haddon Hall. Chatsworth's baroque was too 'modern' and the house was still being extended by the 6th Duke of Devonshire in the neo-classical style.

86 *Hathersage. Drawn and engraved by Thomas Hofland, 1823. Turner stayed here at Brookfield House, the home of his friend James Holworthy, the watercolourist, during his tour of the Peak, 1831.*

87 *Castleton. Pencil sketch by J.M.W. Turner, 1831, who made some 35 sketches of the town, castle and cave.*

Haddon was considered one of the finest baronial halls of 'the olden times'; its great hall, in particular, inspired Scott in describing banquets in *Ivanhoe* and *Peveril of the Peak*. The house inspired the architectural watercolourist, George Cattermole, who had toured Scotland in 1830 to produce illustrations for Scott's *Waverley Novels*. His drawings of Haddon Hall[30] in turn influenced Samuel Rayner who produced his celebrated *History and antiquities of Haddon Hall* in 1838 with Cattermole's and his own lithographs of the building. These occasionally include figures in 'Elizabethan' costume and allusions are made to the recently concocted tale of Dorothy Vernon's elopement with John Manners.

More lithographs of Haddon followed in 1842 when Douglas Morison published *Twenty-Five Views of Haddon Hall*. Morison's work was not as competent as that of Cattermole or Rayner; he over-emphasised the trees in his pictures in order to accentuate the drama and mystery of the house.[31]

Artist after artist felt compelled to relive and record history at Haddon. Philip Reinagle captured hunting and hawking in the park as did David Cox, who sketched regularly in Derbyshire throughout the 1830s and concentrated on the pastoral setting of his favourite house.[32]

The climax of all this musing about 'the olden times' is to be found in the work of Joseph Nash. He was a fine architectural draughtsman who had been trained by Augustus Charles Pugin, father of the famous gothic revivalist, A. W. N. Pugin. Nash surpassed Cattermole and Rayner in his interpretation of historical scenes. Between 1839 and 1849 he published a hundred lithographs under the title of *Mansions of England in the olden time*. Among the most celebrated of these was his rendering of Christmas festivities in the great hall at Haddon. The room is hung with evergreens among armorial banners and the resident waits play lustily from the minstrels' gallery. Below is a chaotic scene as the family and servants join the riotous merriment of jesters, mummers, morris dancers, a giant, a crocodile and a monkey.[33]

Such Yuletide scenes delighted the Victorians and this particular Tudor-gothic extravaganza was reproduced with even more exaggerated variations in Reynolds's *Miscellany* in 1867.

It was from a revel such as this, on her sister's wedding day, that Dorothy Vernon is said to have slipped away on the evening of her elopement. Judith Millais captured her in 1861, attired in a Victorian ball gown, her head and shoulders covered with a shawl, as she furtively escaped into the garden.[34] Axel Haig chose to paint her at the moment she left the gardens to meet John Manners at the little bridge across the Wye (see plate 70, p.138).[35] Such scenes were a far cry from John Constable's delicate drawing of this last location, devoid of figures, in 1801, or indeed of Thomas Smith's first portrait of the Hall in 1743. Nostalgia and an untrammelled urge to relive the past had taken over and the Duke of Rutland was under increasing pressure to allow more and more visitors to enjoy the experience.

16

Writers in the Dales

Derbyshire's celebrated dales are those tortuous gashes in the Peak's limestone plateau, gouged by torrential streams. Their secluded worlds of tree-lined pools, crags and caves, pierced by flashing shafts of sunlight, contrast markedly with the wider, gentler dales beneath the gritstone moors. The Dove and the Wye, both rising near Buxton, are the two main streams on the limestone; the former winding down to its confluence with the Trent near Burton; the latter slipping out of the dales at Bakewell and entering the Derwent at Rowsley.

The best location from which to visit Dovedale was, and still is, the elegant market town of Ashbourne. Unlike the villages and market towns of the High Peak, Ashbourne by the late 18th century was, with the exception of its church and grammar school, largely a red-brick Georgian town typical of those to the south on the Midland clays. Set amid gentler pastures and more fertile arable fields, its market was quite prosperous and had the added attraction of being provisioned by exotic goods from the London wagons. However, the carping trencherman, John Byng, moaned that he could not obtain fruit, wine or fish equal to that in London, complained that venison was unavailable out of season and turtles were nowhere to be found![1]

The parish church of St Oswald with its fine steeple and peal of bells was the focal point of the town. Byng was not impressed by it. Dr Johnson, on the other hand, admired the church and Boswell considered it 'one of the largest and most luminous that I have seen in any town of the same size'.[2]

Johnson was the foremost literary person to visit Ashbourne, which attracted writers from Lichfield and Derby, some of whom, such as Erasmus Darwin, were associated with the scientific circles of the Midlands. Ashbourne Hall, the home of the Boothbys, was one of the cultural meeting places. Here Johnson befriended Mrs Hill Boothby, sister of the squire, Sir Brooke Boothby. Into this circle came the Sewards of Lichfield, Anna, the overrated poetess, and her father, a canon of Lichfield Cathedral. Johnson perhaps found the canon somewhat tedious and pretentious; he told Boswell that the canon's ambition was 'to be a fine talker; so he goes to Buxton, and such places, where he may find companies to listen to him'.[3]

Johnson disliked the artificialities of the spa and found greater inspiration in Dovedale. In September 1777 he and Boswell travelled from Ashbourne to Ilam to see the hall and grounds which had once belonged to the Congreve family, one of whom had been in Johnson's class at school. The beautiful setting appealed to Johnson, who amazed Boswell by his vivid description of the 'romantick scene'. Boswell subsequently described the occasion:

> I recollect a very fine amphitheatre, surrounded with hills covered with woods, and walks neatly formed along the side of a rocky steep, on the quarter next the house, with recesses under projections of rock, overshadowed with trees; in one of which recesses, we were told, Congreve wrote his *Old Bachelor.* We viewed a remarkable natural curiosity at Islam; two rivers bursting near each other from the rock, not from immediate springs, but after having run for many miles under ground. Plott, in his *History of Staffordshire*, gives an account of this curiosity; but Johnson would not believe it, though we had the attestation of the gardener, who said, he had put in corks, where the river Manyfold sinks into the ground, and had catched them in a net, placed before one of the openings where the water bursts out.[4]

Perhaps to Johnson and other writers who came to this magical place, its name, as spelt on maps and signposts of the day – Islam – conjured up Eastern associations. These illusions were translated from the village of Ilam itself to the wondrous enclosed world of Dovedale.

Johnson must have explored the lower reaches of the dale, though we have no account of this, and one cannot believe that he toiled beyond the point where the path narrowed and the going became difficult. Some have said that he was highly elated by its idyllic scenery and that it inspired his oriental novel *Rasselas, Prince of Abyssinia*, which he wrote in a week in 1759 to pay for his mother's funeral. Was the 'happy valley' described in the novel, where the prince lived so blissfully, really inspired by Dovedale? Davies was but one of many who was transported by it, declaring that 'the loneliness and silence that are here, entitle it to the appellation of the Vale of Fancy or another Vaucluse; and as there is but one rugged, narrow footpath, it has more the air of being the haunt of imaginary beings than human ones'.[5]

The Dove, which forms a good part of the boundary between Derbyshire and Staffordshire, snakes out of the dale between two abrupt hills (see plate 81, p.154), Thorpe Cloud (943 ft) and Bunster (1,000 ft). To those proceeding upstream these were referred to as the 'Gates' and, having approached from Ashbourne by the village of Thorpe, the traveller crosses St Mary's Bridge to the Staffordshire bank in order to pass through the 'Gates'. Once through, the

88 *Ashbourne Church from the south. Lithograph by S. Rayner, 1839. Dr Johnson and James Boswell worshipped here.*

stepping stones take the walker back again to the Derbyshire side. The five-mile walk upstream to the village of Hartington then begins, passing through gorges of pinnacles and crags by clear, limpid pools and swift currents flanked by cascades of trees. To many 18th-century writers this dale was quintessentially picturesque. To some its upper reaches were sublime, to others the treeless stretches of Patterdale in Cumbria were considered of grander sublimity.

By the early 18th century, at least, local people, together with visiting writers and artists, had given names to the many curious rock formations in Dovedale, just as they had to those in Peak and Poole's Caverns. These names, still used today, have gothick connotations. Immediately through the 'Gates' is a limestone outcrop, Dovedale Castle, and opposite, and inevitably in a landscape of cliffs, Lovers' Leap. Similarly-named features occur on the limestone precipices of Matlock Dale, Middleton Dale and near Buxton. The next features are the Twelve Apostles and then Tissington Spires (the latter owe their name to the nearby village and church of Tissington) followed by Dovedale Church.

Caves are an important feature of the Dale, especially Reynard's Cave and the Dove Holes, a secret refuge for Cotton from his creditors and a haven for Byng in a downpour. Here anglers walked the banks or waded the pools, fishing for brown trout under the gaze of the overhanging Lion's Head Rock, Ilam Rock, Pickering Tor and Raven's Tor.

89 *Ashbourne. West entrance showing the Grammar School. Lithograph by S. Rayner, 1839. Dr Taylor's house, where Johnson and Boswell stayed, is the pedimented building on the right. The London waggon is entering the town.*

Further upstream, past the Nabs, the rocky gorge opens out until one reaches the village of Milldale. Here the river is spanned by Viator's Bridge referred to by Cotton in *The Compleat Angler*. Indeed, as one passes from Wolfscote Dale into Beresford Dale, this is the very heart of Cotton's lonely, contemplative realm. Here once stood his family seat, Beresford Hall, near the Pike Pool (named after a rock, not a fish) where he and Walton cast their flies and smoked their pipes in the little riverside temple whose exclusive inscription proclaimed its *piscatoribus sacrum*. The passer-by could take his own refreshment at the Duke of Devonshire's village of Hartington before proceeding higher towards the river's source or leaving the Dale for the Ashbourne-Buxton road at Newhaven.

The blissful serenity of the spot near Reynard's cave is still remembered for a tragedy that was reported in the newspapers in July 1761. A house party from nearby Longford Hall had ridden into Dovedale to picnic. Among the guests were the Reverend Langton, Dean of Clogher and a Miss La Roche. As they prepared to return the Dean, with a bravura remarkable in a prominent man of the cloth, decided he would ride his horse up the valley side and make a short cut over the top to Tissington. Miss La Roche relished the challenge and he lifted her up behind him. His horse strove valiantly upwards but was then directed along a narrow sheep track which suddenly rose too abruptly before it. Unable to turn about the poor animal lost its footing and cascaded with its passengers back down the valley. The lady was knocked senseless and was only saved from a worse fate by her hair, which became entangled in a bush. The Dean paid dearly for his rashness and died a few days later. He was interred in Ashbourne church a week or so after he had ominously preached in All Saints, Derby, on the text, 'It is appointed unto all men once to die'. His horse survived the calamity.

Poets were naturally drawn to Dovedale. Thomas Gray and his close friend and biographer, William Mason, were contemporaries of Johnson, though by no means part of his Ashbourne–Lichfield circle. They were friends of Horace Walpole and were somewhat distasteful to Johnson, who joked that Mason was a prig as well as a Whig and, although he liked aspects of Gray's famous *Elegy*, did not consider Gray a first-rate poet.[6]

Gray's love of nature was more intense than Johnson's. He was an inveterate tourist seeking inspiration in the landscape and was one of the foremost pioneers of picturesque travel. He sometimes stayed with Mason, a precentor at York Minster, at his rectory at Aston, between Sheffield and Rotherham. From this base Gray could make journeys into the Peak. These were not always inspirational. In December 1762, for instance, he left Sheffield for Chatsworth, climbing across the gritstone moors. He declared, 'I entered the Peak, a countrey beyond comparison uglier than any other I have seen in England, black, tedious, barren and not mountainous enough to please one with its horrors'.[7]

90 *The Dean of Clogher's fatal fall in Dovedale. Engraved for the* Gentleman's Magazine, *1794.*

Visiting Aston again in June 1767, he was jestingly euphoric and enthused, 'Here we are ... in a wilderness of sweets, an Elysium among the coalpits, a terrestrial heaven ... Tomorrow we visit Dovedale and the wonders of the Peaks'.[8] He was well acquainted with the literature on the Peak by Hobbes, Cotton, Leigh and Pilkington[9] and found much to delight him and revise his pejorative comments made five years earlier.

The visit of Gray and Mason to Dovedale had the added attraction of meeting Jean Jacques Rousseau. It was perhaps no coincidence that the greatest 18th-century analyst of Nature should seek isolation close to the natural elysium of Dovedale. Fleeing imagined persecution in France, he and his mistress, Thérèse le Vasseur, were invited to England by the Scottish philosopher, David Hume, in January 1766. Through Hume's good offices, Rousseau was domiciled at Wootton Lodge, the seat of the Davenports, five miles south-west of Ashbourne on the Staffordshire side of the Dove. Here he strove to live the life of a recluse, occasionally venturing forth to commune with Nature. According to William Howlett, the locals called him Roos Hall or Dross Hall and remarked upon his Armenian dress of furred cap and striped caftan as he pursued his botanical interests in Dovedale. He collected plant specimens, planted seeds and announced, 'Here I have at last arrived at an agreeable and sequestered asylum where I hope to breathe freely and at peace'.[10]

'Rasselas', it seemed, had truly arrived in Dovedale, but Johnson was unhappy about his asylum and castigated Boswell for having sought Rousseau's acquaintance earlier in Switzerland. 'Sir', he growled,

> I think him one of the worst of men; a rascal who ought to be hunted out of society as he has been ... and it is a shame he is protected in this country. [He] is a very bad man. I would sooner sign a sentence for his transportation than of any felon who has gone from the Old Bailey these many years. Yes, I should like to have him work in the plantations.[11]

Yet Rousseau made friends and drew numerous admirers who wished to meet him. The Delanys of nearby Calwich Abbey invited him there and the young Duchess of Portland shared his botanical enthusiasm. Erasmus Darwin, whose botanical interests were yet to be expressed in verse, failed to lure Rousseau from his retreat. He contrived to meet him by accident whilst out walking and managed to engage him on the subject of botany. Rousseau was civil but suspicious and did not renew the acquaintance.[12]

William Mason fared better. Through his patron, Lord Harcourt, who was devoted to Rousseau, Mason came to admire the latter's sentimental appreciation of nature and its presence in the garden. Over the entrance to the flower

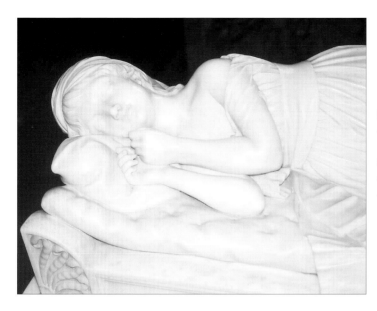

91 *The monument of Penelope Boothby, 1793. The most admired work of Thomas Banks, RA, St Oswald's Church, Ashbourne.*

garden at Nuneham that Mason designed in 1772 for Viscount Nuneham, later 2nd Earl Harcourt, he inscribed a quotation from Rousseau – 'If the Author of Nature is great in great things, he is very great in the smallest'. Rousseau's bust was placed in the garden and Mason completed his homage by translating Rousseau's lyrical work, *Pigmalion*, in 1775.[13]

Despite Johnson's strictures, Rousseau had admirers in Ashbourne and especially the new 22-year-old squire of Ashbourne Hall, Brooke Boothby. Although in 1767 the philosopher left Wootton and England after 15 months, as peremptorily as he had arrived, he did not forget Boothby. This minor poet of Derbyshire visited Rousseau in Paris some years later, on his return from Italy, and was entrusted with his *Dialogues*. He published these in Lichfield in 1780, two years after Rousseau's death.

The sequel to the Dovedale 'affair' was unveiled in 1781 when Joseph Wright of Derby painted one of the great full-length portraits in British art. It depicts a melancholic Sir Brooke Boothby reclining beside a brook in a sylvan landscape which might well represent Dovedale. In his left hand is a vellum-bound volume inscribed *Rousseau*.[14]

Boothby, who succeeded his father as the last baronet of his line, has left in Ashbourne parish church one of the most visited and tragic works of art of the Romantic era. This is the exquisite monument to his infant daughter and only child, Penelope. This sparkling, winsome little girl had beguiled the ageing Sir Joshua Reynolds, who painted her portrait. Her premature death in 1793 prompted her distraught father to commission from Thomas Banks, RA,

92 *Wootton Lodge. Lithograph by S. Rayner, 1839. Jean Jacques Rousseau sought solitude here.*

what has been acclaimed as his greatest sculpture. The little girl is carved in white marble reclining and relaxed as in sleep. Edmund Burke is said to have been moved to compose this epitaph:

> She was in form and intellect most exquisite. The unfortunate parents ventured their all on this frail bark, and the wreck was total.

This poignant monument of dead innocence, the maquette for which is in Sir John Soane's Museum, has drawn thousands to Ashbourne over two centuries. It also inspired subsequent artists such as Sir Francis Chantrey and Sir John Millais in their celebrated studies of children.

Magnetic as Dovedale was, no one of note had written anything inspiring about it until Wordsworth. He came in 1788 as a young undergraduate returning to Hawkshead from St John's College, Cambridge on his first long vacation. Having enjoyed Cotton's poetry and the *Compleat Angler*, it was something of a pilgrimage when he broke his journey at Ashbourne. He recorded his experience in prose as follows:

> Saw nothing particularly striking till I came to Ashburn. Arrived there on Sunday evening – and rode over to Dovedale. Dovedale is a very narrow valley somewhat better than a mile in length, broken into five or six distinct parts, so that the views it affords are necessarily upon a small scale. The first scene that strikes you on descending into the valley is the River Dove, fringed with sedge and spotted with a variety of small tufts of grass, hurrying between two hills, one of which about six years ago was cloathed with wood; the wood is again getting forwards; the other had a number of

cattle grazing upon it. The scene was pleasing – the sun was sinking behind the hill on the left – which was dark – whilst his beams cast a faint golden tinge upon the side of the other. The River in that part, which was streamy, had a glittering splendor which was pleasingly chastized by the blue tint of intervening pieces of calm water, the fringe of sedge and the number of small islands, with which it is variegated. The view is terminated by a number of rocks on the side of one of the hills of a form perfectly spiral. [15]

This delightful, painterly description illustrates well the picturesque entry to the Dale and 'what is essentially Wordsworthian, the contrasts in the scene'. [16]

Though this was but a brief evening excursion as far as Tissington Spires, Dovedale had a lasting impact on the young poet. He referred to this visit again and to 'Dovedale's spiry rocks' in his autobiographical poem, *The Prelude*, and some scholars maintain that his poem *Lucy* was inspired by the Derbyshire river:

> She dwelt among untrodden ways
> Beside the springs of Dove[17]

But more and more travellers trod the ways beside the Dove. In 1810, Wordsworth's sister, Dorothy, came, like her brother, having broken her journey at Ashbourne.[18] Byron wrote to his friends, and biographer, the poet Tom Moore, 'Was you ever in Dovedale? There are things in Derbyshire as noble as Greece or Switzerland'. The Irish poet laureate and song writer responded to Byron's question by going to live there. He moved to a cottage in Mayfield, a small village on the Staffordshire side of the Dove, two miles west of Ashbourne, and lived and wrote there from 1813 to 1817. Whether the valley inspired oriental fantasies in Moore, as it is said to have done in Johnson, is not known, but during his time at Mayfield he published *Lalla Rookh* (1817). This, his most popular work, is a series of oriental tales in verse linked by a prose narrative.[19]

Byron had gone abroad in 1816, never to return. He corresponded with Moore who named his daughter Olivia Byron in memory of his friend. When Moore decided to leave Mayfield, following the death of Olivia, Byron wrote nostalgically, 'I don't know whether to be glad or sorry that you are leaving Mayfield. Had I been at Newstead during your stay there … we should have been within hail, and I should like to have made a giro of the Peak with you. I know that country well, having been all over it when a boy.'[20]

Moore returned in 1827 to visit his young daughter's grave. Lord Byron, too, was dead. His memories of past times in Dovedale and the pealing bells in Ashbourne steeple are no doubt the inspiration for these fine lines, *Evening Bells.*

Those evening bells! Those evening bells!
How many a tale their music tells
Of youth and home and that sweet time
When last I heard their soothing chime.

Those joyous hours are passed away;
And many a heart that then was gay
Within the tomb now darkly dwells
And hears no more those evening bells.

And so 'twill be when I am gone;
That tuneful peal will still ring on
While other bards shall walk these dells
And sing your praise, sweet evening bells.

Dovedale continued to inspire minor local writers, none of whom equalled Cotton's devotional verses on its river or the fresh, quick sketch of the young Wordsworth's prose. In 1766, for instance, the Reverend Samuel Bentley, born beside the river at Uttoxeter, wrote a 'lyric pastoral' in which he traced the river from its source at Dove Head to its confluence with the Trent at Tutbury. It is a dull topographical poem in that it records the river's course by recounting the villages and towns through which it flows.[21] Equally ordinary, though more elaborate and florid, was the poem by John Edwards of Derby who traced the Dove in the opposite direction. His verse enjoyed brief notice at the beginning of the Victorian and the end of the romantic period.[22]

The hyperbole used about the Dale seemed boundless. The artist, Edward Dayes, held that Dovedale 'possesses an union of grandeur and beauty not to be equalled by anything I ever beheld'.[23] De Loutherbourg painted it as an Alpine scene (see plate XI) inspired by such notions contained in Edmund Burke's *A Philosophical Enquiry into the Sublime and the Beautiful*. Davies was transported to Egypt when he viewed 'the huge pyramids of rock' and declared that 'if divested of its woods' Dovedale would be reminiscent of 'the neighbourhood of Cairo'.[24]

The writer who rivalled Gray as a tourist in search of the picturesque was the Reverend William Gilpin. He first coined the phrase 'picturesque beauty' as he travelled through England and Wales, focusing on particular scenes which illustrated Nature's ragged and random treatment of water and verdure, crags and trees. His visits to the Peak were fleeting and his analysis of its beauties terse and particular.[25] His language in comparison with that he employed in describing his native Cumbria was curt and disappointing to Ebenezer Rhodes who considered he had 'treated Derbyshire with apparent indifference'.[26]

Gilpin found the hills known as the 'Gates' of Dovedale too shorn and bald to be picturesque though, writing of the Dale as a whole, he exclaimed 'it is, perhaps, one of the most pleasing pieces of scenery of the kind we anywhere meet with. It has something peculiarly characteristic. Its detached perpendicular rocks stamp it with an image entirely its own, and for that reason it affords the greater pleasure. For it is in scenery as in life: we are most struck with the peculiarity of an original character, provided there is nothing offensive in it'. Gilpin accompanied his comments with quick sketches of the

93 *Tom Moore's cottage at Mayfield. Engraved by J. Garforth, 1839.*

scenes and the one he made of Dovedale was copied by the young student J.M.W. Turner before his first visit to Dovedale and Matlock in 1796.[27]

Gilpin also singled out for particular attention Middleton Dale, a defile between jagged rock precipices, whose drama was heightened by the explosions in its quarries and the palls of smoke and dust created by the limestone burners. Turner again was lured to this place on his sketching tour of 1831.[28]

Rhodes, too, admired parts of Middleton Dale (see plate 84, p.160) though he confessed that 'some travellers have either felt or affected a contempt of its pretensions to picturesque beauty'.[29] Some, like Arthur Young, for instance, felt that it lacked a sufficient flow of water.

No such criticism could be levelled at the chain of magnificent dales watered by the Wye between Buxton and Bakewell – Cheedale, Millers Dale, Monsal Dale and their offshoots. They were not, as now, passable on foot along their whole length and entry was only possible from nearby villages (see plate x). Cheedale, for instance, could be reached from Wormhill and Millers Dale from Tideswell and Litton, the latter approaches being improved considerably in the late 18th century following the construction of Litton and Cressbrook Mills. Monsal Dale was served by a convergence of tracks from Wardlow Mires, Ashford, Litton, Cressbrook and the Longstones. These led the tourist to Monsal Head, one of the great 'surprise view' vantage points in England.

These dales along the Wye were opened further in 1810 when the Ashford-Buxton turnpike was laid for much of its length along the Wye and one could alight at Topley Pike and walk downstream to reach a loop in the river beneath

the towering face of Chee Tor. This great outcrop rivalled and surpassed High
Tor at Matlock, especially when the latter became too thronged with tourists.
William Adam considered Chee Tor 'one of the most remarkable Tors in
Derbyshire, both for its form and position'.[30]

As the 19th century dawned Monsal Dale had become the most popular of
the limestone dales. If Dovedale was the Peak's 'elysium', Monsal Dale was its
'arcadia'; a gorge where the Wye meandered in a narrow fertile plain between
steep craggy slopes. Small farmsteads dotted the valley bottom and sheep and
cattle grazed along the banks. From Monsal Head the viewer looked down
on an elbow in the river as it flowed towards Ashford over a rock and tufa
waterfall which Smith and Vivares captured as an anglers' paradise, in 1740
(see plate 80, p.152). Above was the collapsed limestone cave known as Hob's
House and higher still the steep dome of Fin Cop. From spring to autumn the
dale abounded with profusions of wild flowers and, in places, still does.

Surprisingly, Adam would have had no compunction in driving the Ashford-
Buxton turnpike through Monsal Dale, Millers Dale, Chee Dale and so to
Blackwell and Topley Pike – 'it would have presented some of the finest scenery,
and formed one of the best drives in the world, at the same time avoiding a
long and formidable hill'.[31] Such magnificent scenery again lured some minds
to oriental associations and the belief that Monsal Dale, not Dovedale, was the
setting where Johnson imagined the wandering Rasselas.[32]

Rhodes, whose writing we are told could occasionally emulate that of Sir
Walter Scott or Samuel Johnson, may have been subconsciously affected by
the latter's *Rasselas* when he recounted the true story of his own encounter
with a wandering Hindu in the vicinity of Bakewell and Monsal Dale. His
narrative has pathos and is as moving as Defoe's graphic description of his
meeting with the lead miner's wife at Brassington a century earlier. In this
case Rhodes and a stranger he had met at an inn were travelling in his gig
when they came upon 'a man clothed in an English great-coat, with a white
turban on his head; his gait and appearance, even at a distance, bespoke him
the native of another country'. Rhodes's companion had apparently served in
India and spoke to the wanderer in his native tongue. He replied, ecstatic with
emotion, that he had not heard his mother tongue since he had left India on
a vessel bound for Hull. On arrival at that port 'he was no longer useful and
therefore discarded'. He was now seeking another ship to take him home. He
spoke no English, had no food and was quite lost. Rhodes's companion wrote
on a card the name of a gentleman in Ashbourne who had resided for some
years in Calcutta and suggested that he would help this lost 'Child of Nature'
to his native land.[33]

What would Wordsworth have made of this romantic encounter? He arrived at Monsal Dale on 5 November 1830 on another of his journeys, this time to Cambridge where he was delivering his daughter's pony. In a letter to his sister Dorothy he described Monsal Dale as graphically as he had Dovedale 33 years earlier.

At Tideswell is a noble Church for its sequestered site; I regretted that my time did not allow me to enter it. Mounted a hill and descended upon the Village of Cressbrook, where is a large Factory – but the Wey, which I here first came in sight of, is singularly beautiful both above and below the village. It winds between green lawny hills and limestone steeps, through a narrow trough and twists its way in some places through slips of meadow-ground as rich in verdure as Nature's bounty can make them. I was charmed with the mile and a half of this Stream along which my road took me, wished for you both a hundred times. I would gladly have continued to follow the river, which I was told was possible, but along a rugged track that might have lamed my Pony, and the day was too far advanced, so I yielded to necessity, and turned up the main road after halting often to look back upon this happy and holy seclusion, for such I could not but think it. I clomb the hill, descended, and joined the Wey again at Ashford; a pretty spot, but twilight was coming on. – The firing of guns startled me every now and the, for it was the fifth Nov: and I thought it prudent to dismount, and walked most of the 2 miles into Bakewell. – rose early – rode down the valley with Haddon Hall in view, and at the point where Wey and Derwent unite, turned up towards Chatsworth – rode a mile, and leaving my pony to bait, walked up the valley and through Chatsworth Park to the House – splendid and large, but growing larger every year. The trees in this valley are still in many places clothed with rich variegated foliage – and so I found many all the way almost to Derby.[34]

Chatsworth moved Wordsworth to write a sonnet on the spot and he included this in his letter to Dorothy. He subsequently polished it and published it in 1835 in this form:

CHATSWORTH! thy stately mansion, and the pride
Of thy domain, strange contrast do present
To house and home in many a craggy rent
Of the wild Peak; where new-born waters glide
Through fields whose thrifty occupants abide
As in a dear and chosen banishment,
With every semblance of entire content;
So kind is simple Nature, fairly tried!

Yet he whose heart in childhood gave her troth
To pastoral dales, thin-set with modest farms,
May learn, if judgment strengthen with his growth,
That, not for Fancy only, pomp hath charms;
And, strenuous to protect from lawless harms
The extremes of favoured life, may honour both.[35]

The contrast between the pomp and the pastoral does not conceal his preference since childhood for the latter. More to his liking was the simple view of Oaker Hill where in 1828 he sat beside the coachman as he passed down Darley Dale to Derby. He was told the story of the two trees planted on the summit of the hill at the final farewell of two parting brothers. His lines are the finest written about this tradition and have helped perpetuate this simple tale for future travellers:

A TRADITION OF OKER HILL IN DARLEY DALE, DERBYSHIRE

'Tis said that to the brow of yon fair hill
Two Brothers Clomb, and, turning face from face,
Nor one look more exchanging, grief to still
Or feed, each planted on that lofty place
A chosen Tree: then, eager to fulfil
Their courses, like two new-born rivers, they
In Opposite directions urged their way
Down from the far-seen mount. No blast might kill
Or blight that fond memorial: – the trees grew,
And now entwine their arms: but ne'er again
Embraced those Brothers upon earth's wide plain;
Nor aught of mutual joy or sorrow knew
Until their spirits mingled in the sea
That to itself takes all, Eternity.[36]

Most tourists and some travel writers still viewed the Peak from the saddle, the seat of a gig or through the window of a coach. Few alighted to explore and describe what today passes for some of the most delightful scenery in the region. Lathkill Dale was virtually unrecorded, though Rhodes gave a vivid description of the River Lathkill from Conkesbury Bridge. Yet there are no descriptions of the mysteries of this delightful stream which issues from a cave near Monyash and disappears and reappears in the limestone fissures below Over Haddon. Similarly Bradford Dale below Youlgreave and the river Bradford, a tributary of the Lathkil, attract little attention. Both these Dales belonged to the Duke of Rutland, contained lucrative lead workings and were closed to intruders, with the exception of the occasional angler.

Historical sites like the plague village of Eyam and Little John's grave in Hathersage churchyard were little known and of small interest to the Georgian traveller. History was not yet a science and the early Victorians spun a web of romantic myth and legend that, especially in the case of Eyam, has proved difficult to disentangle.

By the beginning of the 19th century travel books on the Peak, together with their accompanying route maps, might have given the impression that there was nothing left to discover. This was not so. The highest and bleakest region of the High Peak, centred on Kinder Scout, was still little known and hardly mentioned in tourist literature. This changed in 1809 when John Hutchinson of Chapel-en-le-Frith wrote his *Tour through the High Peak of Derbyshire, including an account of the natural and subterranean curiosities of that country; the beautiful crystallised cavern, lately discovered at Bradwell; and the romantic scenery of the Woodlands, never before described.* Dedicated to the Marquess of Hartington (later the 6th Duke of Devonshire) and published in Macclesfield, it was illustrated with charming, if naïve, woodcuts.

Hutchinson set off from Sheffield to explore the Dark Peak, the dour landscape so disliked by Thomas Gray. Having climbed the East Moor he descended by the Millstone Edge into Derwent Dale and crossed the river at the hamlet of Grindleford, passing through scenery 'uniting every idea of wild, beautiful and sublime'. He passed in awe through Middleton Dale with its 'stupendous rocks … rising perpendicular' and arrived at the *George Inn* in Tideswell. The following day he visited the newly discovered 'crystallised cavern' at Bradwell – 'a grotto of paradise' and pressed on to Castleton to view Peak Cavern. From here he set out for the wild hills and moors beyond. Standing on the ridge of hills comprising Mam Tor, Back Tor and Lose Hill, which separates Castleton and Hope Dales from Edale, he surveyed the latter – 'this little retired world watered by the River Now'. Edale lay below Kinder Scout, the highest prominence in the Peak, and Hutchinson pondered the task of skirting its base to penetrate the Woodlands and the remotest parts of the parish of Hope (see plate 78, p.149). Then he intended to climb Kinder Scout, cross its grim plateau and descend into Hayfield (see plate 94, p.188). His ultimate aim was to map the tracks, hamlets and homesteads in this previously 'untrodden district'.

He and his young son, accompanied by a servant with a packhorse, undertook this challenge on foot. They took a compass for guidance and a flask of spirits 'as a corps de reserve'. This was a very sparsely populated region; there were hardly any inns, and the natives had little to offer them beyond milk, water and oatcakes.

Yet Hutchinson enthused repeatedly about the picturesque Woodlands and their quaint inhabitants. 'Everyone', he declared, 'who is fond of observing the wild and sublime scenery of nature, who wishes to visit man nearly unassociated with man, the scattered houses of about forty families in a circuit of thirty miles, will flee to the Woodlands for solitude and contemplation.'

His Rousseauesque language became more tense as he left this realm of the 'noble savage' and struggled up to Alport Crags on the way by Ashop Dale to Derwent village (see plate 102, p.198). The small party emerged on to the boggy peat moors and travelled for a whole day without encountering anyone apart from 'a miller's boy and a Scotchman who was visiting the lonely houses with his pack'. Eventually, winding down from Derwent Edge, they crossed the river and entered the hamlet and its welcome inn.

Here was the 'back of beyond', a place where Celia Fiennes, Defoe, Byng and all the other tourists in the Peak would never have ventured. Even Rowlandson's eccentric dilettante, Dr Syntax, could hardly have been envisaged in this terrain.

Derwent's inn was an oasis in the wilderness of crags, bogs and heather. The party returned here the next night having spent the day exploring Toothorn Field and Crookhill in lower Ashop Dale. Undaunted, they struck out next day to cover the 14 miles to the mill town of Glossop.

The going was now the most arduous they had encountered and they were barely covering a mile within an hour. The peat bogs, or groughs as they were known locally, were narrow and frequent at first and they and their horse leapt them. Eventually the horse could go no further and was sent back with their servant to find the hamlet of Woodhead by a lower, easier route.

Meeting a local shepherd, they recruited him as a guide and battled across the spongey morass in torrential rain to reach the partial shelter of Grinow Stones. Here they stayed for two hours and considered themselves fortunate to witness an electric storm of 'such singular sublimity'.

They left their haven elated, only to encounter groughs above twenty feet wide whose storm-laden peat often sucked them in to their thighs. Eventually they reached Woodhead and regained their servant and horse, 'drenched with rain, dropping with sweat and covered with dirt'. Most irritating were the bites inflicted by the swarms of mosquitoes which had plagued them. Their trials were not over; the landlady at the inn refused them beds for the night and they were compelled to plod a further eight miles to an inn at Mottram.

Reinvigorated and still undeterred they rose the next day, travelled to Mellor and traversed the plateau summit of Kinder Scout (see plate 97, p.192) with its 'extensive prospect of the vicinities of Manchester, Liverpool and North Wales'. They took the rugged path down to Hayfield and then travelled by road from Chapel-en-le-Frith to Buxton.

Hutchinson had blazed a trail through the last unconquered and unrecorded fastnesses of the Peak. Defoe's 'howling wilderness' had at last been tamed.

By the beginning of the 19th century the old associations of horror and evil in the Peak had largely passed into folklore. They were aroused for the last time in William Blake's mystical poem *Jerusalem: the Emanation of the Giant Albion* (1804-20). As far as is known, Blake does not appear to have visited Derbyshire and relies for his topographical references to the underworld on the works of Drayton, Hobbes and Cotton. Was it the Peak that he had in mind when in *Milton* (1804-8) he contrasted England's 'pleasant pastures' and 'mountains green' with her 'dark satanic mills'? John Ruskin took up Blake's cry in a later and different context. He loved Scotland, the Lake District and the Alps but the Peak had a special place in his heart. Here he found a different solace in a haven where the grandeur was not overwhelming and where he could draw and paint the minutiae of lichens, flowers and foliage. Viewing with dismay the threats to the region, he has left us, perhaps, the best short descriptions of it:

> Much as I love Thirlemere and Helvellyn, there are in other climes lovelier lakes and sweeter strands ... But ... I ... can't find anything like Derbyshire anywhere else. [It's a fine thing] to scale the Wengern Alp with Manfred – to penetrate with Faust the defiles of the Brocken:- the painlessly accessible turrets of Matlock High Tor, the guiltlessly traceable Lovers' walks by the Derwent, have for me still more attractive peril and a dearer witchery. Looking back to my past life, I find, though not without surprise, that it owes more to the Via Gellia than the Via Mala – the dripping wells of Matlock than the dust-rain of Lauterbrunnen.
>
> Enough said in my own cause. I now ... take up that of the public ... That little heap of crystalline hills, white over with sheep, white under with dog-tooth spar, is a treasure alike to them all ...
>
> Learned traveller ... think what this little piece of mid-England has brought into so narrow a compass, of all that should be most precious to you. In its very minuteness it is the most educational of all the districts of beautiful landscape known to me. The vast masses, the luxurious colouring, the mingled associations of great mountain scenery, amaze, excite, overwhelm, or exhaust – but too seldom teach; the mind cannot choose where to begin. But Derbyshire is a lovely child's alphabet; an alluring first lesson in all that's admirable, and powerful chiefly in the way it engages and fixes the attention. On its miniature cliffs a dark ivy leaf detaches itself as object of importance; you distinguish with interest the species of mosses on the top; you count like many falling diamonds the magical drops of its petrifying well; the cluster of diamonds in the shade is an Armida's garden to you. And the grace of it all! and the suddenness of its enchanted changes, and terrorless grotesque ... It was a meadow a minute ago, now it is a cliff, and in an instant is a cave – and here was a brooklet, and now it is a whisper under ground; turn but the corner of the path, and it is a little green lake of incredible crystal; and if the trout in it lifted up their heads and talked to you, you would be no more surprised than if it was in the Arabian Nights. And half a day's work of half a dozen navvies, and a snuff-box full of dynamite, may blow it all into Erebus, and diabolic Night, for ever and ever.[37]

17

The End of the Idyll

The French Wars at the end of the 18th century closed Europe to British travellers and induced more of them to discover their native land. The Peak began to lose its mystique. New roads and the coaching network, together with a steadily increasing flow of printed information, historical, topographical and scientific, eroded its secret identity. The coming of the railways and their waves of passengers scarred its beauty and shattered its peace. The new maps of the late 18th century, culminating in the Ordnance Surveys of the Victorian era, provided the traveller with new information. For Derbyshire, Burdett's excellent *Survey*, begun in 1762 and completed in 1791, superseded all its predecessors and opened the Peak to the traveller.

Peter Perez Burdett was a member of the Derby Philosophical Society and a remarkable polymath – a mathematician, surveyor, cartographer, topographical artist and print maker. He was a friend of Joseph Wright who painted a splendid portrait of him and his wife in 1765.[1] The sitters are posed against the rocks and hills of the Peak and Burdett holds an attribute – a telescope – to denote his status as a cartographer. The portrait was, no doubt, painted to celebrate the forthcoming *Survey of Derbyshire* in 1767, for which Burdett had been awarded a prize by the Society for the Encouragement of the Arts. Burdett's was the first map of the county to be based on a completely new survey since that of Christopher Saxton in 1577, and its inset plan of Derby the first new survey since John Speed's in 1610. Considerable changes were made in the copper plates before the definitive edition was published in 1791. Recorded on the scale of one inch to the mile, the map, Burdett claimed, contained 'the exact situation of every place, remarkable or curious in the said County, as Towns, Villages, Churches, Noblemen and Gentlemen's seats, extraordinary mountains; the Origin and Course of Rivers, Bridges, Ferries, Towns, Fords, Mills, all Main and Cross Roads with their Measure by the Perambulator' (see plate 94, p.188).[2]

Such a map was a work of reference which had a place in gentlemen's libraries. The writers of tours and guides, like Ward, derived their own route maps from it, giving the distances laid down by Burdett. However, Burdett's 'extraordinary Mountains' were still not measured by contour lines and the steepness of hills and dales was, as always, indicated by the intensity of hatched shading.

Burdett's map eclipsed the *Accurate Map of the County of Derby* which had been published about 1760 by Emanuel Bowen, Geographer to King George II. Bowen claimed it was 'drawn from the best authorities'. However, it was still executed in the style of the maps from Saxton's time and persisted in filling the margin with decorative detail – in this case descriptions in italic print – of the Seven Wonders of the Peak.

Burdett did record some, though not all, of the new industrial sites, but not enough to indicate how increasingly industrialised Derbyshire, especially the Peak, was becoming. Having initially marvelled at the new factories, the late 18th-century tourist was beginning to question their impact on the landscape and on traditional rural life. John Byng provides a good example of this early ambivalence. We have seen him wondering at the romantic effect of Arkwright's Mills by day or night. On his second visit to Cromford in 1790 his comments sound a note of alarm that was to become a crescendo that still resounds.

> I dare not, perhaps I shou'd not, repine at the increase of our trade, and (partial) population; yet speaking as a tourist, these vales have lost all their beauties; the rural cot has given place to the lofty red mill, and the grand houses of overseers; the stream perverted from its course by sluices, and aqueducts, will no longer ripple and cascade. – Every rural sound is sunk in the clamours of cotton works; and the simple peasant (for to be simple we must be sequester'd) is changed into the impudent mechanic: – the woods find their way into the canals; and the rocks are disfigured for lime stone.
>
> So that the intention of retirement is much lost here; and the citizen or the tourist, may soon seek in vain for quiet, and wild scenery: – for it will quickly become as noisy as Cashalton [*sic*], or Merton in Surrey.
>
> I well know that a peasantry maintain'd by their own ground, or by the cultivation of others ground, must abide; but a fear strikes me that this (our over stretch'd) commerce may meet a shock; and then what becomes of your rabble of artisans!! – The bold rock opposite this house is now disfigur'd by a row of new houses built under it; and the vales are every way block'd up by mills.
>
> I saw the workers issue forth at 7 o'clock, a wonderful croud of young people, made as familiar as eternal intercourse can make them; a new set then goes in for the night, for the mills never leave off working. – Rocks, mills and water 'in confusion hurled'.[3]

More concern was being expressed about the effects of industrial development on health by the beginning of the 19th century. The mortality rate among those working in the lead mines had long been a cause of concern and to this was added the dangers to life and limb of children employed in factories; but now more attention was being drawn to the deleterious effects of limestone burning. The impact of the smoke and dust, especially in Middleton Dale, had drawn the romantic writer and artist to depict their effect on the scenery in terms of gloom and horror. By 1836, however, a doctor from Eyam, Richard Furness, was writing verse which implied a threat from the limestone industry to humanity as well as the landscape:

> The smouldering lime-kilns lent a flickering ray,
> And through the darkness cast a dubious day;
> By fits the flame threw sombre horror round,
> On pine-clad cliff and tor with foliage crown'd;
> The restless winds were still, nor breath'd a breath
> All living lay in temporary death,
> Rocks, hills, and vales were clad in fearful gloom,
> And nature slumber'd on her marble tomb.[4]

Air pollution, affecting a greater area than Middleton Dale, is now a not infrequent summer visitor to the Peak. Ruskin commented on it as early as June 1871, whilst he was staying at the *New Bath Hotel*, in Matlock Bath. He was probably sickening for a serious illness that confined him to his room there for most of July. This indisposition, prompted by a tendency to overstate, was to some extent responsible for the following outburst:

… It is the first of July, and I sit down to write by the dismallest light that ever yet I wrote by; namely, the light of this midsummer morning, in mid-England [Matlock] in the year 1871.

For the sky is covered with grey cloud; – not rain-cloud, but a dry black veil, which no ray of sunshine can pierce; partly diffused in mist, feeble mist, enough to make distant objects unintelligible, yet without any substance, or wreathing, or colour of its own. And everywhere the leaves of the trees are shaking fitfully, as they do before a thunder-storm; only not violently, but enough to show the passing to and fro of a strange, bitter, blighting wind. Dismal enough, had it been the first morning of its kind that summer had sent, but during all this spring, in London, and at Oxford, through meagre March, through changelessly sullen April, through despondent May, and darkened June, morning after morning has come grey-shrouded thus.

And it is a new thing to me, and a very dreadful one. I am fifty years old, and more; and since I was five, have gleaned the best hours of my life in the sun of spring and summer mornings; and I never saw such as these, till now …

It looks partly as if it might be made of poisonous smoke; very possibly it may be: there are at least two hundred furnace chimneys in a square of two miles on every side of me. But mere smoke would not blow to and fro in that wild way. It looks more to me as if it were made of dead men's souls – such as them as are not gone yet where they have to go …

You know, if there *are* such things as souls, and if ever any of them haunt places where they are hurt, there must be many about us, just now, displeased enough!

You may laugh, if you like. I don't believe any one of you would like to live in a room with a murdered man in the cupboard, however well preserved chemically; – even with a sunflower growing out of the top of his head.[5]

Yet pollution there was. If Ruskin exaggerated the cause and location of it within two miles of his hotel, he omitted to mention the more distant and encircling sources – the steelworks of Sheffield, the mills of Manchester, Derby and Nottingham together with the Staffordshire potteries.

The very place where Ruskin had so often stayed, since his first visit in 1830 – Matlock Bath – had undergone the most rapid change. Beside the 'bold rock' in Cromford, which Byng had considered 'disfigured', was the picturesque Scarthin Rock (see plate 33, p.64); this fell victim to the turnpike road which linked Cromford and Matlock Bath. Ward mourned its demolition by gunpowder and recorded that 'it has often been mentioned as a subject of regret that in doing this, the rock was not merely perforated and a rude arch left over the passage; since such a vestibule to this romantic dale [Matlock Bath] would have been extremely appropriate, and have produced a very happy effect'.[6]

Matlock Bath was flourishing – or declining – as a beauty spot under the joint pressures of settlement and tourism. Like Buxton, it was drawing more visitors than its hotels, inns and boarding houses could accommodate. Davies, like Ward and other writers, looking back to barely a century ago, when the Matlocks were a wild, secluded place of peace and solitude, reflected that 'some have thought that Matlock … was infinitely more deserving of admiration than since the increase of its buildings and its having become the resort of the gay and fashionable visitors'.[7]

The poets and painters came less frequently as their silent haunts were gradually invaded by sightseers and trippers. The decline of landscape painting, generally, was symptomatic of the waning Romantic Movement. The discovery of photography provided a shock to those who plied the pencil and the brush. In the second half of the 19th century these usurping 'artists' took to the railways with their equipment. Ruskin bemoaned the sunless images they produced as a negation of nature and harangued them thus:

… You think it a great triumph to make the sun draw brown landscapes for you. That was also a discovery, and some day may be useful. But the sun had drawn landscapes before for you, not in brown, but in green, and blue, and all imaginable colours, here in England. Not one of you ever looked at them then; not one of you cares for the loss of them now, when you have shut the sun out with smoke, so that he can draw nothing more, except brown blots through a hole in a box.[8]

We have an early account of a party of photographers 'rambling' through the Peak with a handcart and an Ordnance Survey map in 1858. They were led by the

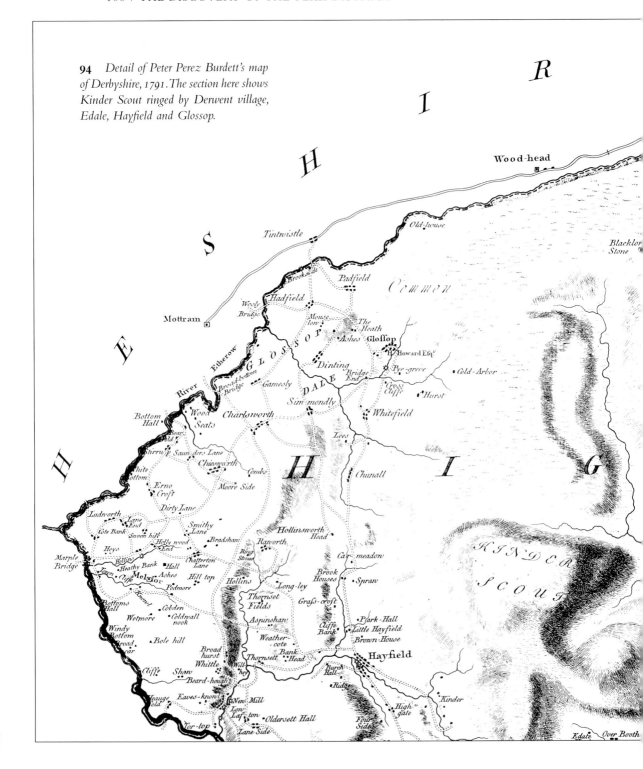

94 *Detail of Peter Perez Burdett's map of Derbyshire, 1791. The section here shows Kinder Scout ringed by Derwent village, Edale, Hayfield and Glossop.*

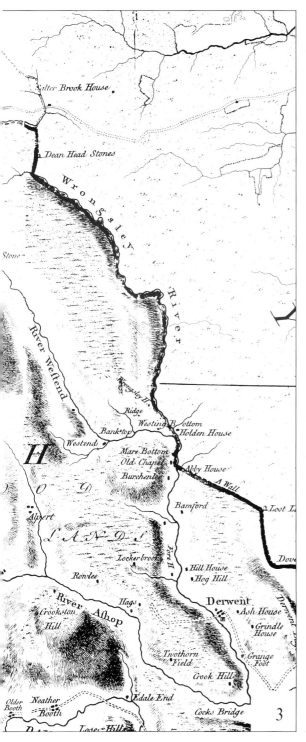

Derby photographer, Richard Keene (see plate 96, p.191), and had travelled by rail as far as Rowsley, the furthest point then reached in the Peak by the Midland Railway. Here they unloaded their equipment. Keene tells us

> our party consisted of A. Warwick, W. Hirst, myself and Tillett, who had charge of the cart, a light iron frame with good springs and large wheels made specially for the work. On this cart was mounted a large box containing our photographic apparatus, waterproof coats etc. closely packed; at one end, outside this box swung a keg of bitter, and at the other was fastened a large water proof packet containing our linen and other matters. The wheels were furnished with drags for descending hills more easily while to the front part of the vehicle were attached ropes for pulling up-hill. The whole outfit would weigh about 3 cwt as near as I can guess.[9]

With this they trundled along roads and tracks and even ascended to Carl Wark on the rough moors above Hathersage.

The visits of Keene and other photographers have left us a record of much of the changing Peak that Ruskin lamented. The 'desecration' of Monsal Dale is among the earliest surviving photographs.

Vandalism inevitably increased in the 18th century. This had been the activity of the souvenir-hunting gentry and aristocracy with Byng himself, as we have seen, a typical example. In the 19th century, as people of all classes journeyed from the surrounding towns and cities so damage, voluntary and involuntary, increased. Stanton Moor and Rowtor Rocks bear testimony to the urge to chisel names and dates on to rocks whose shapes had been formed by glaciation and the elements. Some rocks had toe-holds cut into them as the early rock climbers left their marks. Juvenile delinquency was displayed in the ravaged rock garden at Rowtor. Adam tells us that at 'the east end' is a vast block weighing about fifty tons, of irregular shape, which could be 'shook with ease, till the mischievous efforts of fourteen young men moved it from its position in 1799'.[10] The Hermit's Cave at Cratcliff Tor, across the valley from Rowtor, had to be protected from vandals with an iron grid.

Litter is a form of vandalism associated with some trippers and picnickers. Its increase by the mid-19th century can be gauged by the growing number of visitors to Chatsworth and the measures taken by the 6th Duke of Devonshire to restrain their excesses. By the 1850s Sir Joseph Paxton reckoned that 60,000 people a year were visiting the house and grounds regularly.[11] This required greater vigilance by the staff and the display of cautionary notices about the gardens and grounds. At weekends and especially on holidays people invaded the grounds like termites. It took ground staff up to two days to clear up the detritus after Bank Holidays.

95 *Cartouche for Burdett's map.*

Of course, the coming of the railways brought people speedily into the Peak and out again at the end of the day. Hence Andreas Cokayne could entitle his guide, *A Day in the Peak*, in the knowledge that people could now visit Chatsworth, Haddon Hall and even Bakewell if they took the carriages that awaited their arrival at Rowsley, Bakewell and Hassop stations.

Many did not welcome the coming of the railway and its army of largely Irish navvies. The Midland Railway had reached Rowsley in 1849 and after an acrimonious debate in the House of Lords as to whether it should pass through Chatsworth Park to Baslow or Haddon Park to Bakewell, the Duke of Rutland agreed

96   *Eyam's Saxon cross. An early photograph by – and including – Richard Keene, 1858.*

to allow its passage through tunnels just behind Haddon Hall. It arrived in Bakewell in 1862. Its controversial course ahead to Buxton, en route for Manchester, necessitated its entering Monsal Dale through a tunnel, crossing the river Wye by a viaduct (see plate 112, p.212) and proceeding up the valley through further tunnels, crossing and recrossing the river on lofty bridges and viaducts.

Some remarkable feats of railway engineering were achieved by ravaging the limestone dales and, just as Wordsworth had abhorred the prospect of the railways coming to Windermere, so Ruskin raged about its coming into the Peak. He wrote as follows about the rape of Monsal Dale:

> There was a rocky valley between Buxton and Bakewell, once upon a time, divine as the Vale of Tempe; you might have seen the Gods there morning and evening – Apollo and all the sweet Muses of the light – walking in fair procession upon the lawns of it, and to and fro among the pinnacles of its crags. You cared neither for Gods nor grass, but cash (which you did not know the way to get); you thought you could get it by what the Times calls "Railroad Enterprise". You Enterprised a Railroad through the valley – you blasted its rocks away, heaped thousands of tons of shale into its lovely stream. The valley is gone, and the Gods with it; and now, every fool in Buxton can be at Bakewell in half-an-hour, and every fool in Bakewell at Buxton ... [12]

Later he could still fulminate about the Midland Railway's Dore and Chinley project to open the northern Peak along the Hope Valley, as a means to linking Sheffield and Manchester:

> ... In almost every other lovely hill-district, and in all rich Lowland, the railway kills little more than its own breadth and a square mile or two about every station, and what it leaves is as good as what it takes. But in Derbyshire the whole gift of the country is in its glens. The wide acreage of field or moor above is wholly without interest; it is only in the clefts of it, and the dingles, that the traveller finds his joy, and in those clefts every charm depends on the alternate jut and recess of rock and field, on the

97 *The plateau of Kinder Scout today. Photograph by Ray Manley.*

successive discovery of blanched heights and woody hollow; and, above all, on the floretted banks and foam-crisped wavelets of the sweetly wilful stream. Into the very heart and depth of this, and mercilessly bending with the bends of it, your railway drags its close clinging damnation. The rocks are not big enough to be tunnelled, they are simply blasted away; the brook is not wide enough to be bridged, it is covered in, and is thenceforward a drain; and the only scenery left for you in the once delicious valley is alternation of embankments of slag with pools of slime.[13]

In his poem *The Bard*, written at the dawn of the Romantic Movement, Gray had depicted the last guardian of Welsh culture fulminating from his mountain fastness against the invading English army of Edward I. Ruskin represents a similar figure at the Movement's end. His powerful words were the epitaph for a vanishing realm of mystery and evocation – a lost idyll.

18

Freedom to Roam

Ruskin may well have cursed the railways which spread their tentacles from Sheffield and Manchester to Buxton, Bakewell, the Matlocks, Hathersage, Hope, Ashbourne and Wirksworth. Yet, ironically, he had contributed to their increasing use. In his lectures to the artisans and workers of Sheffield, Manchester and the northern industrial towns he exhorted them to seek the fresh air, to ramble in the hills and to look enquiringly not only at the broader landscape but at the minutiae of flora and fauna. Such athleticism and aestheticism, away from the mills, mines and furnaces, would enrich the body, mind and spirit. *Mens sana in corpore sano* need not be the preserve of the Victorian public schools.

Much of William Morris's views on the nobility of labour and the honesty of craftsmanship was in tune with the anti-capitalist and anti-industrialist views of Ruskin. Edward Carpenter, who forsook a Cambridge fellowship and a vicarage to continue the teaching of Ruskin and Morris, settled near Chesterfield on the edge of the Peak District and worked for some years as an influential university extension lecturer in the neighbouring towns. The ideas of these eminent Victorians became the fountainhead of the so-called 'outdoor movement', which was increasingly prominent at the end of the 19th century.[1]

Although rambling and scrambling in the hills and dales often had political overtones, especially in Lancashire and Yorkshire, the earliest ramblers were groups of friends usually of middle-class origins. Their equipment consisted of stout hob-nailed boots, a waterproof, knapsack and an Ordnance Survey map. Their social activity in no way derived from Dr Johnson's 'ramble in a post chaise' and they had progressed from the solitary wanderings of Wordsworth in the Lakes or Rousseau in Dovedale. As we have seen, John Hutchinson and his companions were the first true ramblers in the Peak, who did not simply visit the old Wonders. They did not contrive to avoid bad weather and to stay at good inns.

98 *The Kyndwr Club at the foot of Kinder Downfall in winter. Photograph by W. Meakin, 1890s.*

Typical of this new breed was James Croston, FSA, a Manchester educationist and writer of *On foot through the Peak, or a summer saunter among the hills and dales of Derbyshire*. Some of the early chapters had appeared during the 1860s in the *Manchester Courier* and had been well received by the public. He tells us his excursion had 'been undertaken solely with the desire of combining healthful recreation with intellectual amusement, and to cultivate a more close acquaintance with the charms of nature'. Whilst not claiming the book as a guide to the Peak District, he hoped 'it may be found an agreeable and useful companion to the tourist'.[2]

Ruskin would have applauded this justification and have approved entirely the 'catalogue of mosses and ferns found in Castleton and the immediate area' at the end of the book's third edition. He would also have endorsed the valedictory opening, 'Adieu to Cottonopolis', though he may have viewed with some dismay the fact that Croston boarded a train to Chapel-en-le-Frith to make his escape!

Croston's attention to historical monuments, as well as natural phenomena, was not surprising in one who was a Fellow of the Society of Antiquaries. Numerous societies and field clubs embraced all these interests as part of their rambling excursions. One such, and typical of many, was the Bakewell Field Club, formed about 1890 by a young graduate of Pembroke College, Cambridge, William Storrs-Fox. Son of a York clergyman, he was the founding headmaster of St Anselm's Preparatory School which still flourishes in Bakewell. He gathered around him the town's medical officer, Dr Evans, a prominent solicitor, Herbert Brooke-Taylor and the town's local antiquary and publisher, Andreas Cokayne. These, with others, rambled in the High Peak, entering caverns, wading in rivers, whilst recording and collecting archaeological, geological and botanical specimens. Storrs-Fox set up a museum in his school house and in the interests of biology contrived to trace and exhume the carcass of a rogue circus elephant which had been shot by the military in Bakewell.

Sheffield and Manchester produced numerous rambling and field clubs. By 1924 there were 24 in Sheffield and some 38 in Manchester.[3] Among their principal concerns were the preservation of ancient footpaths, rights of way and the freedom to roam. Such concerns, still burning issues today, date back to test cases near Glasgow and in Lancashire and Yorkshire in the 1820s.

At the end of the 19th century the journalist Robert Blatchford took up the ramblers' cause in the *Manchester Sunday Chronicle*. He was a socialist and founder member of the Manchester Fabian Society. Having left the *Sunday Chronicle* in 1891 he, together with his brother and three colleagues, launched the socialist weekly, *The Clarion*. It urged city dwellers to enjoy and reclaim the countryside. Rambling was not the only way. *The Clarion* particularly

99 *The Kyndwr Club exploring Eldon Hole. Photograph by H. Eggleston, 1900s.*

encouraged the formation of cycling clubs. Clarion clubs sprang up in the Pennine towns and as far west as Liverpool. Blatchford's articles in *The Clarion* were published in 1893 as *Merrie England*.

Another socialist writer who was extremely influential in the 'outdoor movement' was G.B.H. Ward, an engineer-fitter from Sheffield. He responded to *The Clarion*'s call to the countryside by organising an outing for Sheffield ramblers on Kinder Scout on 2 September 1900. This first organised excursion served as the beginning of the most active of all the rambling clubs, the Sheffield Clarion Club. Moreover, in traversing Kinder Scout it was as though it was serving notice of the famous mass trespass which was to take place 32 years later. Ward was involved with the Sheffield Clarion Club until his death in 1957. He edited its *Handbook* which recorded meticulously what was seen and discovered on hundreds of rambles.[4] Perhaps he, more than any other single person, discovered the hitherto unrecorded facts and details of the Peak's ancient landscape. He kept a wary eye on the activities of the landowners, whether they were wealthy aristocrats like the Duke of Rutland, the Sheffield City Corporation, or the various water boards.

The last were involved in one of the greatest transformations of the landscape of the High Peak. In 1899 the corporations of Derby, Leicester, Nottingham, Sheffield and the county council of Derbyshire were incorporated to form the Derwent Valley Water Board. Land had been purchased from the Duke of Norfolk covering the source of the Derwent in the remote moors of Bleaklow down to the village of Bamford. In accordance with the

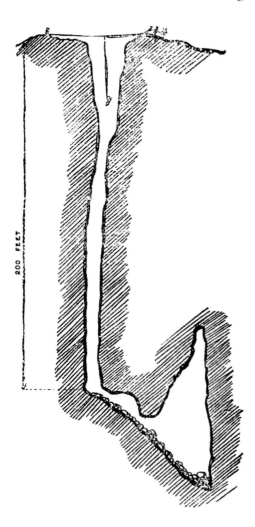

100 *Sectional diagram of Eldon Hole. Pen drawing by Arnold Bemrose, MA, FGS.*

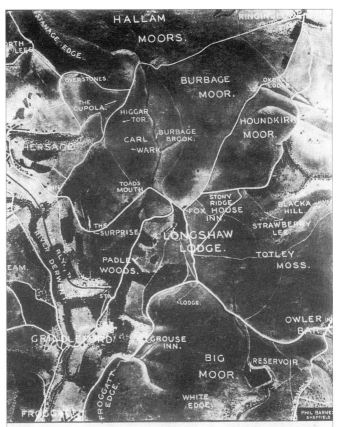

THE LONGSHAW ESTATE & SURROUNDING COUNTRY.

AN APPEAL IS BEING MADE FOR £15000 TO PURCHASE 747 ACRES OF THIS ESTATE. TO BE HELD FOR EVER BY THE NATIONAL TRUST AS AN OPEN SPACE. THE AREA IN QUESTION EXTENDS FROM THE SURPRISE TO THE GROUSE INN AND FROM FOX HOUSE AND THE WOODEN POLE ALMOST TO GRINDLEFORD STA.

CHEQUES &c. SHOULD BE SENT TO MR. SAMUEL OSBORN J.P. HON. TREASURER OF LOCAL COMMITTEE. LONGSHAW APPEAL FUND. 84 WEST ST. SHEFFIELD. ALL PROFITS FROM THE SALE OF THIS CARD WILL BE GIVEN TO THE PURCHASE FUND.

101 *Postcard appeal on behalf of the National Trust for the purchase of part of the Duke of Rutland's Longshaw Estate.*

Derwent Valley Water Act of 1898 and its modification of 1901, three reservoirs were planned with dam walls. The highest was excavated at Howden (see plate xv) and opened in 1912, followed by the Derwent Dam in 1916 and finally the Ladybower Dam, begun in 1935.

This area had been one of the delights of the rambler since it was first described by Hutchinson and many tears were shed as the hamlet of Ashopton with its famous inn was submerged beneath the waters. The larger village of Derwent, including its church, its fine manor house and woodlands, suffered the same fate. For almost fifty years the area was closed to walkers. Arthur Mee

102 *Derwent Village before its destruction.*

visited Derwent village in the early 1930s and found it 'perhaps the saddest village in Derbyshire, lying under the shadow of death'. He concluded hopefully that 'though it is sad to think so much loveliness must go, the new lake will have a beauty of its own'.[5]

W.A. Poucher came just before the war and took some haunting photographs of Derwent church and hall before the dam consumed them. He wrote:

> I did not know this valley before its metamorphosis, so that when I visited it I was unable to draw any comparisons between its natural and changed aspects. I do, however, like the glint of water in the landscape and I love trees, so that in consequence I found the upper part of the valley enchanting and reminiscent of a Scottish glen with its conifers coming right down to the water's edge … This prospect was therefore reassuring after the sad sight of the shattered Derwent village and I can only hope that in years to come the new reservoir will assume an equally attractive appearance.[6]

Indeed it has. The ladder of lakes, in the words of Pevsner, 'form[s] a splendid enhancement of the natural beauties of Derbyshire'.

Trying to save the Derwent Valley was a battle that could never have been fought or won and although the lovers of the Kinder region mourned, there was still much to explore and protect.

The interest in climbing and caving had grown considerably at the end of the 19th century. Prominent among the early clubs was the Kyndwr Society which chose as its title the pre-English name of Derbyshire's highest hill. Its first president was the Reverend David Macdonald, MA, BD, who typified the professional men from the universities who have always been part of the English climbing and mountaineering fraternity.

The society found scrambling and climbing underground almost as exhilarating as scaling the crags in the open air (see plate 98, p.194). This is clearly evident in the book by one of their members, Ernest Baker, entitled *Moors, Crags and Caves of the High Peak and Neighbourhood*. The old Wonders of the Peak were re-visited and in 1902 the Society decided to see how far its members could penetrate into Peak Cavern. Equipped with alpine ropes and ladders they passed the limits of public access and probed considerably further than had a Frenchman, one Monsieur Martel, who explored the cave in the 1890s. Eventually the fear of rising water drove them back.

Having tackled Speedwell Cavern, Bagshawe Cavern and the Blue John Mine, they had assembled before Eldon Hole on Boxing Day 1900 equipped with long alpine ropes, lamps and a telephone. A stout cable with a pulley was stretched above the Hole and a bosun's chair fixed on the end of the rope. The expedition failed to find the fabled passage by which Cotton told us that a goose made its way into Peak Cavern. The cavers claimed that the passage, if it ever existed, had been blocked by debris over the centuries. However, many of the local folk from Castleton still believed, as had Defoe, that there was a route to the centre of the earth!

At least below the ground there was no question of trespassing; above it on the sheep runs and the grouse moors it was a constant irritant. Baker tells us how two of his party unwittingly strayed out of bounds during a traverse of Kinder Scout from Edale to the *Snake Inn*.

Two of the five had recently been caught in an innocent act of trespass by a redoubtable farmer, who had been dissuaded only by bribery from walking them off to Bakewell police-court. With their nerves unsteadied by this experience, they listened with quaking hearts to our talk about fierce and implacable gamekeepers; and then it was pointed out that, as a queer coincidence, the brow we were ascending is called 'the Nab', the omen struck them as full of terrible significance. Little was said about a certain document one of us carried, which was supposed to be a powerful talisman for softening the obdurate hearts of keepers.[7]

103 *Derwent Hall.*

However, it was at Haddon and Bakewell, not Kinder, that the first major confrontation over rights of way in the Peak took place.

The context was the economic pressure on the aristocracy before, and especially after, the First World War. Rising prices and increasing taxation – especially Lloyd George's death duties – had far reaching effects. Many landowners were selling off their estates and abandoning their country seats. In Derbyshire alone one third of the landed estates had been broken up by 1930. The Duke of Rutland decided to sell off some of his peripheral Derbyshire holdings in order to consolidate the estate around his old seat of Haddon Hall as the Haddon Estate Company. This was to be vested by deed in his son, John Manners, Marquess of Granby, on his coming of age in 1921 and was obviously a precaution against death duties.[8]

In 1920 he sold his property and manorial rights in Bakewell and followed this in 1927 by disposing of Longshaw Lodge and its surrounding grouse moors to the National Trust and Sheffield and Chesterfield corporations.

The Marquess of Granby had, as a boy, dreamed of returning to live in Haddon Hall which his ancestors had vacated for Belvoir Castle two centuries earlier. During that absence the park had been converted to sheep enclosures and the woods had been somewhat neglected. First the townsfolk of Bakewell and then the numerous rambling clubs had established a network of paths over the property. Some passed by the very walls of the Hall and its gardens.

In what became a painstaking restoration of the Hall, the Marquess at first encouraged visitors and raised the admission fees to help offset the cost of the work. However, he was unable to cope with the droves of visitors and the concomitant parking problems. He reduced the opening hours at the Hall and stopped the footpaths across the estate, complaining that visitors 'left litter about and behaved like so many worthy people of a certain class behaved themselves when on holiday'.[9]

The battle over the footpaths now began, and was taken up by Bakewell Urban District Council supported by the Bakewell Rural District Council and local rambling clubs. Having, out of courtesy, informed the Marquess's agent in the town of their intention to unstop the footpaths, the town clerk and the surveyor mustered eight workmen armed with pickaxes, shovels, crowbars and wire-cutters. They assembled on Bakewell bridge and were joined by some two hundred ramblers and townsfolk. In the course of an eight-mile tramp, completed in three hours, they uprooted notices, threw down walls and fences, cut barbed wire and cropped bolts. The local and national papers, especially the *Manchester Guardian*, literally had a field day in highlighting the matter.

The Marquess sued and the case was heard in the Chancery Division of the High Court. His counsel readily demonstrated that he had precedent in his favour with regard to the footpaths in the immediate vicinity of Haddon Hall. These had been stopped up in 1799 and again in 1813. However, he could find no such instances to protect the others. The Marquess was advised to settle out of court and leave these footpaths open.[10]

Nevertheless, following his Pyrrhic victory the Marquess screened Haddon Hall from the A6 road and nearby paths with swathes of trees and tall spike-topped iron railings. Following his succession to the ducal title in 1925, he finally occupied the Hall in 1927 and promptly closed it to the public save one day a year for charity.

No obvious political motives were evident in the Bakewell 'rising'. Indeed the two councils, like the Marquess, were Tory in sympathy. This was not the case with other gatherings which drew in socialist elements. Such was the thriving Sheffield Clarion Club which was to the fore in the defence of rights of way and greater moorland access. Its efforts were strengthened in 1924 following the formation of the Sheffield Cooperative Ramblers who were affiliated to the Cooperative Party. Among their successes was the concession by the landowner of the Dore to Hathersage right of way in 1928.

MPs in Pennine constituencies were lobbied to press for legislation and attention was focusing on the Peak District. The Sheffield Clarion Club called for a mass rally in the Winnats Pass, near Castleton, proclaiming that 'every rambler is expected to be at the annual demonstration in the Winnats Pass at 3 pm Sunday, June 26th 1932'. An estimated three thousand gathered there to be addressed by Professor C.E.M. Joad, G.B.H. Ward and Tom Stephenson, open air correspondent of the *Daily Express* and editor of *The Hiker and Camper*. The gathering, which was to meet annually here until the war, pressed for an Access to Mountains Bill to be set before Parliament.

The Country Landowners' Association steeled itself for a possible social revolution culminating in the nationalisation of land. Its fears were not allayed when a group of young activists among the Sheffield Clarion ramblers pressed for mass trespass and in 1932 advertised that they would assert their right to walk freely over the grouse moors of Kinder Scout on Sunday, 24 April. They duly rallied their supporters at Edale whilst several hundred from Manchester gathered at Hayfield to the strains of the *Red Flag* and the *Internationale*.

Both parties ascended to the summit where they greeted one another in triumph. A few from each party had left the footpath and there were scuffles with gamekeepers. Some of the latter had their sticks taken from them and one sustained minor injuries. It was hardly a mass trespass! [11]

On the way down on the Hayfield side police arrested six of the ringleaders who were imprisoned overnight and subsequently brought before the Derby

104 *Hayfield memorial plaque.*

105 *Re-enactment of the 'Mass Trespass' to commemorate its 50th anniversary, 24 April 1982.*

Assizes. Five were given sentences of up to six months in prison on charges ranging from riotous assembly, trespass and committing bodily harm.

The Manchester papers dramatised the occasion with headlines such as 'Mob law on the moors', 'Sunday's attack on Kinder' and 'Free fight with gamekeepers on mountain'. In fact the trouble caused was slight and was provoked by a few *agents provocateurs* who found little sympathy in the rambling fraternity. Although those taken into custody were never hailed as martyrs, the event has become a landmark in the history of the struggle for access. Its 50th anniversary was marked by a ramble in 1982 and this has been repeated every year since.

The 'mass trespass' made little immediate change in the opening of the Peakland moors. Even today, following the Countryside and Rights of Way Act in 2000, there are still disputed areas. Nevertheless, rallies in the Winnats Pass continued and new approaches to the problems were mooted as war loomed.

The first of these was raised by Tom Stephenson in 1935 and concerned the possibility of a Pennine Way for ramblers. He pressed the idea at rallies and in his newspaper articles that a continuous footpath could be opened along the spine of England from Edale in the Peak to Wooler in Northumberland.

106 *Derwent church steeple in the waters of Ladybower Dam.*

This aroused considerable attention and in 1938 the Pennine Way Association was founded at a conference of all interested parties. Most of the proposed route, stretching some 250 miles, was along agreed rights of way, but about seventy miles still needed to be negotiated with landowners. It was not until 1965 that Britain's first and most famous long-distance walk was officially opened. Thereafter the once quiet little village of Edale was crowded with walkers beginning and completing this exciting new challenge.

The second proposed new way to allow greater discovery of the Peak District was to designate it as a National Park.

19

Britain's First National Park

The Peak District was no longer a totally 'unspoilt' area. Its towns were growing, changing and encroaching along the improved roads and into the landscape. As the cotton mills declined in the face of more up-to-date technology in Lancashire, other industries replaced them in the last third of the 19th century.

In modern terminology, the spa towns could be described as having 'service industries'. Though Bakewell had failed to compete, Buxton and Matlock Bath enjoyed their greatest prosperity as spas from the 1850s until the First World War. An important factor in their expansion was the development of the hydropathic institutions. Known as 'hydros', these huge hotels catered for the tourist and the visitor in general but particularly provided for the needs of the infirm and those who had come to take the waters. Some of the elderly and wealthy invalids made these institutions their homes to the end of their days.

Buxton, under the waning patronage of the Dukes of Devonshire, was striving to become a holiday centre in its own right. The northern Lancashire resorts such as Blackpool attracted the Pennine mill workers. Buxton drew their employers and a strongly middle-class clientèle.

Apart from its stolid Victorian villas, its boarding houses and hotels, the spa was enjoying a building boom. In 1853 its Thermal Baths and Natural Baths were begun. Ten years later a fine double station was opened for the increasing number of visitors. This served the Midland Railway and the London and North Western line. Just behind it in 1968 the huge *Palace Hotel* was erected in a French château style. Buxton was exhibiting a confident swagger not seen since the days of Carr and the 5th Duke of Devonshire.

The next development by Edward Milner of London, born near Bakewell and a pupil of Paxton, was the creation of the Pavilion and Winter Garden in front of the newly landscaped riverside gardens. Around this complex were added a fine domed Concert Hall (1876), a theatre, subsequently known as the Hippodrome or Playhouse (1889) and finally an opulent Edwardian Opera House (1903).

107 *The Thermal Baths, Buxton. Anonymous watercolour, c.1850.*

Nor were the less well-off invalids forgotten. The town had always afforded some relief for the poorer visitors. New hospital accommodation was needed and attention was focused on Carr's Great Stable which was now leased by a small livery company. Eventually the Duke of Devonshire agreed to its conversion into the Devonshire Hospital. The architect, R.R. Duke, in 1881 raised on its octagonal base a dome which at that time was the largest in the world.[1]

In that year, too, Buxton's first hydro was established by Dr Samuel Hyde, a water physician who had taken up the practice of hydropathy. This process of alleviating internal ailments by the various external applications of water was developed in Germany in the 1830s. Its great advantage was that it was not dependent on the mineral waters of the spa. Any good source of clean water could be used, which meant that the new hydros did not have to be located over the natural mineral springs. Having founded the Buxton Hydropathic Company Limited, Dr Hyde began to build his hydro at Buxton House on Terrace Road (now the Buxton Museum and Art Gallery) and in 1887 renamed it the Peak Hydropathic Establishment.[2]

Matlock Bath, confined beside the river Derwent in its rocky defile, could not expand in the manner and style of Buxton. Although the splendid *Royal Hotel* was erected, and behind it the Pavilion, hydros were built well upstream at Matlock Bank. The largest and most prestigious of these was Smedley's Hydropathic Establishment, built by John Smedley, a hosiery manufacturer at nearby Lea Mills, in 1867. It was enlarged in 1885. This vast establishment contained every amenity for the luxurious comfort of guests who came from around the world. Two resident physicians supervised all the latest water treatments including Turkish baths, Russian baths, vapour baths, electric baths and various forms of massage. Matlock was indeed the hydro town; some 13 further hydros were built on the Bank extending as far as the neighbouring villages of Darley Dale and Tansley.[3]

All these fashionable trappings of cure and recuperation in Edwardian England came to a rather abrupt end with the First World War. Afterwards the cures afforded by modern medicine and advanced hospital treatment saw the decline of the hydros and the loss of thousands of jobs that had helped to maintain them.

Buxton and Matlock ceased to be spas and lost their old lustre. Arthur Mee particularly deplored what, in his view, had happened to Matlock:

> It has sold its beauty for a mess of pottage, or for a pot of message. We remember it as one of Nature's lovely places; it has sunk to the level of many hoardings, cheap houses and mean sights. Its glory has often been sung ... but that long ago, and it has spoiled itself.[4]

The encroachment of light industry and especially the growth of mineral extraction by quarrying were eroding the Peak landscape. Wirksworth, once the lead-mining capital, was now a quarry town. Whole hills and edges were consumed for building, road and motorway foundations and the manufacture of cement. As the railways declined, so the increasing products of the quarries were removed in heavy lorries along the A6 and its feeder roads. This was the new industrial landscape of the Peak District in the 20th century. Could this be an integral part of a proposed national park?

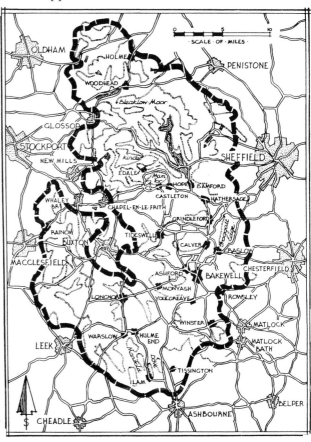

108 *Map of the Peak District National Park, 1953.*

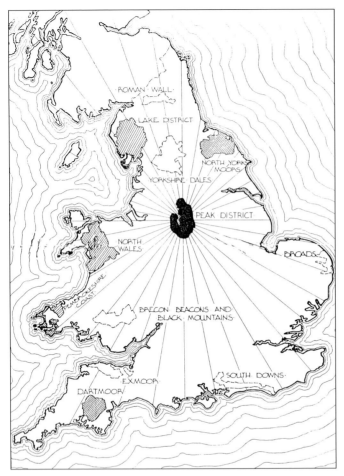

109 *Map indicating further National Parks, designated and recommended, 1953.*

In 1945 a Report on National Parks in England and Wales listed the Peak District as one of the six areas considered worthy of national-park status. A second Report (by the Hobhouse Committee) two years later recommended the Peak District, along with the Lake District, Snowdonia and Dartmoor as a first instalment of 12 suggested National Parks. By 1949 the National Parks Commission, established by the National Parks and Access to the Countryside Act, agreed that priority should be given to the Peak District, the Lake District and Snowdonia. Thus, in 1950 the Peak District was designated Britain's first National Park.

There was considerable debate about its size and boundaries at a widely attended public meeting in Buxton in March 1951. Following this the then Minister of Local Government and Planning confirmed the boundaries as first proposed by the Hobhouse Committee.

It is a common misconception that the Peak District and the Peak District National Park are synonymous and coterminous. They are not. The National Park incorporates parts of the old hundreds of the High and the Low Peak of Derbyshire and also part of the Staffordshire Moorlands. However, it also includes parts of Cheshire, South Yorkshire and Sheffield. In all it covers 542 square miles and is about 39 miles long and 24 wide.[5]

Its foetal shape on the map is due to the exclusion of a long enclave of land central to the old High Peak. This extends from around and including Buxton and forms a corridor along the A6 to Chapel-en-le-Frith, Whaley Bridge and New Mills. This area was considered incompatible within the Park chiefly on account of its industrial development and the existence of long-standing, active quarries. Glossop, a declining mill town in the High Peak, was also excluded, as were the Matlocks and Wirksworth in the Low Peak, together with the town of Ashbourne. Just beyond lay the ring of industrial cities and towns – Sheffield, Chesterfield, Nottingham, Derby, Stafford, Stoke, Stockport and Manchester. Approximately half the population of England and Wales lives within a 60-mile radius of the centre of the National Park. Its headquarters were established at Aldern House in Bakewell from where its 18 members representing the five councils took on its complex administration.

The general aims and objectives of the National Parks are found in the Act of 1949. The pre-eminent one is to maintain and enhance each Park as an area of natural beauty and to promote its enjoyment by the general public. Each National Park had powers of granting or withholding planning consent for development within its area to enable it to control building in towns and villages. Likewise it could control landscape development, protect woodland and encourage tree-planting schemes. Old and derelict buildings could be removed whilst those of architectural and historical importance could be protected.

It was a widely held belief that the formation of the Peak District National Park would give visitors an unrestricted right of access to the land within it. This was not and is not so. The inclusion of land and estates within the Park's boundaries in no way changes the rights of ownership or the rights of access. The Peak, both within the Park and without, has always been a working and developing landscape of farms, country estates, moors for grazing sheep and shooting grouse, industries for mineral extraction and so on. From the outset the Park's authority has negotiated with landowners and has appreciably increased rights of access, not least on Kinder Scout. At the same time it has striven to protect flora and fauna.

The principal landowner within the National Park is the National Trust which, in the hundred years since its foundation, has acquired considerable tracts of outstanding landscape in three important areas. Following the break-up of the Duke of Rutland's shooting estate at Longshaw, the Trust acquired a wide area of moorland, woods and farmland only ten miles from the centre of Sheffield. The Trust also owns a vast area of the highest and wildest terrain in what is known as its High Peak Estate. This 'stretches from the heather-clad moors of the Park Hall to the gritstone of Derwent Edge, and from the peat bogs of Bleaklow to the limestone crags of the Winnats Pass'. The third area, known as the South Peak estate, straddles the Staffordshire and Derbyshire borders at Ilam Park and runs along both banks of the River Manifold with spectacular views towards Dovedale. All told the National Trust cares for over twelve per cent of the Peak District National Park.[6]

In the half century of the Park's existence more and more visitors have come to the area. Among them are considerable numbers of trippers and picnickers who in the summer choose to make small explorations on easy tracks and paths, usually not too distant from their cars. The results in Dovedale and elsewhere have led to the need for car parks, toilets and the repair of eroded footpaths. Mountain bikers have invaded some footpaths and woodland areas, though the 'trails' provided on the disused Midland Railway and the High Peak Railway have satisfied the needs of many cyclists and 'gentle' walkers.

More alarming are the inroads of scrambling bikes and especially the four-track vehicles that are beginning to probe, legally as well as physically, old bridle ways and cart tracks. Matlock Bath has become one of the chief rallying points in England for the fast modern motor cyclists. They congregate in their hundreds at weekends, seated on their expensive, brightly coloured machines, clad in boldly blazoned leather armour and sporting black-vizored helmets. Their gatherings resemble a medieval muster such as might have been witnessed on the medieval tournament ground at Castleton. Sadly, these 'knights of the road' increasingly maim and kill themselves by reckless driving. The result is another newcomer to the Peak, the police helicopter that tracks them along the A6!

As for the motor car, this has become the major nuisance. It contributes in no small way to the pollution of the air and greedily demands more and more parking space. In the summer, and especially on bank holidays, it clogs the narrow roads. This has become so serious in the case of the road to Derwent Dams that Derbyshire County Council is currently considering the imposition of the first rural traffic tolls in England.

Conversely, local authorities raise considerable income from parking fees and businesses, large and small, especially tourist shops, profit from car-borne custom. Napoleon dubbed Britain 'a nation of shopkeepers'; today sociologists

110   *Parking in the Winnats Pass, 1973.*

111   *Queueing for the new toilets, Dovedale, 1976.*

112 *The Monsal Dale Railway viaduct, which appalled Ruskin, converted to a walkers' and cyclists' trail, 1981.*

suggest it is a nation of 'shopaholics'. Tourism for many is synonymous with shopping and towns and villages, country houses, museums and gardens all respond to the shoppers' wants. At Rowsley, just outside the National Park, a new 'Peak Village' simply consisting of shops has been erected. In the old villages the pubs, post offices and local stores are increasingly threatened. The cost of housing, especially in the Park, has soared and cottages are being bought as holiday homes by wealthy outsiders.

The landscape itself is being invaded, not just by tourists, but by television and radio masts and now by the latest erections – telephone masts. Wind farms have not yet arrived! However, quarrying, now the Peak's chief industry, carries on both inside and outside the park and the huge Blue Circle cement works raises its lofty chimney, like a smoking gun, in the Hope Valley. A new breed of troglodites has appeared; not the old lead miners and limestone burners who lived in their workings, caves and spoil-heaps, but Greenpeace's eco-warriors. On Stanton Moor they are encamped in tree-houses and tunnels in an endeavour to halt quarry working as it encroaches on one of Britain's most important prehistoric sites, including the famous henge, the Nine Ladies' Circle.

So new generations will come to discover the Peak. Millions arrive annually and the National Park is now the second most visited in the world after Japan's Mount Fujiama.

Notes

CHAPTER 1 – 'IN MONTE VOCATO PEC'

1. *Thraliana, The Diary of Mrs Hester Lynch Thrale, 1776-1809*: Ed. K.C. Balderston, Oxford, 1957, vol. II (1784-1809), p 689.
2. This oil painting is in the City Art Gallery, York.
3. Samuel Johnson and James Boswell, *A Journey to the Western Islands of Scotland* and *The Journal of a Tour to the Hebrides*. Ed. P. Levi, London, 1984, p15.
4. J. Moore, *The Letters and Journals of Lord Byron*, 1830, vol. III, p.369.
5. C. Leigh, *Natural History of Lancashire, Cheshire and the Peak in Derbyshire*, Oxford, 1700.
6. W. Stukeley, *Itinerarium Curiosum*, London, vol. I, 1724, p.51.
7. E. Rhodes, *Peak Scenery; or the Derbyshire Tourist*, London, 1824, pp.192-4.
8. Revd R. Warner, *A Tour through the Northern Counties of England and the Borders of Scotland*, London, 1802, p.166.
9. *Chronicles and Memorials of Great Britain and Ireland during the Middle Ages*, vol. 66, 1857. Appendix to preface p.xxxi.
10. William Camden, *Britannia*, London, 1586.
11. *Ibid.*
12. For a discussion of this interpretation of 'Peak' see the *New English Dictionary*. For the broader interpretation see K. Cameron, *The Place-Names of Derbyshire*, Nottingham, 1933, Part 1, pp.1-2.
13. John Speed, *The Theatre of the Empire of Great Britaine*, 1611, Book 1, Fol. 67-8.

CHAPTER 2 – THE HAZARDS OF THE WAYS

1. E. Moir, *The Discovery of Britain: The English Tourists 1540-1940*, London, 1964, p.xiii.
2. See R. Gough, *British Topography*, London 1780 and E.S. Parsons and Sir F. Stenton (eds.), *The Map of Great Britain c. A.D 1360, known as the Gough map*, OUP, 1958.
3. *The Works of the Late Edward Dayes: containing an excursion through the Principal parts of Derbyshire and Yorkshire*, London, 1805, p.10.
4. 'Extracts from the Commonplace Book of Sir Thomas Browne', *The Reliquary*, Vol XI, No 42, Oct 1870, pp.73-8.
5. C. Morris (ed.), *The Illustrated Journies of Celia Fiennes c.1682-c.1712*, London 1984, p.107.
6. From *The New and complete British Traveller*, cited in T. Brighton, 'Chatsworth's 16th-century Parks and Gardens', *Journal of Garden History*, Vol. 23 No. 1, 1992, pp.45-6.
7. W. Stukeley, *op.cit.*, p.27.
8. W.A. Carrington, 'Selections from the Steward's Accounts Preserved at Haddon Hall for the years 1549 and 1564'. *Derbyshire Archaeological Journal*, Vol. XVI, 1896, p.75.
9. See D. Hey, *Packmen, Carriers and Packhorse Roads*, Leicester University Press, 1980.
10. T. Brighton, 'Bakewell Stone and the Building of Chatsworth House', *Journal of the Bakewell and District Historical Society*, vol. 24, 1997, pp.14-16.
11. D. Defoe, *A Tour through the whole Island of Great Britain*, London, 1983, p.459.
12. For guide stoops in the Peak see D. Hey, *op.cit.* Chapter 2. A.E. and E.M. Dodd, *Peakland Roads and Trackways*, Moorland Publishing Company, 1974. J. Simpson, 'Ancient Guide-Posts' *DAJ* vol. XXXVI, 1914, pp.97-100.
13. I. Walton and C. Cotton, *The Compleat Angler*, Chapter II (First Day).
14. J. Buxton (ed.), *Poems of Charles Cotton*, London, 1958, pp.27-38.
15. T. Brighton, 'The King of the Peak goes to London in 1553', *JBDHS* No. 7, 1980, pp.66-7.

16. F. Brodhurst, 'Sir William Cavendish', 1557, *Derbyshire Archaeological Journal*, Vol. 29, 1907, pp.98-9.
17. *Illustrated Journeys of Celia Fiennes, op.cit.*, p.108.

CHAPTER 3 – THE PEAKRILS

1. G.H. Healey (ed.), *The Letters of Daniel Defoe*, Oxford, 1909, pp.380-1.
2. I. Ousby (ed.), *James Plumptre's Britain. The Journals of a Tourist in the 1790s*, London, 1992, pp.59-60.
3. Camden, *Britannia, loc.cit.*
4. *Ibid.*
5. Revd R. Warner, *op.cit.*, pp.160-1.
6. *The Illustrated Journies of Celia Fiennes, op.cit.*, pp.107-8.
7. Defoe, *op.cit.*, p.407.
8. C. Glover and P. Riden (eds.), 'William Woolley's History of Derbyshire', *Derbyshire Record Society*, Vol. VI, 1981, p.179.
9. James Plumptre, *op.cit.*, p.69.
10. W. Page (ed), *Victoria County History of Derbyshire*, London, 1905-7, Vol. II, p.184.
11. *Ibid.*, p.431; these figures are perhaps exaggerated.
12. L. Jewitt, *The Ballads and Songs of Derbyshire*, Derby, 1867, pp.280-1.
13. Defoe, *op.cit.*, p.475.
14. *Ibid.*
15. *The Illustrated Journies of Celia Fiennes, op.cit.*, p.110.
16. E. Rhodes, *op.cit.*, pp.92-3.
17. *Ibid.* Rhodes cites B. Faujas de Saint-Fond, *A Journey through England and Scotland to the Hebrides in 1784*, 2 vols., ed. Sir A.Geikie, Glasgow, 1907.
18. L. Jewitt, *The History of Buxton*, London, 1811, p.xxv. *See also* J.T. Leach, 'Grin Hill, Buxton: a major limestone quarry', *DAU*, cxvi, 1996, pp.101-34.
19. T. Brighton, 'John Constable's Sketching Tour in the Peak, 1801', *JBDHS* no. 22, 1995, pp.59-71.
20. *Compleat Angler, op.cit.*
21. W. Fitzherbert, *Husbandry*, 1523, Chapter 13. Cited in the *OED*.
22. See J.P. Carr, 'Open Field Agriculture in Mid-Derbyshire', *DAJ*, LXXXIII, 1963.
23. T. Brighton, 'In search of mediaeval Chatsworth', *JBDHS* no. 23, 1996, p.22.
24. A.Young, *A Six Months Tour through the North of England*, London, 1770, Vol.I, pp.213-17.
25. T. Brighton, 'Wordsworth in Derbyshire', *JBDHS* no. 19, 1992, p.37.
26. J.Farey, *A General View of the Agriculture and Minerals of Derbyshire*, Vol.I, 1811, p.96.

CHAPTER 4 – WONDER OF WONDERS

1. Leland's *Itinerary* was first published by the historical antiquary, Thomas Hearne (1678-1735) in 1710-12.
2. P Kinder, *The Historie of Darbyshire*, Bodleian Library, Ashmole MS 788.
3. *Britannia, op.cit.*
4. See J. Buxton (ed.), *Poems of Michael Drayton*, London 1967 (2nd edn.) vol. 1. Lines on the Peak, pp.685-90.
5. John Aubrey's *Brief Lives* contains a biography of Hobbes whom he knew as a fellow native of Wiltshire.
6. Anon. *Ducis Devoniae Sedes Vocata Chastworth* [sic] (The Duke of Devonshire's seat called Chatsworth) (n.d.) Dept. of Mss and Special Collections, University of Nottingham.
7. T. Brighton (ed.), 'A Mid-Georgian Tourists Poem on the Wonders of the Peak', *BDHS* No. 25, 1998, pp.11-29.
8. Defoe, *op.cit.*, pp.469-79.
9. *Four Maps of Great Britain Designed by Matthew Paris about 1250*, London 1928. Only the first map (B.L., Cotton Ms Claudius DVI fol 12v) gives any Derbyshire places. 'Aeolian' is a classical allusion to Aeolus, god of the winds.
10. *The Map of Great Britain … known as the Gough Map, op.cit.*
11. For a description and brief history of the castle see B. Morley, *Peverel Castle*, English Heritage, London, 1990.
12. As with the cavern, legends survive about the castle, such as the great joust held there to provide a suitable husband for Pain Peverel's daughter. See J. Pilkington, *View of the Present State of Derbyshire*, Vol II, London, 1789, p.397.
13. Sir Philip Sidney, *The Seven Wonders of England*, Sonnet IV. London, 1593.
14. *Cocke Lorelles Bote*, a popular verse satire partly imitating the *Ship of Folys*, was printed by Wynkyn de Worde in about 1515.
15. Hobbes, *De Mirabilibus Pecci.*

16. Cotton, *The Wonders of the Peak, op.cit. BEING THE WONDERS OF THE PEAK IN DARBYSHIRE commonly called The Devil's Arse of Peak. In English and Latine. The Latine written by Thomas Hobbes. The English by a Person of Quality*, London, 1678.
17. Leigh, *Natural History, op.cit.*
18. T. Wright *et al.*, *A Tour Through England in 1750* published in *The Reliquary* Vol XV, 1875, p.218.
19. N. Scarfe, *Innocent Espionage. The La Rochefoucauld Brothers Tour of England in 1785*, 1995, p.59.
20. T. Moore, *The Letters and Journals of Lord Byron*, London, 1830, p.30.
21. Revd R. Warner, *op.cit.*, pp.171-3. Could the anonymous baronet have been the celebrated Sir Francis Dashwood, 2nd Bart, of West Wycombe in Buckinghamshire? He made the largest artificial caves in England incorporating a 'River Styx' and a 'Banqueting Chamber' for the infamous Hell-fire club.
22. Blasts were the charges of gunpowder placed in boreholes in the rock and ignited for effect.

CHAPTER 5 – A PIT, A MOUNT AND A WELL
1. J.M. Hedinger, *A Guide through Peak's Hole with a Description of the Curiosities of Castleton*, Stockport, 1805, pp.7-8.
2. Miners were sent down to search for the bodies of missing people. See Revd D.P. Davies, *A New Historical and Descriptive View of Derbyshire from the Remotest Period to the Present Time*, Belper, 1811, p.680.
3. S. Markham, *John Loveday of Caversham. The Life and Tours of an 18th Century Onlooker*, London, 1984, p.184.
4. See *Philosophical Transactions* No. 2, p.7 and Vol. 61, p.250.
5. Revd D.P. Davies, *op.cit.* pp.676-7, J. Britton and E.W. Brayley, *The Beauties of England and Wales or Delineations, Topographical, Historical and Descriptive of each County*, Vol III, London, 1802, pp.470-7.
6. See Cameron, *op.cit.*, pt. 1, pp.55-6.
7. Cameron gives its origin as Tide's stream.
8. W. Mavor, *The British Tourist*, Vol.V, 'Journal of a Three Week's Tour through Derbyshire to the Lakes by a Gentleman of the University of Oxford,' London, 1800.
9. Farey, *op.cit.*, vol. 1, p.288.
10. L. Jewitt, *History of Buxton*, London, 1811, pp.170-6 and pp.142-3.

CHAPTER 6 – THE WELLS AND THE CAVERN AT BUXTON
1. It was one of the Roman towns listed in the seventh-century *Ravenna Cosmography* (see *Archaeologia*, XCII, p.23).
2. J. Leach, *The Book of Buxton*, Buckingham, 1987, pp.27-34.
3. Cameron, *op.cit.*, I, p.53.
4. J. Nasmith (ed.), *Itineraria Willelmi de Worcestre*, Cambridge, 1778, p.357.
5. T. Ford and D. Allsop, *The Story of Poole's Cavern*, Buxton, 1984, pp.22-5.
6. Cited in M. Langham and C. Wells, *Buxton Waters: a History of Buxton the Spa,* Derby, 1986, pp.34-5.
7. *Ibid.*, p.36.
8. R. Thorne and J. Leach, 'Buxton Hall', *DAJ*, CXIV, 1994, pp.29-53.
9. J. Jones, *The Benefits of the Auncient Bathes at Buckstones*, London, 1572, f.3.
10. E. Axon, 'Historical notes on Buxton, its inhabitants and visitors', *The Buxton Advertiser*, 1934-1947.
11. J. Jones, *loc.cit.*
12. 'Extracts from the Commonplace Book of Sir Thomas Browne', *op.cit.*, p.77.
13. J. Floyer, *An enquiry into the right uses and abuses of the hot, the cold and temperate Baths in England*, London, 1697, p.144.
14. Hobbes, *op.cit.*, p.48.
15. H. Kelliher, 'Donne, Jonson, Richard Andrews and the Newcastle Manuscript' in *English Manuscript Studies 1100-1700* ed. P. Beal and J. Griffiths, Vol. 4. See A. Fowler, *The Country House Poem*, Edinburgh UP, 1994, pp.159-69.
16. Richard Andrews, *The Muse to Chatsworth*, British Library, Harl. Ms 4955, f.172r.
17. *Ibid.*, ff.1641-1711.
18. J. Paget, 'A visit to Derbyshire in 1630', *DAJ* IX, 1887, p.54.
19. Defoe, *op.cit.*, p.469.

CHAPTER 7 – THE TOURIST INVASION
1. *Journal of the House of Commons*, XX (1722-27), p.363 and XXI (1727-32), p.435. For the road improvements in the Peak see J. Radley, 'Peak District roads prior to the turnpike era', *DAJ* LXXIII, 1963, pp.39-50 and J. Radley and S.R. Penny, 'The Turnpike Roads of the Peak District', *DAJ* XCII, 1972, pp.165-74.

2. S. Markham, *op.cit.*, p.185.
3. Rhodes, *op.cit.*, p.212.
4. *Ibid.*, p.5.
5. Rev. D.P. Davies, *op.cit.*, p.52.
6. C. Bruyn Andrews (ed.), *The Torrington Diaries, containing the Tours through England and Wales ... of the Hon. John Byng between the years 1781 and 1794*, 4 vols., London, 1934-38. The tours through Derbyshire in 1789 and 1790 are contained in vol. I, pp.25-65 and pp.184-201.
7. Special clothing designed by the Italian aeronaut, Vicenzo Lunardi (1759-1806).
8. James Plumptre, *op.cit.*, p.59. Nankeen was a yellow cotton fabric originally made in Nanking.
9. Carl Philip Moritz, *A Walking Tour in England in 1782* (trans. and introd. by R. Nettel), London, 1983, p.166.
10. *Ibid.* p.79.
11. *Torrington Diaries*, I p.187.
12. T. Brighton, 'Chatsworth's 16th Century Parks and Gardens', *Garden History*, Vol. 23 No. 1 (1992), p.44.
13. D. King-Hele (ed.), *The Letters of Erasmus Darwin*, CUP 1981 p.170.
14. The famous haulage firm of Pickford had its origins in the mid-17th-century packhorse business established by James Pickford of Adlington, Cheshire.
15. J.P. Malcolm, 'A Journey from Chesterfield to Matlock', *The Gentleman's Magazine*, Vol. 63, 1793, pp.505-8.
16. Rev. R. Warner, op.cit. pp139 and 156.
17. Rhodes, *op.cit.* pp.222-3.
18. G. Challenger, 'White Watson (1760-1835)', *JBDHS* No. 8, 1981, pp.27 and 33.
19. *Ibid.* p.23.
20. Rhodes, *op.cit.* pp.89-90.
21. Cited by A.E. Dodd and E.M. Dodd, *op.cit.* p.125.
22. S. Smith, 'The Greaves family and the Royal Mail in Bakewell', *JBDHS*, No. 29, 2002, pp.89-96.
23. Sir G. Head, *Home Tour through the Manufacturing Districts of England in the Summer of 1835*, London, 1836, pp.95-6.
24. *Ibid.*
25. L. Jewitt, *op.cit.* p.188.
26. *Ibid.* pp.208-9, Rhodes, *op.cit.* p.127.

CHAPTER 8 – GEOLOGY, COMMERCE AND TOURISM

1. Defoe, *op.cit.*, p.468
2. W. Watson, *A delineation of the Strata of Derbyshire*, Sheffield, 1811, p.68.
3. L. Jewitt, *History of Buxton*, 1811, p.147.
4. Farey, *op.cit.*, p.442.
5. T. Brighton, 'White Watson's Memorabilia', *BDHS* Vol.21, 1994, p.27.
6. T. Brighton, 'The Ashford Marble Works and Cavendish Patronage, 1748-1905', *Bulletin of the Peak District Mines Historical Society*, Vol.12, No. 6, Winter 1995.
7. J. Howe, *Trifles light as air*, Sheffield, 1816, pp.19-20.
8. 'White Watson's Memorabilia', *op.cit.* pp.26-7.
9. W. Adam, *The Gem of the Peak*, 4th edn. 1845, p.398.
10. 'White Watson's Memorabilia', *op.cit.*, p.28. For other explanations of the term 'Blue John' see T.D. Ford, *Derbyshire Blue John*, Landmark Publishing, Ashbourne, 2000, p.7.
11. *Ibid.*
12. M. Craven, *John Whitehurst of Derby, Clockmaker and Scientist, 1713-88*, Ashbourne, 1996, p.243.
13. W. Watson, *op.cit.*, p.ii.
14. *Torrington Diaries*, I, p.46.
15. E.R. Meeke, *White Watson*, Vol 1 (Diaries) privately printed 1996, p.130 (copy in Matlock Local Studies Library and the Old House Museum, Bakewell).
16. Craven, *op.cit.*, p.221.
17. *Ibid.*, p.90.
18. *Torrington Diaries*, I, p.42.
19. D. King-Hele, *op.cit.*, 1981, p.128.
20. Craven, *op.cit.*, p.75.
21. *Ibid.* Plate VI/13, p.98.
22. Kedleston Archives cited in R. Gunnis, *Dictionary of British Sculptors, 1660-1851*, 1964, p.64.
23. Craven, *op.cit.*, p.77.

24. *Ibid.*, p.76.
25. T. Brighton, 'Marble Works on the Wye at Ashford and Bakewell', *BDHS*, Vol 24, 1997, pp.45-70.
26. 'The Ashford Marble Works and Cavendish Patronage …', *op.cit.*, p.63.
27. See T.D. Ford, 'White Watson and his Geological Tablets', *Mercian Geologist*, Vol.13, No.4, pp.157-64.
28. For Ashford marble see T.D. Ford, 'The Black Marble Mines of Ashford in the Water', *Bulletin of the Peak District Mines Historical Society*, Vol.2, No.4, 1964, pp.179-88 and 'The Inlaid Black Marble of Ashford in the Water, Derbyshire', *Petros* (Leicester) Vol. 32, 1994, pp.24-5. J.M. Tomlinson, *Derbyshire Black Marble*, Peak District Mines Historical Society Special Publication No. 4, 1996.
29. W. Adam, *op.cit.*, pp.408-9.
30. Tomlinson, *op.cit.*, p.62.
31. Rhodes's daughter was certainly a painter and exhibited at the RA in 1811-13. Rhodes himself, however, in his *Derbyshire Tourist Guide* of 1837, says: 'Diamond engraving on black marble was introduced by a lady from Sheffield who was then on a visit to Matlock … Her subjects were chiefly moonlights, for which this kind of engraving seems to be peculiarly adapted.'
32. See Tomlinson, *op.cit.*, engraving of Chatsworth, p.23.
33. W. Adam, *op.cit.*, p.79.

CHAPTER 9 – ANTIQUARIES, BARROW OPENERS AND ECCLESIOLOGISTS

1.   For the sketch see Bodleian Library, Ms, Top. Gen. E61 Fol. 11p.
2.   See Stukeley's drawing, 'The Hermitage, Stamford, 1738' in J. Dixon Hunt, *The Figure in the Landscape*, London, 1976, p.3.
3.   Chatsworth Library, *The Correspondence of Hayman Rooke* (Ms copies of letters) f.172.
4.   Vol.VI, 1782 pp.110-115, Plates XI-XVIII 'The Druidical Remains in Derbyshire' (paper read 6 April 1780).
5.   The printer had set Mr Eyre as 'Mr Ashe' in the text. This was another reason why Stukeley's description, which does not name the garden's location, has mystified subsequent readers.
6.   John Aubrey (1626-97) was the first person to claim Stonehenge for the Druids but his work was not published until 1862. Stukeley appears to have known nothing of Aubrey's claims apart, perhaps, from Gibson's brief statement of Aubrey's opinion in Camden's *Britannia* in 1695.
7.   Speaking generally of the Druids, Rooke says their sacred groves have long since given way to cultivation. 'The Druidical Remains in Derbyshire', *op.cit.*, p.115.
8.   Stukeley missed these stones by not proceeding beyond the hermit's cell.
9.   'Rooter or Roo-Tor Rocks, Derbyshire,' by Thomas Allom, engraved by J. Saddler and published by Fisher, Son and Co., London and Paris.
10. James Plumptre, *op.cit.*, p.73.
11. W. Adam, *The Gem of the Peak*, London, 1845, pp.296-97.
12. J. Radley, 'The origin of Arbor Low henge monument', *DAJ*, LXXXVIII, 1969, pp.100-03.
13. This henge was first recorded by J. Pilkington in 1789 (*A View of the Present state of Derbyshire*) who noted that only one of its stones remained. See J. Barnatt and A. Myers, 'Excavations at the Bull Ring hence … 1984-85', *DAJ*, CVIII, 1988, pp.5-26.
14. Mander had published his discoveries in a barrow on Winster Common in *Archaeologia II*, p.274, Richard Gough described him as 'an attorney at Bakewell, an excellent antiquary, who shewed great civility to Mr [Thomas] Pennant, 1775, and gave him large extracts from his numerous and valuable collections for this county [Derbyshire], which his declining health will not permit him to arrange'. *British Topography,* Vol 1, London, 1780, p.295.
15. See *Archaeologia*, Vol VII, 'A Disquisition on the Lows or Barrows in the Peak of Derbyshire, particularly that capital British Monument called Arbelows'.
16. *Correspondence of Hayman Rooke*, f.76.
17. S. Pegge, *Sketch of the history of Bolsover and Peak Castles … illustrated with various drawings by H. Rooke,* London, 1785, and *An historical account of Beauchief Abbey*, London, 1801.
18. S. Glover, *History and Gazetteer of the County of Derby*, *op.cit.*, Vol. I, p.66.
19. G.A. Lester, 'Thomas Bateman, barrow opener', *Derbyshire Archaeological Journal* XCIII, 1973, pp.10-22. Bateman was not an FSA but a member of the newly formed British Archaeological Association. In its *Journal* he published his articles. His two most important works are *Vestiges of the Antiquities of Derbyshire*, London, 1848, and *Ten years' 'Diggings'*, London, 1861.
20. L. Jewitt, Thomas Bateman's obituary, *Reliquary II* (1861-62), pp.87-97.
21. Sandby's oil painting is in the collection of the Society of Antiquaries and a watercolour is in Derby Museum and Art Gallery. An engraving of the former painting was published in Francis Grose's *Antiquities of England*

and Wales, 6 vols., 1773-77.

22. J. Mordaunt Crook, 'John Carter and the mind of the Gothic Revival', Vol. 17 of occasional papers from the *Society of Antiquaries of London*, 1995, p.31.

23. Buckler's sketch book is in the British Library, Add. Ms. 36361 61B. Further drawings of Bakewell church are in Add. Mss 36979 and 36401. The first sketch book also contains drawings of Ashbourne Church, Kedleston Church and Hall, Haddon Hall, Hardwick Old and New Halls. Sketches of Wingfield Manor, Youlgreave and Brassington churches are dated 1830.

24. J.T. Brighton, 'The Architects' debate: the restoration of Bakewell Church', *JBDHS*, VI, 1979, pp.35-65. See also J.T. Brighton, 'Architectural Drawings for the restoration of All Saints Church, Bakewell', *JBDHS*, IV, 1977, pp.19-42.

25. The Turner drawings are in his *Worcester and Shrewsbury Sketchbook* (1829-30) pp.30a, 31 and 31a in the Tate Gallery. The Revd Jean Louis Petit's sketches are in Buxton Art Gallery and the Victoria and Albert Museum (watercolour 93 c18). A copy of Morison's lithograph is in the Old House Museum, Bakewell.

26. 'The Architects' Debate …' *op.cit.*, pp.50-1.

27. On Bateman's death some of the items were purchased by Weston Park Museum, Sheffield; others were returned to the church.

28. 'William Flockton's lecture to the Society of Antiquaries, 1842', *JBDHS*, No. VII, 1980, pp.48-65.

29. By Weightman and Hadfield of Sheffield and by G.G. Scott the younger.

CHAPTER 10 – THE SATANIC MILLS AND THEIR SECRETS

1. For an account of the mill see H E Bullerton, *Silk Mill*, 1991.

2. F.D. Klingender, *Art and the Industrial Revolution*, edited and revised A. Elton, 1968, pp.10-11.

3. H.E. Bullerton, 'For Arkwright read Lombe'. Chapter 10 of *The Seven Blunders of the Peak*, ed. B. Robinson, Cromford, 1994.

4. Defoe, *A Tour …* 4th Edn., 1748.

5. J.G. Macqueen, 'An unpublished 18th century poem on the Derby Silk Mill', *Derbyshire Miscellany*, Vol. 10, Spring 1985, pt 5, pp.146-9.

6. Stephen Glover tells us 'these premises were occupied for many years by Mr Swift who made many additions to the machinery'. *History of the Borough of Derby*, 1843, p.77.

7. N. Scarfe, *op.cit.*, p.38.

8. *Ibid.*, p.39.

9. T. Brighton, 'The Watsons: some further notes on Derbyshire's ingenious family of craftsmen', *JBDHS*, No 28, 2001, p.52. J.P. Polak, 'The production and distribution of peak millstones from the 16th to the 18th centuries', *DAJ*, CVII, 1987, pp.59 and 68.

10. His funeral procession is described by J.P. Malcolme, 'A Journey from Chesterfield to Matlock', *The Gentleman's Magazine*, Vol. 63, 1703, pp.505-6.

11. *Torrington Diaries*, I, p.40. The name of Arkwright's Castle was Willersley, not Wensley.

12. *Ibid.*, p.196.

13. N. Scarfe, *op.cit.*, p.62.

14. E. Darwin, *The Botanic Garden, 1789-1791*. He declared that 'the general design … is to enlist imagination under the banner of science'.

15. J. Egerton, *Wright of Derby*, Tate Gallery, 1990, pp.198-200 and pl.127. B. Nicholson, *Joseph Wright of Derby, Painter of Light*, 2 vols., 1968, No. 312, pl.331.

16. *Torrington Diaries*, I, p.196.

17. H. Clarke, 'The Cotton Industry of Great Longstone', *JBDHS*, 1997, No. 24, pp.35-44.

18. *Torrington Diaries*, I, p.190-1.

19. *Rhodes, op.cit.*, p.73.

20. M.H. Mackenzie, 'The Bakewell Cotton Mill and the Arkwrights' *DAJ*, LXXIX, 1959, pp.72-3. For further information on the mill *see* R. Thornhill's, 'The Arkwright cotton Mill at Bakewell' in the same volume of the *DAJ*, pp.80-7.

21. See M H Mckenzie, 'Calver Mill and its owners', *DAJ*, LXXXIII, 1963, pp.24-34, and LXXXIV; also V Parker, 'The Calver Mill Buildings', LXXXIII, pp 35-8.

22. Mary Sterndale was one such writer; see J. Bunting, 'Give a Man a Good Name', Chapter 4 in *The Seven Blunders of the Peak* (ed. B. Robinson, 1994). Bunting discusses the reputation of William Newton and the paeans of praise lavished on him by Sterndale.

23. Rhodes, *op.cit.*, pp.113 and 115.

24. *Ibid.*, p.114.

25. *Ibid.*
26. *Ibid.*, p.112
27. For a description of Cressbrook and Litton mills and the debate about the reputations of William Newton and Ellis Needham see the following:
    i.   M.H. Mackenzie, 'Cressbrook and Litton Mills, 1779-1835', 1968, part 1, *DAJ*, LXXXVIII, pp.1-25.
    ii. 'Cressbrook Mill 1810-1835', *DAJ*, XC 1970, pp.60-71.
    iii. 'Cressbrook and Litton Mills: a reply', *DAJ*, XC 1970, pp.56-9.
    iv. S.D. Chapman, 'Cressbrook and Litton Mills: an alternative view', *DAJ*, LXXXIX, 1969, pp.86-90.

CHAPTER 11 – GATEWAY TO THE SPAS

1. *Four topographical letters written in July 1755 upon a journey thro … Derbyshire … etc. From a gentleman of London to his brother and sister in Town.* Newcastle upon Tyne, 1757, p.42.
2. Anon., *The Matlocks and their past.* Derbyshire County Library, 1977.
3. Defoe, *op.cit.*, pp.461-2.
4. Rhodes, *op.cit.*, pp.89-90.
5. Cited by A.E. Dodd and E.M. Dodd, *op.cit.*, p.125.
6. Davies, *op.cit.*, p.504 *et seq.*
7. Warner, *op.cit.*, p.140.
8. Young, *op.cit.*, p.211.
9. Cited in Davies, *op.cit.*, pp.468-9.
10. For details on Ecton Mine see J.A. Robey and L. Porter, *The Copper and Lead Mines of Ecton Hill, Staffordshire,* Moorland Publishing Co. And Peak District Mines Historical Society, 1972.
11. T. Althin, 'Eric Geisler and his journey abroad of 1772', *Med. Hammare och Fackla,* XXVI, 1972.
12. See I. Hall, *Georgian Buxton, a sketch of Buxton's architectural history in Georgian times,* Derbyshire Museum Service, 1984.
13. N. Pevsner, *The Buildings of England: Derbyshire*, London, 1986, p.114.
14. *Torrington Diaries* I, pp.186-7.
15. J.M.W. Turner's Worcester and Shrewsbury Sketch Book, ff.56a and 58, Tate Gallery, London.
16. These are the comments from two of Arbuthnot's letters in BL Add. MSS vol. 3559, ff.229 and 251. They are cited by J. Black, 'Buxton in 1787', *Derbyshire Miscellany*, vol. 10, Spring 1985, pt. 5, pp.145-6.
17. *Torrington Diaries* I, pp.186-7.
18. L. Jewitt, *op.cit.*, pp.148-9.
19. Bodleian Library, *Lady Macartney's Accounts of her Expenses at Buxton*, Ms. Eng. Misc. e880.
20. Dr Johnson's Birthplace Museum, Lichfield. *Letter of Anna Seward to Mary Powys, 22nd October, 1808.* Ms 38/23.
21. Sir George Head, *op.cit.*, pp.95-6.
22. T. Brighton, 'An early 18th century landscape and garden in the Peak District', *Journal of Garden History*, Vol.4 No.4, 1983, p.362.
23. J. Lowe, 'The Town of Bakewell in Derbyshire Described', *The Royal Magazine,* 1765, pp.234-7.
24. 'A Journal of a Three Week Tour in 1797 through Derbyshire and the Lakes', cited in Mavor, *British Tourists,* Vol.5, p.224.
25. For details of White Watson see E.R. Meeke, *White Watson 1760-1835*, privately printed 1996 (Matlock Local Studies Library).
26. W. Watson, *The Strata of Derbyshire*, Sheffield, 1811, pp.35-6.
27. See S. Glover, *History & Gazetteer of the County of Derby,*Vol.2 (1829), pp.225-6.

CHAPTER 12 – THE RISE, DECLINE AND RISE OF CHATSWORTH

1. Many visitors to the house came to see the wood carvings by Grinling Gibbons as described by Horace Walpole and others. However, it has now been shown that Gibbons never worked there. See T. Brighton, 'Samuel Watson, not Grinling Gibbons at Chatsworth'. *The Burlington Magazine,* Dec. 1998, pp.811-18; also 'A monument to Samuel Watson', *JBDHS,* No. 26, 1999, pp.34-56.
2. J.E. Heath, 'A Bishop's Summer Journey into the East Midlands in 1708', *Derbyshire Miscellany,* vol. 9, Autumn 1980, p.44.
3. T. Brighton, 'Haddon Hall Gardens', *Journal of Garden History,* Vol. 6, No. 3, 1986, pp.247-50.
4. For a reconstruction of the floor plans of Elizabethan Chatsworth on which the new Chatsworth was based see M. Girouard, 'Elizabethan Chatsworth', *Country Life,* Nov. 22, 1973, p.1668 *et seq. See also* T. Brighton, 'Elizabethan Chatsworth and its 1601 Inventory', *JBDHS,* No. 29, 2002, pp.15-50.

5.   Cotton, *op.cit.*, p.93.
6.   *Ibid.*, p.88.
7.   *Illustrated Journeys of Celia Fiennes, op.cit.*, p.106.
8.   *Ibid.*, p.106.
9.   *Ibid.*, p.105.
10. Defoe, *A Tour ...* p.475.
11. Anon., *Iter Boreale. or a Journey into the Peakes,* No. 97 of the MSS of E.P. Shirley of Ettingham Hall, Warwicks. See HMC Report, Vol.V, 1876, p.366.
12. S. Markham, *op.cit.*, p.193. The Thornhill paintings are now fixed to the ceiling of the Theatre.
13. A. Young, *op.cit.*, vol. 1, p.213.
14. Chatsworth MSS 644; cited in A. Foreman, *Georgiana, Duchess of Devonshire,* London, 1998, p.28.
15. 'Notes Queries and Gleanings', The *Reliquary,* April 1864, p.249.
16. T. Cunningham (ed.), *The Letters of Horace Walpole,* London, 1891, Vol. III, p.337.
17. J. Boswell, *Life of Johnson, op.cit.*, p.844.
18. 'Horace Walpole's Journals of Visits to Country Seats, etc.' *Walpole Society,* Vol. XVI (1927-28), p.65.
19. A. Young, *op.cit.*, p.212.
20. *Torrington Diaries* I, pp.37-8. Vanbrugh did not design the chapel.
21. E. Rhodes, *op.cit.*, p.151.

CHAPTER 13 – HADDON AWAKES

1.   The date of the marriage of Dorothy Vernon and John Manners is unknown. It probably took place in the early 1560s and certainly before the death of her father, Sir George, in 1565.
2.   T. Brighton, 'In search of Mediaeval Chatsworth', *JBDHS,* 1996, No. 22, p.22.
3.   Haddon was spared an account of the Earl of Rutland's loyalty to Parliament.
4.   *Illustrated Journeys of Celia Fiennes, op.cit.*, p.107.
5.   T. Brighton, 'Haddon Hall Gardens: facts and fancies', *Journal of Garden History,* Vol.6, No. 3, 1986, p.252.
6.   *Ibid.*
7.   'Haddon Hall Gardens ...', *loc.cit.*
8.   Much of the superfluous furniture at Haddon was sold, left to rot in barns or reduced to firewood. G. Le Blanc Smith, *Haddon* (1906), p.77.
9.   *Torrington Diaries* I, p.44.
10. P. Cunningham (ed.), *Letters of Horace Walpole,* vol. 3 (1891), p.338.
11. E. King, 'Observations on Ancient Castles', *Archaeologia,* VI (1782).
12. T. Gray, *The Traveller's Companion in a Tour through England and Wales,* London, 1773, p.23.
13. E. Rhodes, *op.cit.*, p.147. He claimed, wrongly, that she was 'a native of Derbyshire' and 'often visited Haddon Hall for the purpose of storing her mind with those romantic ideas, and impressing upon it those sublime and awful pictures which she so much delighted to pourtray: some of the most gloomy scenery of her *Mysteries of Udolpho* was studied within the walls of this ancient structure'.
14. What Scott knew about the Peak was minimal. In *Peveril of the Peak* he mentions the odd local feature such as Elden Hole, but his footnote to a description of a passage linking the chapel and the kitchen at the fictional Martindale Castle is pure invention: 'This peculiar collocation of apartments may be seen at Haddon Hall ... where, in the lady's pew in the chapel, there is a sort of scuttle, which opens into the kitchen, so that the good lady could ever and anon, without much interruption of her religious duties, give an eye that roast-meat was not permitted to burn, and that the turnbroche did his duty.'
15. J.M.W. Turner, *Worcester and Shrewsbury Sketchbook,* Tate Gallery, London, pp.24-30.
16. British Library, Add MS 36361, 61B.
17. R. Lockett, *David Cox 1783-1859,* Birmingham Museum and Art Gallery. Bicentenary Exhibition Catalogue, 1983, pp.29-33. *See* De Wint's sketchbook (1842) in the Victoria and Albert Museum.
18. The print is inscribed 'Drawn on the stone by Rayner from a drawing by Oakley. Printed by Lefevre and Kohler, Newman Street, Oxford'.
19. *Torrington Diaries* I, p.44.
20. W. Watson, *A Tour of Haddon Hall ... in September 1805.* Printed in *JBDHS,* 10 (1983), pp.64-7.
21. *Torrington Diaries* I, pp.43-4.
22. *See* A. Cunningham, *Tales of the English and Scottish Peasantry* and 'The King of the Peak, a Derbyshire Tale', *London Magazine,* March 1822.
23. *Haddon Hall,* the libretto by Sydney Grundy, sets the Dorothy Vernon story in the time of the Civil War!
24. P. Zenner, *The Shakespeare Invention,* Bakewell, 1999, pp.103-5.

CHAPTER 14 – EARLY CONCEPTS OF LANDSCAPE: DRAWINGS, PAINTINGS AND PRINTS

1. G. Vertue, 'Notebooks' 1-6, *The Walpole Society*, Vols 18, 20, 22, 24, 26, 29 & 30, 1930-55, I, p.23.
2. R. Tyler, *Francis Place, 1647-1728*, York Art Gallery, 1971, p.21.
3. T. Brighton, *Henry Gyles, Virtuoso and Glasspainter of York, 1645-1709*, Yorkshire Architectural and York Archaeological Society, 1984, p.9.
4. Tyler, *op. cit.*, pl. 73.
5. Vertue, Vols 1, p.75; 2, p.35 and 6, p.71.
6. M. Clarke, *The Tempting Prospect: a social history of English Watercolours*, British Museum, 1981, p.30.
7. T.H. Fokker, *Jan Siberechts, peintre de la paysanne flamande*, Bruxelles et Paris, 1931, pp.10-11.
8. Rijksmuseum, Amsterdam. Printroom Inv. No. 13-58, Fokker, *op.cit.*, pl. 43, dates the sketch 1694.
9. Catalogue by E. Croft-Murray and P. Hulton, *British Drawings*, British Museum, 1960. Vol. 1, No. 2, p.477 and Vol. II, p.259.
10. Collection Frits Lugt, Paris, Inv. No. 9335. See *Flemish Drawings of the 17th century*, catalogue of exhibition at the Victoria and Albert Museum, 1972, pl. 101; pp.123-4.
11. Fokker, *op cit.*, pl. 38.
12. W.G. Constable, *Richard Wilson*, London, 1953, p.172, pl. 31b. J. Harris disagrees with Constable's attribution in *The Artist and the Country House*, London, 1970, pp.75 and 172.
13. Fokker, *op cit.*, p.11.
14. J. Harris and G. Jackson-Stops (eds.), *Britannia Illustrata*, 1984; introduction, pp.6-7.
15. Private Collection (see plate 79, p.151).
16. F. Thompson, 'A Lost Painting of Chatsworth', *Country Life*, 26 March 1952, p.915. The smoke is not from Calver leadmine but from the lime kilns at Stoney Middleton. S.W. Bray, cited by Thompson in *A History of Chatsworth*, p.100.
17. F. Thompson, *A History of Chatsworth*, p.190.
18. L. Binyon, *Catalogue of Drawings by British Artists and artists of foreign origin working in Great Britain … in the British Museum*, IV 1907, p.188.
19. Thornhill's Sketchbook, 1699, British Library, MS 595602 f.16r.
20. Ibid.
21. *Ibid.*, f.18
22. *Ibid.*, f.17 and f.17r. There is also one Derbyshire sketch from outside the Peak. It is a distant view of Wingfield Manor (f.l6r).
23. Bodleian Library, Ms Gough Maps, 4 fol 31r. *The Devils Arse 'th Peak drawn from ye life July 22nd, 1707, by J Thornhill.*
24. There is only one topographical view by Thornhill, that of Castleton, surviving on the ceiling of the Theatre. There are some imaginary landscapes by Thornhill together with architectural paintings by Louis Chéron.
25. *See* R Raines, 'Peter Tillemans' life and work with a list of representative paintings', *The Walpole Society*, vol. 47 (1978-80). Tillemans also drew a number of views for a proposed history of Northamptonshire. *See* B.A. Bailey (ed.), *Northamptonshire in the early 18th century. The Drawings of Peter Tillemans and others*, Northampton, 1996.
26. Bodleian Library: *Pools hole in Derybsh'* [*sic*] *26th July 1725*, Ms Top. Gen. d 14 f.18r; *Prospect of Buxton July 27 1725, Ibid.* f.19r; *The Cascade at Chatsworth July 26 1725, Ibid.* f.18r.
27. Sheffield City Library, Local Collection, Bagshawe MS 779.
28. There is a signed ink, sepia and wash drawing by Samuel Buck in Buxton Museum and Art Gallery. It is inscribed *The South View of Alfreton in the County of Derbyshire 29 June 1727*. It is labelled 'seat of Rowland Morewood Esq'.'
29. E. Miller, *Landscape Prints by Francis Vivares 1709-1780*, exhibition in the Prints Gallery of the Victoria and Albert Museum, 1992. Review by L. Herrmann, Journal of the Royal Society of Arts, March 1992, pp.274-5.
30. The poet, Thomas Gray, met Smith, Vivares and William Bellers painting Gordale Scar in Yorkshire. J. Dixon Hunt, *The Figure in the Landscape*, John Hopkins UP, 1976, p.166.
31. For information on Boydell *see* H.A. Bruntjen, *John Boydell 1719-1804. A study of Art Patronage and Publishing in Georgian London*, New York 1985; also K. Garlick and A. Macintyre (eds.), *The Diary of Joseph Farington*, Yale UP, 1978, II pp.1414-15. H.A. Bruntjen, *John Boydell … p.38.*

CHAPTER 15 – A PLETHORA OF ARTISTS

1. For comprehensive coverage of Wright's Derbyshire landscapes *see* B. Nicholson, *Joseph Wright of Derby: Painter of Light*, 2 vols, London, 1968 and J. Egerton, *Wright of Derby*, Tate Gallery Exhibition catalogue, 1990.
2. *The Diary of Joseph Farington, op.cit.*, I p.685.

3. Pilkington, *op.cit.*, p.25.

4. Mrs Thrale's letter to Dr Johnson, 17 July 1770. R. W. Chapman (ed.), *The Letters of Samuel Johnson*, Oxford, 1952, vol. 1, p.242.

5. D. Cosgrove and S. Daniels (eds.), *The Iconography of Landscape*, CUP, 1988, Chapter 6 by D. Fraser, 'Fields of radiance: the scientific and industrial scenes of Joseph Wright', pp.124-7.

6. The pair is now in a private collection. The former was illustrated in *Landscape in Britain c.1750-1850*. Tate Gallery Exhibition catalogue, 1973, p.50, pl. 83. Davies (*A New Historical and Descriptive view of Derbyshire, op.cit.*) attributed these landscapes at Kedleston to Zuccarelli.

7. See K. Sloan, 'A Cozens Album in the National Library of Wales, Aberystwyth', *Walpole Society* vol. LVII, 1993-94.

8. L. Hermann, *Paul and Thomas Sandby*, London, 1986, pp.43-5. Thomas Sandby kept a journal of a *Tour through part of Yorkshire and Derbyshire*. This includes drawings of Derbyshire scenes including Peak Cavern, *ibid.*, p.57.

9. *Barber and Hofland's Views ... from original drawings taken on the Spot ... engraved by J. Bluck ... Nottingham: printed by E. B. Robinson in the Poultry and published by T. Barber and T. Hofland, MDCCCV.*

10. If Thomas Girtin came to the Peak little evidence of his work there has survived. The Victoria and Albert Museum possesses a watercolour of *A House at Winster, Derbyshire* which is attributed to him (157 − 1890). John Sell Cotman does not appear to have visited the Peak, though others of the Norwich School did. John Crome exhibited Matlock scenes at the Norwich Society Exhibition in 1811. He was probably accompanied on his tour of the Peak by his brother-in-law, Robert Ladbrooke, who exhibited *A view near Buxton* at the Royal Academy in 1812. Peter de Wint's visits are well represented by oils, watercolours and drawings of Haddon, Youlgreave, Wingfield Manor etc in the Victoria and Albert Museum.

11. F.A. Barrett and A.L. Thorpe, *Derby Porcelain,* 2nd edn, Cirencester, 1973, pp.56-8.

12. *Ibid.*, pp.81-2, 92-3 and colour plate F1.

13. The original painting of Beauchief Abbey is in the collections of the Society of Antiquaries of London. Another is in Derby Museum and Art Gallery. The view of Chatsworth was taken from an oil painting (F. Thompson, *A History of Chatsworth*, p.100 and pl.39) and was engraved by Michael Angelo Rooker, 1775 and W. Walls, 1780. It appeared in the *Ladies' Magazine* and other journals.

14. L. Hermann, *op.cit.*, pp.54-6 and fig.18. A watercolour by Sandby, *View in Sir Nigel Gresley's Park*, is in Derby Museum and Art Gallery. Drakelow Hall was demolished in 1934 and the painted wall was acquired by the Victoria and Albert Museum where it can still be seen in the Costume Court.

15. E. Rhodes, *op.cit.*, p.19.

16. L. Hermann, *Turner Prints: the Engraved work of J.M.W. Turner*, Oxford, 1990, p.11 and pls. 3 and 4. See also Hermann's amended version of W.G. Rawlinson's list of Turner's engravings, *ibid.*, p.260.

17. Moore also published *Picturesque Excursions from Derby to Matlock Bath and its vicinity: being a descriptive Guide ... Illustrated with twelve etchings by H M* (Derby, 1818). Engravings of Derby by him were also included in Glover's *History of Derby* (1829).

18. *The Diary of Joseph Farington, op.cit.*, I, p.1593. His pen, ink and wash sketch, *High Tor, Matlock Bath* (Bradford Art Galleries and Museum) was almost certainly made on this tour in 1791 and is related to his sketchbook of the tour in the Victoria and Albert Museum (p.81-1921). See *Joseph Farington: watercolours and drawings*, Exhibition Catalogue, Bolton Museum and Art Gallery, 1977. His *West of England and Derbyshire Sketchbook, 1810-1812* is in the Victoria and Albert Museum (p.71-1921).

19. Turner's *Matlock* sketch book (1794), Tate Gallery, TB XIX, p.4.

20. *The Diary of Joseph Farington, op.cit.*, I, p.1591.

21. See R. Sappien, *Philippe Jacques de Loutherbourg, RA.* Catalogue of Exhibition at Kenwood House, pubd. by The Greater London Council, 1973, Introduction.

22. H. N. Greatorex, 'The Wonders of Derbyshire: a setting for a Drury Lane Pantomime', *Derbyshire Life and Countryside*, vol. 40, No. 72, Dec. 1975, p.55.

23. *Ibid.*

24. Two maquettes relating to this pantomime are of the inside of Peak Cavern. See *Landscape in Britain c.1750-1850*, *op.cit.*, p.67.

25. T. Brighton, 'John Constable's sketching tour of the Peak in 1801', *op.cit.*, p.69.

26. *Matlock* sketch book, *op.cit.*, p.4.

27. M. Butlin and E. Joll, *The Paintings of J.M.W. Turner*, 2 vols, London 1977. Revised edn, 1986, No. 240, p.246.

28. For the way Holworthy discovered this isolated estate see his *Book of Memoranda* in Derby Central Library, MS 9668.

29. J. Gage (ed.), *Collected Correspondence of J.M.W. Turner*, Oxford, 1980. See p.2601 for brief notes on Holworthy and index of Turner's letters to him. A further letter to Holworthy in 1821 is printed in J. Gage, 'Further

Correspondence of J.M.W.Turner', *Turner Studies*,Vol.6, No.1, Summer 1986, p.2. The correspondence extended until 7 Nov. 1830 and contains no evidence to suggest Turner had visited him at Hathersage by that date.

30. These were published as lithographs in *The History and Antiquities of Haddon Hall*, London, 1867.

31. Morrison was more highly esteemed in his own day. The Prince Consort, for instance, commissioned him to produce a similar folio of the Palaces and Hunting Lodges of Saxe-Coburg and Gotha.

32. Cox loved three Derbyshire houses in particular, Bolsover Castle, Hardwick Hall and Haddon Hall. The last was his favourite which he referred to as 'dear old Haddon'. He and Copley Fielding illustrated L. A. Twamley's *An Autumn Ramble by the Wye* (1838). He particularly enjoyed staying at the *Peacock Inn* at Rowsley from where he would have his midday meal sent over to the Great Hall at Haddon where he could ponder on the ancient feasts held there. See R. Lockett's introduction to *David Cox 1783-1859*, Bicentenary Exhibition Catalogue, Birmingham Museum and Art Gallery, 1983, pp.29-33.

33. A criticism of Nash, as of Morison, was that he accurately portrayed the architecture as it was but often peopled the scene with figures in costume of an indeterminate period. Thus, in Haddon's banqueting hall, he records post-medieval panelling and a bad 18th-century replacement roof, whilst his figures are part medieval and part early Tudor in their dress.

34. This picture, privately owned, was painted in 1861 and published as a front cover to Sheridan le Fanu's *Uncle Silas*, OUP, 1981.

35. J. Mordaunt-Crook and C.A. Lennox-Boyd, *Axel Haig and the Victorian Vision of the Middle Ages*, London, 1984, p.28; pl. 33.

CHAPTER 16 – WRITERS IN THE DALES

1. *Torrington Diaries* I, p.49.
2. J. Boswell, *Life of Johnson*, op.cit., p.860.
3. *Ibid.*, p.838.
4. *Ibid.*, pp.865-6.
5. Rev. D.P. Davies, op.cit., p.434.
6. J. Boswell, *op.cit.*, p.600.
7. P. Toynbee and L. Whitley (eds.), *Correspondence of Thomas Gray*,Vol. II, p.785.
8. *Ibid.*, vol III, p.964.
9. T. Gray, *The Traveller's Companion, in a Tour through England and Wales, containing a catalogue of the Antiquities, Houses, Parks, Plantations, Scenes and Situations ...* London, 1773, pp.21-45 (Derbyshire).
10. Rev. D.P. Davies, *op.cit.*, p.440 (citing *Correspondence avec M Peyron*, Tom. II, Lettre 45).
11. J. Boswell, *op.cit.*, p.359.
12. Rhodes, p.327.
13. B. Barr and J. Ingamells, *A Candidate for Praise; William Mason 1725-97, Precentor of York*, York Art Gallery and York Minster Library, 1973, pp.35-6 and 72.
14. J. Egerton, *op.cit.*, pl. 59; pp.116-18.
15. W.J.B. Owen and J. Worthington Smyser (eds.), *The Prose Works of William Wordsworth*,Vol. 1, 1974, pp.5, 10-11 and 15.
16. K.R. Johnstone, *The Hidden Wordsworth*, 2000, p.103.
17. Some maintain the reference is to the River Dove in Yorkshire or that in Cumbria.
18. A.G. Hill (ed.), *Letters of William and Dorothy Wordsworth*,Vol. II, 1979, pp.417 and 432.
19. A woodcut of Moore's curious cottage appears in *The History and Topography of Ashbourne ...* (Anon.) 1839, p.209.
20. *Ibid.* citing Moore's *Life of Byron*.
21. *The River Dove : a lyric pastoral.*
22. J. Edwards, *The Tour of the Dove, a Poem*, 1821 (Dedicated to Jesse Watts Russell, Esq, MP, of Ilam Hall).
23. *The Works of the Late Edward Dayes: containing an excursion through the Principal Parts of Derbyshire and Yorkshire*, London, 1805, p.10.
24. Rev. D.P. Davies, *op.cit.*, p.433.
25. William Gilpin's comments on the Peak and Dovedale are chiefly found in Section XXIX of *Observations, Relative Chiefly to Picturesque Beauty, Made in the Year 1772, on Several Parts of England ...* 2 vols. London, 1786.
26. E.D. Mackerness, 'The Harvest of Failure: Ebenezer Rhodes (1762-1839)', *DAJ*, CI, 1981, p.112.
27. Tate Gallery, Turner Collection, Sketchbook (TB, I,H).
28. *Ibid.* Worcester and Shrewsbury Sketchbook (TB CCXXXIX).
29. Rhodes, pp.28-9.
30. W. Adam, *op.cit.*, pp.339-40.

31. *Ibid.*, pp.173-4.
32. cf Adam, *ibid.*
33. Rhodes, pp.137-9.
34. A.G. Hill (ed.), *The Letters of William and Dorothy Wordsworth*, 2nd Edn, Vol V, 'The Later Years', Part II (1829-1834), Oxford, 1979, p.353.
35. E. De Selincourt and H Darbishire (eds.), *The Poetical works of William Wordsworth*, OUP, 1954, pp.49 and 434.
36. *Ibid. See* T. Brighton, 'Wordsworth in Derbyshire', *JBDHS*, No. 19, 1992, pp.35-42.
37. J. Ruskin, *Fors Clavigera*, Letter 4, 7 April 1884.

CHAPTER 17 – THE END OF THE IDYLL

1. The portrait hangs in the National Gallery, Prague. *See* Egerton, *op cit.*, pp.87-91 and pl. 40. Burdett also appears in *The Orrery* by Wright (Derby City Art Gallery), *ibid.*, p.18 and fig.14.
2. *Derby Mercury*, 24 April 1767. *See* J.B. Harley, D.V. Fowkes and J.C. Harvey (introduction), *Burdett's Map of Derbyshire*, Derbyshire Archaeological Society, 1975.
3. *Torrington Diaries* I, p.195.
4. R. Furness, *Medicus – Magus*, Sheffield, 1836, p.34.
5. J. Ruskin, *Fors Clavigera*, 5 Vols, 1871-84; Letter, 8 June 1871.
6. Ref. R. Ward, *A Guide to the Peak of Derbyshire,* 7th edn, Birmingham (nd), p.44.
7. Rev. D.P. Davies, *op.cit.*, p.468.
8. Ruskin, *op.cit.*, 1 May 1871.
9. R. Keene, 'A Six Days' Ramble over Derbyshire Hills and Dales in the Year 1858', *DAJ*, VI, 1884, pp.111-12.
10. H. Lees-Milne, *The Bachelor Duke*, London, 1991, p.211.
11. Adam, *op.cit.*, p.297.
12. Ruskin, *loc.cit.*
13. *Ibid.* Letter 7, 13 April 1884.

CHAPTER 18 – FREEDOM TO ROAM

1. For the latest study of the outdoor movement see H. Taylor, *A Claim on the Countryside. A History of the British Outdoor Movement*, Keele University Press, 1997.
2. J. Croston, *On Foot through the Peak*, 3rd Edition, Manchester, 1876.
3. H. Taylor, *op.cit.*, chapter 7, 'A substantive Interwar Outdoor Movement'.
4. *See* D. Sissons (ed.), *The Best of the Sheffield Clarion Ramblers' Handbooks: 'Ward's Piece'*, Tiverton, 2002.
5. A. Mee, *The King's England: Derbyshire, the Peak Country*. London, 1937, reprinted 1990, pp.110-11.
6. W.A. Poucher, *The Backbone of England*, London, 1946, p.98.
7. E.A. Baker, *Moors, Crags and Caves of the High Peak and Neighbourhood*, London (n d), pp.19-20.
8. P. Mandler, *The Fall and Rise of the Stately Home*, YUP, 1997, pp.248-50.
9. *Ibid.* p.249.
10. T. Brighton, 'The Battle for the Haddon Footpaths in 1924', *Journal of the Bakewell and District Historical Society*, No. 23, 1996.
11. R. Smith, 'Forgive us our Trespassers', Chapter 6 of *The Seven Blunders of the Peak*, B. Robinson (ed.), Wirksworth, 1994.

CHAPTER 19 – BRITAIN'S FIRST NATIONAL PARK

1. M. Langham and C. Wells, *The Architect of Victorian Buxton: A Biography of Robert Ripon Duke*, Derbyshire Library Service, 1996, pp.173-91.
2. *Ibid.*, pp.197-200.
3. Anon., *Famous Derbyshire Health Resorts. The Matlocks and Bakewell*, Brighton, 1893, pp.12-21.
4. A. Mee, *op.cit.*, pp.184-5.
5. *First Annual Report of the Peak Park Planning Board,* November 1951 to April 1953, pp.1-2.
6. *The National Trust Handbook*, March 2004 to February 2005, pp.224-5 and 233, 235, 237.

Bibliographical and other Sources

I. Primary Sources: manuscripts, drawings, prints and paintings

A. Bakewell Old House Museum: prints by Vivares, Morison and Godfrey. Ashford marble exhibition.

B. Birmingham Museums and Art Gallery: sketches and watercolours of Haddon Hall and the surrounding area by David Cox.

C. Bodleian Library, Oxford: Lady Macartney's Accounts of her Expenses at Buxton. Ms Eng Misc e880. Sketches and notes by William Stukeley, Sir James Thornhill etc.

D. British Library, London: poems by Richard Andrews on Derbyshire Country Houses and Poole's Cavern (1630s), Harl. Ms 4955. Sir James Thornhill's sketchbook, 1699, Ms 595602, J C Buckler's sketchbooks 1812-1820, Add Mss 36361 (61B), 36401 & 36979.

E. Buxton Museum and Art Gallery: sketches, paintings and prints by de Loutherbourg, Petit, R. Reinagle etc. Ashford marble exhibition.

F. Chatsworth House Library: William Senior's *Book of Surveys*, c. 1617. Christopher Saxton, *Atlas*. White Watson, *Collections for a History of Derbyshire*, 4 vols. Paintings, prints and drawings by Siberechts, Knijff and Kip, T. Smith, Tillemans, Wyatville, etc.

G. Derbyshire Archaeological Society's Library, Derby. An anonymous sketchbook of Peakland scenes and watercolour, prints and paintings of Derbyshire. 1786-87.

H. Derbyshire County Record Office, Matlock: collection of paintings, prints and photographs.

I. Derby City Library (Local Studies): collection of prints and photographs.

J. Derby City Museum and Art Gallery: sketches and paintings by Farington, T. Smith, Wright etc.

K. Fitzwilliam Museum, Cambridge: works by Cox, Crome, Cumberland and Wright.

L. Lichfield, Dr Johnson's Birthplace Museum: letter of Anna Seward to Mary Powys, 22 October 1808. Ms 38/23.

M. Manchester, Whitworth Art Gallery: sketch by Constable. Watercolour by John Webber.

N. Národni Galerie, Prague: Joseph Wright's portrait of Peter Perez Burdett and wife.

O. Peak Park Planning Board, Aldern House, Bakewell. Photographic archive.

P. Rijksmuseum, Amsterdam. Jan Siberecht's watercolour of Chatsworth Park.

Q. Sheffield Museums and Art Galleries: prints and paintings by Chantrey, Creswick, De Wint, J.M.W. Turner etc.

R. Sheffield City Library (Local Collections): early 18th-century letters, poems and landscape sketches concerning the Peak among the Eyre papers. Bagshawe Mss 313, 314 and 779.

S. Statens Museum for Kunst, Copenhagen. Sketches by Constable in Dovedale.

T.   Society of Antiquaries of London: prints and drawings by Basire, Carter, Godfrey, Rooke, P. Sandby etc. in the Red and the Brown Portfolios.
U.   Tate Gallery, London: sketchbooks by J.M.W. Turner:
XIX (Matlock sketchbook)
XXXIV (North of England sketchbook)
CCXXIX (Worcester and Shrewsbury sketchbook)
Joseph Wright, Portrait of Brook Boothby.
V.   Victoria and Albert Museum, London: sketches and paintings by Constable, de Wint, Farington, Nash etc.

1. PRIMARY SOURCES IN PRINT

Adam, W., *Gem of the Peak,* London, 1845
—, *Description of Buxton, Chatsworth, Haddon Hall and Castleton* (abridged from *Gem of the Peak*), Derby, n.d.
Aikin, Dr J., *A Description of the High Peak*, London, 1800
Anon., *A Description of Buxton and the adjacent country*, Manchester, 1799
—, *Famous Derbyshire Health Resorts. The Matlocks and Bakewell,* Brighton, 1893
—, *Four Topographical Letters written in July 1755,* Newcastle on Tyne, 1757
—, *Journal of a Three Weeks Tour in 1797 through Derbyshire to the Lakes by a Gentleman of the University of Oxford,* paraphrased in Vol. 5 of William Mavor's *The British Tourists: or Traveller's Pocket Companion* … 6 volumes, London 1798-1800
—, *Letters Home; or sketches by the Way. Being a series of consolatory epistles to Beatrice during a short ramble in Derbyshire by her next and most faithful friend, Benedict.* Oldham, 1838
—, *A Treatise on the Nature and Virtues of Buxton Waters … by a Physician*, London, 1761
—, *A Month at Buxton; or, a description of the town and neighbourhood*, 14th edn, Bakewell, 1829
—, *The History and Topography of Ashbourn and the Valley of the Dove*, 1839.
Barker, E.A., *Moors, Crags and Caves of the High Peak and Neighbourhood*, London (n.d.).
Barker, H., *The Panorama of Matlock and its environs … with the Tour of the Peak*, 2nd edn, London, 1828
Bateman, T., *Vestiges of the antiquities of Derbyshire*, London, 1848
—, *Ten Years' Digging*, London, 1861
Bentley, Rev. S., *The River Dove; a lyric Pastoral*, London, 1768
Black, A. and C., *Black's Picturesque Tourist and Road-Book of England and Wales.* Edinburgh, 1843
—, *Black's Picturesque Tourist and Road and Railway Guide Book through England and Wales*, 4th edn, Edinburgh, 1862
—, *Black's Guide to Derbyshire*, ed. L. Jewitt, Edinburgh, 1872
Boswell, J., *Life of Johnson*, ed. R. W. Chapman, Oxford UP, 1976
Boydell, J., *Eight of the most extraordinary Prospects in the most mountainous Parts of Derbyshire and Staffordshire commonly called the Peak and the Moorlands*, London, 1769
Boydell, J. and J., *The Seats of the Nobility and Gentry in a Collection of the most interesting Views, engraved by W. W. Watts from drawings by the most eminent Artists with descriptions of each view*
Bradwell, J., *A Description of Bagshawe's Cavern at Bradwell in the Peak of Derbyshire*, Manchester, 1822
Bray, W., *Sketch of a Tour into Derbyshire and Yorkshire*, London, 1778
Britton, J. and Brayley, E.W., *The Beauties of England and Wales, or Delineations Topographical, Historical and Descriptive of each County embellished with engravings.* Vol. III (Derbyshire) London, 1802
Browne, Sir T., *Journal of a Tour in Derbyshire in 1662.* In *Works* of Sir Thomas Browne. Vol. I Norwich, 1836

Buck, N. and S., *Buck's Antiquities*, London, 1772

Byng, J., *The Torrington Diaries: containing the Tours through England and Wales of the Hon. John Byng (later 5th Viscount Torrington) between the years 1781 and 1794*. Ed. C. Bruyn Andrews, 4 vols., London, 1934–38

Byrne, W., *Britannia Depicta: a series of views with brief descriptions of the most interesting and picturesque objects in Great Britain, engraved from drawings by Messrs. Hearne, Farington etc.* London, 1818

Camden, W., *Britannia, sive florentissimorum Regnorum Angliae, Scotiae, Hiberniae et Insularum adiecentium, ex intima antiquitate chorographica descriptio*, London, 1586

—, *Britannia … In English with large additions and improvements by Edmund Gibson*, London, 1695

Cary, G. S., *The Balnes, or, An Impartial Description of all the popular Watering Places in England*, London, 1799

Cattermole, G., *The History and Antiquities of Haddon Hall*, London, 1867

Cokayne, A. E., *A Day in the Peak*, 5th edn, Bakewell, 1902

Cooke, G. A., *The Modern British Traveller; or, Tourist's Pocket Directory*, Vol. IV (Derbyshire), London, 1802–1810

Cotton, C., *The Poems of Charles Cotton*, J. Buxton ed., London, 1958

Croston, J., *On Foot through the Peak*, 3rd edition, Manchester, 1876

Cunningham, A., *Tales of the English and Scottish Peasantry*, London, 1822 (including *the King of the Peak*, published anonymously in *The London Magazine*, March 1822)

Davies, Rev. D. P., *A New Historical and Descriptive View of Derbyshire from the Remotest Period to the Present Times*, Belper, 1811

Darwin, E., *The Botanic Garden*, London, 1789–91

—, *The Letters of Erasmus Darwin*, Ed. D. King Hele. Cambridge UP, 1981

Dayes, E., *The Works of the late Edward Dayes: containing an excursion through the Principal parts of Derbyshire and Yorkshire*, London, 1805

De Loutherbourg, P. J., *Picturesque Scenery of Great Britain in Colours*, London, 1801

—, *The Romantic and Picturesque Views of England and Wales*, London, 1805

Denman, Dr J., *Observations on the Effects of Buxton Water*, London, 1794

Drayton, M., *The Poems of Michael Drayton*, Ed. J. Buxton, 2 vols, London, 1967.

Edwards, J., *The Tour of the Dove, a Poem*, London, 1821

Farey, J., *A General View of the Agriculture and Minerals of Derbyshire*, 3 vols, London, 1811–1817

Farington, J., *The Diary of Joseph Farington*, Ed. K. Garlic and A. Macintyre, Vol. II, January 1795–August 1796, Yale UP, 1976

Ferguson, J., 'Description of the Devil's Cave at Castleton in the Peak of Derbyshire', *Gentleman's Magazine*, Vol. 42, 1772

Fiennes, C., *The Illustrated Journeys of Celia Fiennes c.1682–c.1712*, Ed. C. Morris, London, 1984

Floyer, J., *An Enquiry into the Right Uses and Abuses of the hot, the cold and temperate Baths in England*, London, 1697

Furness, R., *Medicus-Magus. A poem in three cantos with a glossary*, Sheffield, 1836

Gibbons, L., *The King of the Peak*, London, 1823

Gilpin, W., *Observations, Relative Chiefly to Picturesque Beauty*, 2 vols., London, 1786

Glover, S., *The Peak Guide, containing the topographical, statistical and general history of Buxton, Chatsworth, Edensor, Castleteon [sic], Bakewell, Haddon, Matlock and Cromford … ed. T. Noble*, Derby, 1820

—, *The History and Gazetteer of the County of Derby drawn up from actual observation and from the best authorities; containing a variety of geological, mineralogical, commercial and statistical information*, 2 vols. Derby, 1831–1832

Grant, J., *A London Journal of a Three Weeks' Tour in 1797, through Derbyshire into the Lakes*. Printed in W. Mavor, *The British Tourists … (q.v.* below), Vol. V, London, 1800

Gray, T., *The Traveller's Companion on a Tour through England and Wales*, London, 1773

—, *A Supplement to the Tour through Great Britain, containing a catalogue of the Antiquities Houses, Parks etc. in England and Wales*, London, 1787

Head, Sir G., *Home Tour through the Manufacturing Districts of England in the Summer of 1835*, London, 1836

Hedinger, J. M., *A Guide through Peak's Hole with a Description of the Curiosities of Castleton*, Stockport, 1805

Henricus, *The Matlock Tourist; and Guide through the Peak. Embracing Matlock Bath, Haddon, Chatsworth and Castleton*, Matlock Bath, 1838

Hobbes, J., *De Mirabilibus Pecci, being the Wonders of the Peak in Derbyshire, commonly called the Devil's Arse of Peak. In English and Latine. The Latine written by Thomas Hobbes. The English by a Person of Quality*, London, 1678

Hofland T. and Barber, T., *Six Views in Derbyshire, Four in Dovedale and Two in Matlock from Original Drawings taken on the spot by T. Hofland and T. Barber and engraved by J. Bluck*, London, 1805

Hutchinson, J., *A Tour through the High Peak of Derbyshire, Including an Account of the Natural and Subterranean Curiosities of that Country; the beautiful crystallized cavern, lately discovered at Bradwell; and the Romantic Scenery of the Woodlands, never before described*, Macclesfield, 1809

Jewitt, A., *The History of Buxton; and Visitors Guide to the Curiosities of the Peak*, London, 1811

—, *The Matlock Companion; and Visitor's Guide to the Beauties of Matlock*, Derby, 1835

Jewitt, L., *The Ballads and Songs of Derbyshire*, Derby, 1867

—, *Chatsworth*, London, 1872

Johnson, S., *The Letters of Samuel Johnson*, Ed. R. W. Chapman, 3 vols, Oxford UP, 1952

Jones, J., *The Benefit of the Ancient Bathes at Buckstones*, London, 1572

Jonson, B., *The Works of Ben Jonson*, Ed. by C. H. Herford, E. M. Simpson and P. Simpson, 11 vols, Oxford UP, 1925-52

Kip, J. and Knyff, L., *Britannia Illustrata or Views of Several of the Queen's Palaces as Also the Principal Seats of the Nobility and Gentry of Great Britain Curiously Engraven on 80 Copper Plates*, London, 1707

—, Privately published edition for members of the National Trust, Ed. by J. Harris and G. Jackson-Stops, Bungay, 1984

Langham, M. and Wells, C., *The Architect of Victorian Buxton: a Biography of Robert Rippon Duke*, Derbyshire Library Service, 1996

Leigh, L., *The Natural History of Lancashire, Cheshire and the Peak of Derbyshire*, Oxford, 1700

Lipscomb, G. A., *A Description of Matlock Bath to which is added some account of Chatsworth and Kedleston*, Birmingham, 1802

Lloyd, J., 'Eldon Hole', *Philosophical Transactions of the Royal Society*, Vol. LXI

Loveday, J., *Diary of a Tour in 1732 through Parts of England, Wales, Ireland and Scotland Made by John Loveday of Caversham. Now for the First Time Printed from a Manuscript in the Possession of his Great Grandson John Edward Taylor Loveday*, Edinburgh, 1890

—, *John Loveday of Caversham. The Life and Tours of an 18th Century Onlooker*, S. Markham, London, 1984

Lowe, J., 'The Town of Bakewell Described', *The Royal Magazine,* 1765

Lysons, D. and S., *Magna Britannia … Vol V, Topographical and Historical account of Derbyshire*, London, 1817

Malcolm, J. P., 'A Journey from Chesterfield to Matlock', *Gentleman's Magazine,* Vol. 63, 1793

Manlove, E., *The Liberties and Customs of the Lead-miners within the Wapentake of Wirksworth in the County of Derby … composed in meeter*, London, 1653

Martin, W., *Petrificata Derbiensia. Figures and Description of Petrifications collected in Derbyshire*, Wigan, 1809

Mawe, J., *The Mineralogy of Derbyshire*, London, 1802

Mee, A., *The King's England: Derbyshire, the Peak Country*, London, 1937

Moore, H., *Picturesque Excursions from Derby to Matlock Bath and its Vicinity*, Derby, 1818

—, *The Romantic Beauties of Dovedale and Ilam*, Ashbourne, 1829

—, *The Stranger's Guide, being a complete Matlock Director and Pilot to the Vicinity*, Derby, 1835

Morison, D., *Twenty Five Views of Haddon Hall*, 1842

Moritz, C. P., *A Walking Tour in England in 1782*, London, 1983

Noble, T., *The Counties of Chester, Derby, Leicester, Lincoln and Rutland illustrated from original drawings by Thomas Allom and Topographical descriptions*, London, 1836

Ogilby, J., *Britannia, Volume the First: or An Illustration of the Kingdom of England and the Dominion of Wales: by a Geographical and Historical Description of the Principal Roads thereof …* London, 1675

—, *The Traveller's Pocket-Book or Ogilby and Morgan's Book of the Roads Improved and Amended in a Method Never Before Attempted*, Fourth edn, London, 1752

Pegge, Rev. S., 'A Disquisition on the Lows or Barrows in the Peak of Derbyshire, particularly the capital British Monument called Arbelows,' *Archaeologia* Vol. VII, 1783

—, *Sketch of the History of Bolsover and Peak Castles … illustrated with various drawings by H. Rooke*, London, 1785

—, *An Historical Account of Beauchief Abbey in the County of Derby*, London, 1801

Pigot, J., *Pigot and Company's London and Provincial New Commercial Directory for 1822-3*, Manchester, 1822

Pilkington, J., *A View of the Present State of Derbyshire*, 2 vols, London, 1789

Plumptre, J., *James Plumptre's Britain; The Journal of a Tourist in the 1790's*, London, 1991

Poucher, N. A., *The Backbone of England*, London, 1946

Price, E., *Twelve Views of Dovedale and Ilam from drawings by Edward Price. With illustrative notes*, Ashbourne, 1845

Rayner, S., *History and Antiquities of Haddon Hall*, 2 vols, London and Derby, 1836

Rhodes, E., *Peak Scenery, or the Derbyshire Tourist*, London, 1824

—, *Derbyshire Tourist Guide and Travelling Companion*, London, 1837

Rooke, H., 'Illustration of some Druidical Remains in the Peak of Derbyshire', *Archaeologia*, Vol. VII, 1783

—, 'Observations on the Stanton Moor Urns and Druidical Temple', *Archaeologia*, Vol. VIII, 1784

Saint Fond, B. F. de, *Voyage en Angleterre, en Écosse et aux Iles Hébrides …* 1784. English translation, 2 vols., London, 1799, 2 vols., Glasgow, 1907

Short, Dr T., *The Natural, Experimental and Medicinal History of the Mineral Waters of Derbyshire, Lincolnshire and Yorkshire …* London, 1736

Simond, L., *Journal of a Tour and Residence in Great Britain during the years 1810 and 1811*, 2 vols., Edinburgh, 1815

—, *An American in Regency England. The Journal of a Tour in 1810-1811 by Louis Simond*, D. C. Hibbert, London, 1968

Spence, E. I., *A Summer Excursion through parts of Oxfordshire … Derbyshire and South Wales*, 2nd edn, 2 vols., London, 1809

Sterndale, M., *Vignettes of Derbyshire*, London, 1824

Stukeley, W., *Itinerarium Curiosum*, London, 1724

Sullivan, R. J., *A Tour through part of England and Wales in 1778 in a series of letters*, 2nd edn, London, 1785

Twamley, A., *An Autumn ramble by the Wye with drawings by Copley Fielding and David Cox*. London, 1838

Walton, I., *The Compleat Angler*, London, 1653, with additions by Charles Cotton in 1676, when it was published as *The Universal Angler*

Ward, R., *A Guide to the Peak of Derbyshire*, 7th edn, Birmingham, 1827

Warner, Rev. R., *A Tour through the Northern Counties of England and the Borders of Scotland*, 2 vols, Bath, 1802

Watson, W., *An Explanation of a Tablet representing the Strata of Derbyshire*, Sheffield, 1791

—, *A Delineation of the Strata of Derbyshire*, Sheffield, 1811

Whitehurst, J., *Enquiry into the Original State and formation of the Earth, deduced from Facts and Laws of Nature*, London, 1778

Wood, W., *The History and Antiquities of Eyam*, 2nd edn, London, 1848

Worcester, W. De, *Itineraria Willelmi de Worcestre*, ed. J. Nasmith, Cambridge, 1778

Wordsworth, W., *The Letters of William Wordsworth*, 5 vols, Oxford, 1979

—, *The Prose Works of William Wordsworth*, Vol. I, 1972, ed. W. J. B. Owen and J. W. Smyser

—, *The Poetical Works of William Wordsworth*, ed. E. de Selincourt and H Darbishire, Oxford UP, 1954

2. SECONDARY SOURCES

A. Articles

Derbyshire Archaeological Journal (DAJ)

Chapman, S. D., 'Cressbrook and Litton Mills: an alternative view', Vol. 89, 1969

Fletcher, J. M. J., 'William Newton, "the Minstrell of the Peak"', Vol. 34, 1912

Keene, R., 'A six days' ramble over Derbyshire hills and dales in the year 1858', Vol. 6, 1884

Kirke, H., 'The Peak in the days of Queen Anne', Vol. 26, 1904

Lester, G. A., 'Thomas Bateman, barrow opener', Vol. 93, 1973

Mackenzie, M. H., 'The Bakewell Cotton Mills and the Arkwrights', Vol. 79, 1959

—, 'Calver Mill and its owners', Vol. 83, 1963

—, 'Calver Mill and its owners, a supplement', Vol. 84, 1964

—, 'Cressbrook and Litton Mills, 1779-1835', Vol. 90, 1970

—, 'The Bakewell Cotton Mill and the Arkwrights', Vol. 79, 1959

Mackerness, E., 'The Harvest of failure; Ebenezer Rhodes (1762-1839)', Vol. 101, 1981

Pagett, J., 'A visit to Derbyshire in 1630', Vol. 9, 1887

Parker, V., 'Calver Mill Buildings', Vol. 83, 1963

Radley, J., 'Peak District Roads prior to the turnpike era', Vol. 83, 1963

Radley, J. and Penny, S. R., 'The turnpike roads of the Peak District', Vol. 92, 1972

Sadler, E. A., 'Dr Johnson's Ashbourne friends', Vol. 60, 1940

Thomas R. and Leach, J.T., 'Buxton Hall', Vol. 114, 1994

Thornhill, R., 'The Arkwright Cotton Mill at Bakewell', Vol. 79, 1959

Whittington, R., 'Poole's Hole; a narrative of an adventure made in that cavern by Mr. R. Whittington, of Stevenage, Herts. On 25th August 1794', Vol. 19, 1897

Journal of the Bakewell and District Historical Society (JBDHS)

Brighton, (J.) T., 'A Guide to Myth and Legend: William Hage at Haddon Hall', No. 18, 1991

—, 'Wordsworth in Derbyshire', No. 19, 1992

—, 'Allan Cunningham's Seven Foresters of Chatsworth', No. 20, 1993

—, 'White Watson's Memorabilia', No. 21, 1994

—, 'John Constable's sketching tour in the Peak', No. 22, 1995

—, 'In search of mediaeval Chatsworth', No. 23, 1996

—, 'The Battle for the Haddon Footpaths in 1924', *Ibid.*

—, 'Bakewell Stone and the Building of Chatsworth House', No. 24, 1997

—, 'Marble Works on the Wye at Ashford and Bakewell', No. 24, 1997

—, 'A mid-Georgian tourist's poem on the Wonders of the Peak', No. 25, 1998

—, 'Elizabethan Chatsworth and its inventory', No. 29, 2002

—, 'Three 18th century antiquaries and the Bakewell Chantry House stone', No. 31, 2004

Clarke, H., 'The cotton industry of Great Longstone', No. 24, 1997

Pierrepont, J., 'Sir Stephen Glynne's notes on Bakewell Church and Haddon Hall', No. 23, 1996

Smith, S., 'The Greaves family and the Royal Mail in Bakewell 1805-1844', No. 29, 2002

Buxton Advertiser

Axon, E., 'Historical notes on Buxton, its inhabitants and visitors', 1934-47

Country Life

Girouard, M., 'Elizabethan Chatsworth', 22 Nov. 1973

Derbyshire Life and Countryside

Greatorex, H. N., 'The Wonders of Derbyshire: a setting for a Drury Lane Pantomime', Vol. 40, No. 72, Dec. 1975

Bulletin of the Peak District Mines Historical Society

Brighton, J. T., 'The Ashford Marble Works and Cavendish Patronage, 1748-1905', Vol. 12, No. 6, Winter 1995

Journal of the Walpole Society

Sloan, K., 'A Cozens Album in the National Library of Wales, Aberystwyth', Vol. LVII, 1993-94

Journal of Garden History

Brighton, J. T., 'An Early 18th-Century Landscape and Garden in the Peak District', Vol. 4, No. 4, 1983

—, 'Haddon Hall gardens: facts and fancies', Vol. 6, No. 3, 1986

Garden History

Brighton, J. T., 'Chatsworth's 16th-century Parks and Gardens', Vol. 23, No. 1, 1992

Peak Park Planning Board, Annual Reports, Nov. 1951 to the present

B. Books

Anon., *The Matlocks and their past*, Derbyshire County Library, 1977

Barnatt, J., *Arbor Low: a guide to the monuments*, Peak National Park, Sheffield, 1996

Brighton, J. T., *Bakewell in old picture postcards,* European Library, Zaltbommel, 2001

—, *Mrs Ann Greaves and the Bakewell Pudding*, BDHS, Matlock, 2000

Brighton, J.T. and Saunders, F., *Recollections of Bakewell: a century of photographs*, BDHS, Bakewell, 1994

Cameron, K., *The Placenames of Derbyshire*, English Placename Society, 3 Vols, Nottingham, 1993

Craven, M., *John Whitehurst of Derby, Clockmaker and Scientist, 1731-88*, Ashbourne, 1996

Craven, M. and Stanley, M., *The Derbyshire Country House*, 2 vols, Nottingham, 1982

Dodd, A. E. & E. M., *Peakland Roads and Trackways*, Moorland Publishing Company, Hartington, 1974. Republished by Landmark Publishing, Ashbourne, 2000

Egerton, J., *Wright of Derby*, Tate Gallery, 1990

Fitton, R. S., *The Arkwrights: Spinners of Fortune*, Manchester UP, 1989

Fokker, T. H., *Jan Siberechts, peintre de la paysanne flamande*, Bruxelles et Paris, 1931

Ford, T. D., *Derbyshire Blue John*, Landmark Publishing, Ashbourne, 2000

—, *Rocks and Scenery of the Peak District*, Landmark Publishing, Ashbourne, 2002

Ford, T. D. and Allsop, D., *The Story of Poole's Cavern*, Buxton, 1984

Ford, T. D. and Gunn, J., *Caves and Karst of the Peak District*, Nottingham, 1990

Ford, T. D. and Rieuworts, J. H., *Lead Mining in the Peak District*, Bakewell, 1970

Fowler, A., *The Country House Poem. A cabinet of 17th century estate poems and related items*, Edinburgh UP, 1994

Hall, I., *Georgian Buxton; a sketch of Buxton's architectural history in Georgian times*, Derbyshire Museums Service, 1984

Henstock, A. (ed.), *A Georgian Country Town, Ashbourne*, 2 vols., Nottingham, 1989 and 1991

Hey, D., *Packmen, Carriers and Packhorse Roads*, Leicester UP, 1980. Reprinted by Landmark Publishing, 2000

King-Hele, D., *Doctor of Revolution*, London, 1977

Klingender, R. D., *Art and the Industrial Revolution*, ed. and revised by A. Elton, 1968

Langham, M. and Wells, S. C., *Buxton Waters: a history of Buxton Spa*, Derby, 1986

Leach, J. T., *The Book of Buxton*, Buckingham, 1987

Lees-Milne, J., *The Bachelor Duke. A life of William Spencer Cavendish, 6th Duke of Devonshire, 1790-1858*, London, 1991

Lockett, J., *David Cox*, Birmingham, Museum and Art Gallery, 1983

Mandler, P., *The Fall and Rise of the Stately Home*, Yale UP, 1997

Mecke, E. R., *White Watson, 1760-1835*, privately printed, Bakewell, 1996

Moir, E., *The Discovery of Britain. The English Tourists 1540-1840*, London, 1964

Morley, B., *Peveril Castle*, English Heritage, London, 1990

Nicholson, B., *Joseph Wright of Derby, Painter of Light*, 2 vols, London, 1968

Ousby, I., *The Englishman's England*, Cambridge UP, 1990

Page. W. (ed.), *The Victoria County History of Derbyshire*, 2 vols, London, 1905-1907

Parsons, E. and Stenton, Sir F., *The Map of Great Britain c. A.D 1360, known as the Gough Map*, Oxford UP, 1958

Porter, L., *The Peak District: pictures from the past*, Moorland Publishing, Ashbourne, 1984

Robey, J. A. and Porter, R., *The Copper and Leadmines of Ecton Hill, Staffordshire*, Nottingham, 1972

Robinson, B. (ed.), *The Seven Blunders of the Peak*, Cromford, 1994

Sappien, R., *Philippe Jacques de Loutherbourg, RA.*, London, 1973

Sissons, D. (ed.), *The Best of the Sheffield Clarion Ramblers Handbooks*, Tiverton, 2002

Smith, G. le Blanc, *Haddon Hall*, London, 1906

Taylor, H., *A Claim on the Countryside. A history of the British Outdoor Movement*, Keele UP, 1997

Thompson, F., *A History of Chatsworth*, Country Life Ltd, London, 1949

Tomlinson, J. M., *Derbyshire Black Marble*, Peak District Mines Historical Society, Matlock Bath, 1996

Turbutt, G., *History of Derbyshire*, 4 Vols, Cardiff, 1999

Wood, A., *The Politics of Social Conflict. The Peak Country 1520-1770*, Cambridge UP, 1999

Index

Numbers in **bold** refer to illustration page numbers.

103, 141, 143, 165, 178

Senior, William (fl. 1617), 125, **129**, 146, V

Seven Wonders of the Ancient World, 31-2

Seven Wonders of the Peak, 31-3, 50, 161, 185

Seward, Anna (1742-1809), 103, 104, 115, 167

Shakespeare, William (1564-1616), 142, 143

Sheffield, 10, 15, 50, 81, 159, 171, 181, 191, 195, 196, 200, 209

Sheffield Clarion Club, 201, 202

Sheffield Cooperative Ramblers, 201

Sheldon, 165

Shelley, Mary (1797-1851), xiii

Sheridan, Richard Brinsley (1751-1816), 161

Shrewsbury, Earl of see Talbot

Siberechts, Jan (1627-c.1697), **7**, 125, **129**, 145-53, **148**

Sidera, 53

Sidney, Sir Philip (1554-86), 36, 54

signposts, **14**, 15

silk mill, 94

Sketch of a Tour into Derbyshire, 90

Sketches of Derbyshire Scenery, 81, 90

Smedley, John, 206

Smith, John Raphael (1742-1812), 56

Robert, 112

Thomas of Derby (d.1767), **135**, 138, **138**, 141, 152-5, **152**, 166, 178, X

Smith and Pennell, 106

Soho Works, Birmingham, 76, 78

Sorocold, George, 94, 97

South Peak Estate, 210

South Yorkshire, 209

spars, 71, 73, 105-21

spas, 47-53, 104-21, 205-7

Speed, John (1552?-1629), 1, **4**, 11, 50, 144, **146**, 184

Speedwell Cavern, 199

spinning (cotton), 93-103

Staden, 47, 83

Stafford, 209

Staffordshire, 1, 8, 19

stalactites, 71, 72

Stamford, 84

Stanedge, 25

Stanhope, Philip, 2nd Earl of Chesterfield (1633-1713), 147

Stanley Moor, 48

Stanton Moor, 87, 88, 212

Stephenson, Tom, 202

Sterndale, Mary, 103

Stockport, 10, 209

Stoke, 209

Stonehenge, 32, 87

Stoney Middleton, 25, 112, 162

Storer, John, 159

Storrs-Fox, William, 194

strata, 74, **75**

Strawberry Hill, 89

Strutt, William (1756-1830), 76

Stubbs, George (1724-1806), 20

Stukeley, William (1687-1765), 52

Sullivan, Sir Arthur (1842-1900), 143

Survey of Derbyshire, 184, **188**, **190**

Sussex, Earl of see Radcliffe

Swift, Mr, 94, 95

Swinscoe Hill, 66

Switzerland, 2

Syntax, Dr, 182

Taddington, 65, 70, 119

Talbot, George, 6th Earl of Shrewsbury (1528?-90), 50, 53, 122

Talman, William (fl.1670-1700), 124, 147, 148

Tansley, 207

Taylor, Dr John (1711-88), 70, **170**

theatre, sets, 161-2

Thirlmere, 183

Thomas, William, 97

Thoresby, Ralph (1658-1725), 56

Thornbridge Hall, 100

Thornhill, Sir James (1635-1734), **27**, **33**, 36, **44**, 46, 53, 123, 130, **131**, **132**, 133, 149-51, **149**

Thornhill, William, 87

Thorpe Cloud, **154**

Thrale, Mrs Hester, 2, 155

Thynne, Sir John, 123

Tideswell, 27, 28, 31, 41, 46, 62, 70, 92, 104, 119, 162, 177, 179, 181

church, 27, 179

George Inn, 70

Tilbury, Gervase of (fl. 1211), 5-6

Tillemans, Pieter (1684-1734), 150-3, VII

Tillet, 189

Timon's Villa, 128-9

Tissington Hall, 89, 170

To my dear and most worthy friend, Mr Isaac Walton, 16

Toothorn Field, 182

Topley Pike, 66, **69**, 177, 178

Tour through the High Peak of Derbyshire, 181

tourism, 9, 59-82, 210-2

trackways, 11, 14

travail, 9-18

traveller's equipment, 62-3

Traveller's Oracle, 63

Treak Cavern, 42, 73

Trent Basin, 8

Tribal Hidage, 7

tufa, 71, 82

Tunbridge Wells, 107

Turnebus, 20

Turner, J.M.W. (1775-1851), **61**, **69**, 91, **91**, 113, 141, 150, 158, 159, 160, **162**

Tutbury, 50

Twelve Prospects in that Part of Derbyshire called the Peak and the Moorlands, 154

Twenty Five Views of Haddon Hall, 165

Universal Magazine, 153

Uttoxeter, 176

vases, **79**, **80**

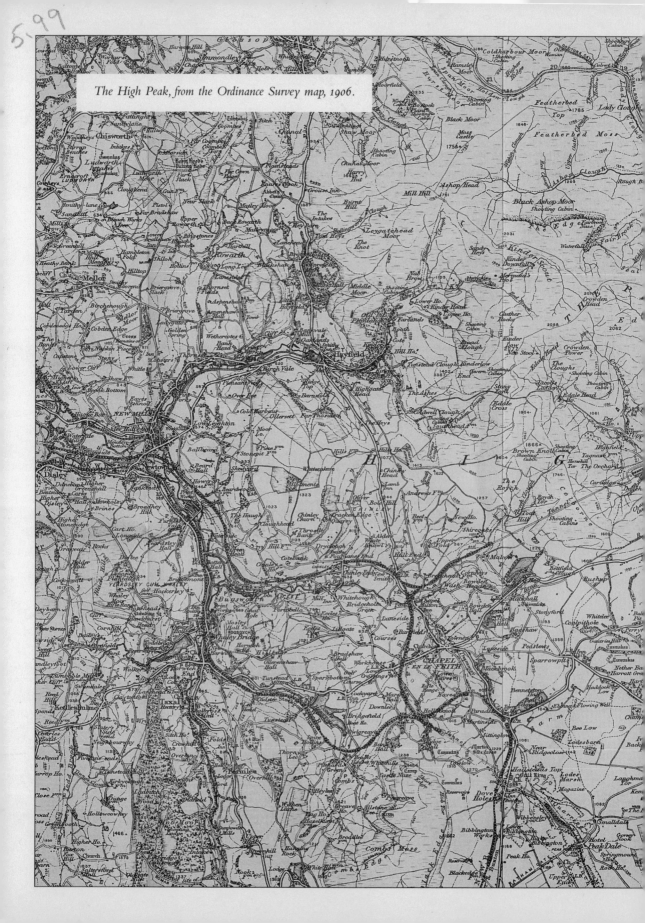

The High Peak, from the Ordinance Survey map, 1906.